dsl∨

500

DATE DUE

D1562373

THE NECESSARY HELL

THE NECESSARY HELL

JOHN AND HENRY LAWRENCE
AND THE INDIAN EMPIRE

MICHAEL EDWARDES

With 8 pages of half-tone illustrations

CASSELL · LONDON

CASSELL & COMPANY LTD
35 RED LION SQUARE
LONDON, W.C.1

and at

210 QUEEN STREET, MELBOURNE
26/30 CLARENCE STREET, SYDNEY
94 WYNDHAM STREET, AUCKLAND
1068 BROADVIEW AVENUE, TORONTO 6
P.O. BOX 275, CAPE TOWN
P.O. BOX 11190, JOHANNESBURG
58 PEMBROKE STREET, PORT OF SPAIN, TRINIDAD
HAROON CHAMBERS, SOUTH NAPIER ROAD, KARACHI
13/14 AJMERI GATE EXTENSION, NEW DELHI 1
15 GRAHAM ROAD, BALLARD ESTATE, BOMBAY 1
17 CHITTARANJAN AVENUE, CALCUTTA 13
P.O. BOX 23, COLOMBO
MACDONALD HOUSE, ORCHARD ROAD, SINGAPORE 9
AVENIDA 9 DE JULHO 1138, SÃO PAULO
GALERIA GÜEMES, ESCRITORIO 454/59 FLORIDA 165, BUENOS AIRES
MARNE 5B, MEXICO 5, D.F.
SANSHIN BUILDING, 6 KANDA MITOSCHIRO-CHO, CHIYODA-KU, TOKYO
25 RUE HENRI BARBUSSE, PARIS 5E
25 NY STRANDVEJ, ESPERGAERDE, COPENHAGEN
BEULINGSTRAAT 2, AMSTERDAM-C
BEDERSTRASSE 51, ZÜRICH 2

Made and printed in Great Britain by
William Clowes and Sons, Limited, London and Beccles
F. 258

FOR
PATRICIA FEAR
AND
VALERIE GRANT

Chamfort, the moralist of rebellion, had already provided the formula 'One must be just before being generous, one must have bread before having cake.' Thus the ethic of luxury will be renounced in favour of the bitter morality of the Empire builder.

The Rebel, by ALBERT CAMUS

PREFACE

THIS BOOK is *not* a biography of two nineteenth-century Empire-builders. The hero is the Indian Empire itself. But John and Henry Lawrence in their lives—and deaths—can give us a view of something that is usually castrated by dates of battles and catalogues of great names—the empty puppets of the school-room. What so many of us know of the Indian Empire in the nineteenth century is only the hagiography of Imperialism, not a living thing emerging out of the laughter and tragedy of those that made it.

'History,' someone has written, 'is the propaganda of the victors.' That is particularly true of the Indian Empire until 1947. Now there is the danger of the propaganda of the defeated. This book grinds no axe but is an attempt to show what the Empire was really like in battlefield, council-chamber, and home. To show the motive as far as is possible behind the act and the result of the act itself. To place nineteenth-century India into the perspective of the British-Indian Empire.

To do this I have used the Lawrences, for to me they represent two facets of the Empire-builder. The almost cold calculation of the 'superior' race, firm of face but always racked by doubts, and the active nostalgia for Indians and their ways of life and thought. They are, of course, not as precise as this, but John and Henry Lawrence have the necessary antagonism of motive to illuminate the structure of nineteenth-century India. Their story is also a drama of excitement, a tragedy fringed with greatness and failure—a story worth telling for its own sake.

But, I must repeat, this is *not* a biography, a calendar of two men's days. For the intimate details, a view through a key-hole, the reader must look elsewhere. This landscape is an impressionist one, concentrating on light and shade; and because of it many details, familiar and unfamiliar, are missing. For this I make no apology. My aim is to give a view of nineteenth-century India, not a portrait of the two Lawrences.

In the Introduction and Epilogue I state my case. In between, the Lawrences and others of their time supply the evidence as well as descriptions of the scene. My sources have been wide and for those who are interested some are noticed in the Bibliography. Thanks are due to the Oxford University Press for permission to quote from P. E. Robert's *History of British India* and also to G. Bell and Son Ltd. for some lines from J. L. Morison's *Lawrence of Lucknow*.

Once again I am indebted for material and aid to the Librarian and staff of the India Office Library and I am particularly grateful for the encouragement and forbearance of my friends, especially those to whom this book is respectfully dedicated.

CONTENTS

LIST OF ILLUSTRATIONS

The miniature is reproduced by kind permission of the Librarian of the India Office Library, Commonwealth Relations Office, London. The remainder of the illustrations are from the Picture Post Library, London.

INTRODUCTION

THE HERO AND THE HISTORIAN

Si j'avais les mains pleines de vérités,
je me garderais de les ouvrir.

BERNARD DE FONTANELLE

THE HISTORY of British India has been confused, not to say falsified, by the necessity of imperial propaganda. An empire must exist in the newspaper headline and the memoir, in the clichés of colonial responsibility and divine providence. There was always (and still is) a breach between what was written about the Empire and what actually happened.

The gap between the idea of the Indian Empire and the realities of that Empire is an important field for study. It is the gap between the historian and the administrator. And until that gap is not so much closed as measured, the true wonder of the Indian Empire and those that made it cannot be assessed. Dazzled by the sun on a sword-blade, overwhelmed by the larger-than-life monument to the Imperial Hero, we can see neither his tragedy nor his achievement.

It is possible for the historian to impose on the vast galli-maufry of men and events that make up the story of British India—virtually any point of view, to enclose it within the rigidities of his particular birdcage. The Indian Empire could be seen as just another alien episode, something like the Mogul's, doctrinaire and exploitive, leaving behind it little more than a few buildings and some poetry. There would be ample evidence for this view. It could be seen as a unique occasion in the world's history, the only empire to end in an immense moral gesture—to leave with the flags still flying. There is evidence for this, too; nor are the two attitudes mutually exclusive. The Empire could be (and has been) written-up as a record of service given unselfishly and with little thought of reward. This is well documented.

So too, with the aid of statistics the exploitive nature of British rule could be made to fill the whole of the canvas. But the history of British India, like any other empire, is not such a simple matter as many historians would have us believe. Looking back on India, we can pretend to see the march of events, governed by all manner of strategical rules and 'forces' only because we are unaware of, or unwilling to consider, the commonplace of these events.

The history of the Indian Empire is an exercise in biography and a study of ideas. It was, until the construction of the Red Sea Telegraph in 1870, an anarchy of decentralized decision, in which the gap between the order and the hand that carried it out was often an unbridgeable gulf. Strong Governors-General and arrogant Law Members formulated in cold prose their majestic, and often magnificently conceived minutes of policy, but the strength of that policy was only as strong as the man in the wilderness. The decision was finally his decision and was distorted by his shortcomings, and by the pressure of local events. The Indian Empire before 1870 was a patch-work quilt of which only length and breadth was subject to the control of 'policy'. The history of India is not a sequence of administrators living in palaces, nor of Acts passed at Westminster.

It is comparatively easy to analyse and tabulate what the Indian Empire was not; it is altogether another matter to show what it *was*. Even the words 'Indian Empire' are essentially meaningless if the attempt is made to apply them to anything but a series of coloured maps. Empires are always more than the cartographer's simplicities, more than legislative boundaries and collections of frontiers. Empires are not merely places existing in the eye. They must also have form that is recognized by the mind.

The only way we have of reconstructing an act or series of actions is to recreate as far as is possible the climate in which they took place. To analyse the motives of men and the pressures of heat and disease. But we must always have in view the striking of a balance. In order to do so we must act as an auditor.

This is all very well if the books have been kept to the accepted rules; if not, and we are not particularly scrupulous, the books will have to be cooked. The twentieth century has seen the books of the British-Indian Empire cooked to rags, and the total has always been different. The Empire lived above its income, the directors were forgers and embezzlers, the company operated wonderful welfare schemes at a loss to the shareholders. . . . All these and more. But the Indian Empire was more than a commercial undertaking, planned, productive, and subject to profit and loss. It was an adventure, a mad, irresponsible adventure, full of pain and tragedy, full of wonder and achievement, and subject only to the logic of adventure which is no logic at all. To convert the Empire into a formula is like carrying water in a paper bag.

The history of India in the nineteenth century is littered, like some dusty museum, with the simulacra of the Imperial Tragedy. All we can see to-day is almost all that could be seen then—the daguerrotype and not the flesh, the memoir and not the act, until the English and India became some sort of representative symbols as rigid and unreal as those of a waxworks.

All empires produce the hero-makers they deserve. Those that populate their private dreams with real people and then tell the story in the Club and the circulating library. The British-Indian Empire was no exception. Back in England, and even in Australia, assiduous clergymen, retired empire-builders, missionaries overflowing with the bowels of some irrelevant compassion, were all hard at work creating the mystique of an Empire. Macaulay, orating in his *Essay on Clive*, of the 'mighty children of the sea' and that 'none could resist Clive and his Englishmen'; John William Kaye, through the cobwebs of India House, constructing his heroes of uncommon clay; the Reverend Fitchett boiling his *Deeds that Won the Empire* as a night-cap for little boys in country vicarages—all buttressing and extending the shrine of the Imperial Hero. But were there any foundations to this Holy Place?

To answer the question at all, one must consider what India meant to the Victorians. Not very much in the great outdoors of ordinary people; and many different things in the closed-room of the upper classes. The English, as a nation, worried little and knew less about their Indian Empire until it ended in 1947. To the Victorian, it was not much different from the idea of India that was widespread only a few years ago. Rascally natives; honest Englishmen; duty; the little mud fort on the frontier; the place where somebody called Carew got involved with unhappy results with a heathen yellow idol to the north of Katmandu. The East

is unchanging only in the unchanging ignorance of the uninquisi-
tive mind.

And the men of affairs? To the business man—business.
Clothes may change in fashion, but motives, never. To the poli-
tician—an administrative headache, or a stick to beat the Government. Lobbies of this interest and that, but in essence India was
never a real *place*. A geographical expression, a problem in
communication, or a subject for legislation; but never a climate
or a physical reality. Except, of course, to those who had lived
there. To them it meant many things—all of them intensely real.
It was a climate that killed the body, and a physical reality that
crushed the soul. These men and their families were caught in
the tragic atmosphere, and sometimes tried to express it in words.
The attempt frequently took the form of poetry, saturated
with an almost hysterical melancholy.

The theme of so much of the 'poetry of empire' is the melancholy of the exile. So much of it, too, is the deliberate addition of
salt to an open wound. Nostalgia for even the fogs of London is
unqualified and the fear of death is always present. It becomes not
the fear of leaving this world but of never seeing the remote green
grass of England again. W. T. Webb, a justly forgotten poet of
Anglo-Indian morbidity, crystallizes this almost pathological
melancholy in 'The Song of Death' (*Indian Lyrics*, Calcutta,
1884):

> My fellow exiles, fill your glasses,
>   We'll sing one song before we die;
> The tiger in the jungle-grasses
>   Has sucked the peasant's life-blood dry...

but even so, the trumpets sound, the price of duty is inescapable,

> Go, bind your sons to exile
>   To serve the captive's need.

The pack must be shouldered and all that is left is the empty
gesture of bad poetry.

But these representatives of the 'Anglo-Indian' tragedy are
drowned by the martial banalities of the hero-makers. In many
cases the retiring administrator, finding himself surrounded with
the contrived aura of the Imperial Hero, soon came to believe in
the myth, and adapted himself to it; the real thing came to
resemble the simulacrum. All this was good for recruiting; the

younger sons of the middle classes saw themselves, sword in hand, carving Empires out of the black lands, bringing Law to the ignorant peasant, shouldering the pack of the white man's burden and marching into a hero's sunset.

How little of the actuality has penetrated into the school-history! Only the 'great' names, cardboard figures of surpassing unreality, are allowed in the class-room. All this is the hangover of the nineteenth century. Of the cult of the Hero obscuring the truth with the thick varnish of the propaganda of Empire.

A Hero is made not born. The Hero is not so much the victim as the creation of propaganda. Because of this, though he can be emasculated, demolished, and thrown on the garbage-pile by the debunkers, the myth can never be totally destroyed. His body, like that of John Brown, persists in marching even when the flesh is shown to be putrifying. Hero-worshippers are the eternal scatophagi, and there is always some hack ready to supply a meal.

But why? Is there some primordial need deep in the gut of Man that demands the figure of the Hero? Some necessity, per-haps, for vicarious adventure? Danger without the sweat or the tears and death without blood, or even death?

The Hero, or rather the image of the Hero, has existed since the organization of society. A little anthropomorphism here, an explanation for misunderstood natural phenomena there, were its foundation. The Hero was the scapegoat, the miraculous person-age who can escape from the web of everyday life and its prob-lems. The Hero can safely be trusted with the cruel weight of lost causes. And who can better support the excuses of failure?

Nineteenth-century England, seeing the hardening of the scaffolding of Empire, and the withdrawal of the climate of adventure as the telegraph lines extended, produced its pantheon of improving 'doers'. The Victorians were great believers in salutary example and as the administration of the Empire became more and more bureaucratic and systematized so the necessity to show the Empire as a great adventure, a moral battlefield popu-lated with knights in shining armour, increased. No one is prepared to fight to the death in defence of a phalanx of memo-randa and despatch-boxes. The adventure is in carving out an Empire, not carving it up into profits for quiet men in the City of London.

These quiet men, the great Victorian bourgeoisie, stuck in the sludge of their counting-house philosophies and moral conceits, knew this well enough. To continue the supply of young men for the services of India, the romance of 'service' and the intoxication of 'duty' must not only be praised as the essential virtues, they must also have their living examples. Hence the creation of the figure of the Imperial Hero.

Though the elements of the Hero had existed before it was necessary to create him, they had mostly been canalized into dull 'official' biographies. But the Imperial Hero in his shining regimentals, strutted his way through the last four decades of the nineteenth century on into the morning of the twentieth. At one end stands John William Kaye, at the other, Rudyard Kipling, whose work is the requiem of the old Imperialism. Of course, the Hero continued to hold an important place in the *dramatis personae* of the novelist and film-writer. The Bengal Lancers still achieved the improbable with a twist of the moustache and the love of the Colonel's daughter. Carruthers, cashiered for something unmentionable, still saved the Pass from the rascally Afghans, but this was the shopgirl's hero. The Hero as recruiting sergeant was *passé*. No one, except a few democrats and some Indians, really cared any longer about the Empire.

But not so in the last forty years of the nineteenth century. Then India was slowly being forced into the mould of Victorian capitalism. The lessons of the Mutiny must never be forgotten. Britain might in 1857 have lost India, if it had not been for the selfless immolation of its Heroes. Under the superficial calm of post-mutiny India lurked the 'crafty Hindu'. Outside its frontiers rumbled the colossus of Russia. The Empire could only be cemented by blood—the blood of young men steeped in its hagiolatry. So said the Hero-makers and professional pantheon-builders. The megalomaniacs, the 'saintly' soldiers, the merely mad, and the frequently bad, suddenly found themselves (if they were not conveniently dead) silver-plated for the edification of the nursery and the public-school.

In some small degree the silver-plate rubbed off on to the men of the Indian Civil Service rushing home to write their memoirs. In them their whole lives have been dedicated to Britain's civilizing mission—the Hero lives even in the battlefield of Simla and the offices of the Secretariat. Every man in India, whatever his position, from Viceroy to junior subaltern, was part of the heroic canvas of Empire. In this they were, ironically enough, quite right, for in the routines of everyday life were dangers far greater than in any real battle. But death by cholera is unheroic. Bubonic plague, curiously unromantic. The Hero is seldom a civilian, for his death, unless he is hacked to pieces by a mob, is without the necessary glamour. The Hero of the nineteenth century was either the missionary (for God was always on the tongues of the Victorians if rarely anywhere else) or the soldier. The missionary Hero was usually confined to places such as Africa, full of objectionable natives and with no immediate prospect of profitable trade. The soldier, frequently with Bible in hand, did God's work in a more realistic way. A sensible and beneficial partnership between God and Mammon.

The Lawrences, especially Henry, supplied suitable material. 'Go out,' said the Hero-makers and the men behind them, 'Be another Henry Lawrence. Do your duty and, if necessary, die for your country.'

All this activity, and it is with us still, obscures and distorts the true tragedy and genuine heroisms of nineteenth-century India.

Now that the Empire is as dead as the Roman we should be able to free ourselves from the blinkers of propaganda and the necessity of keeping a stiff upper lip, and expand the melodrama of the Imperial Hero into the tragedy of British India.

I

THIS MELANCHOLIOUS COUNTHRY

Mary, Mother av Mercy, fwat the devil possist us to take an' kape this melancholious counthry? Answer me that, Sorr.'

Private Mulvaney in 'With the Main Guard', from *Soldiers Three* by RUDYARD KIPLING

WHO THEN IS THE CONQUEROR?

INDIA! Elephants, Rajas, diamonds, belly-dancers, little mud forts on the Frontier (on which the sun never set but the Afghan often did). The Bengal Lancers, luxury and vice, sinister and strangely reprehensible goings-on in the inner recesses of mysterious temples. The whole in Technicolor and probably Cinemascope and, surprisingly enough, not altogether untrue. And yet, this simultaneous view of some of the possible Indias only obscures the real India, for it heightens the exotic and the alien at the expense of the vivid, and tragic, improbabilities of everyday life in the India of the men and madnesses that make up this book.

John and Henry Lawrence—and the Empire—must stand against a backcloth, for from it, and it alone, they take on meaning and life. What was India like when the Lawrences first appeared on the stage of the nineteenth century? What climate and thought moulded by their pressures the men and events that raised the Indian Empire to its greatest heights?

> But who, then, is the conqueror, who the sovereign of this immense empire over which the sun extends so gloriously his glittering rays, that has arisen on the continent of Asia as if by enchantment, and now rivals in extent that of Alexander, Tamerlane, or Nadir Shah?
> Why, on a small island in another quarter of the globe, in a narrow street, where the rays of the sun are seldom able to penetrate the thick smoke, a company of peaceable merchants meet; these are the conquerors of India; these are the absolute sovereigns of this splendid empire.

So wrote Count Bjornstjerna in his book: *The British Empire in the East*, published in 1840.

If we are to know the materials and the colours that make up the scene we must examine Bjornstjerna's question, though simply and without too much of the belches of history, the footnote and the party bias. How, briefly, did the Indian Empire come about?

The founder of it all might be said to be Ralph Fitch, the only survivor of a small group of merchants who set out for the India of Akbar in the reign of the first Elizabeth. This led to the foundation of the East India Company in 1600. Holding a charter from Queen Elizabeth, it was known under the grandiloquent title of 'The Governor and Company of Merchants of London, trading to the East Indies'.

Why did these presumably hard-headed men indulge in such a fantastic gamble? To send their flimsy matchwood ships out into virtually uncharted waters; to risk the supremacy of the Portuguese in the eastern seas, they accepted a myth that has stayed with the Orient until the present day. That illusion was 'the wealth of the Indies'; wealth just for the tapping.

In 1608, in order to establish a trading post in India, the Company received permission from the Mogul Emperor Jehangir to settle at the town of Surat, then the chief port of Western India. Later, in order to keep the favour of the court at Delhi, Sir Thomas Roe was sent as the ambassador of both the Company and of King James I. This remarkable man: solemn, somewhat prudish, was described by his chaplain as 'a Joseph in the court of Pharaoh, for whose sake all his nation seemed to fare the better'. He was an aristocrat at a court which, though cruel and drunken, was seldom coarse, and could recognize a 'gentleman' when it saw one. Before him, the Company had been known only by its merchants and its seamen: tough, adventurous men without finesse or subtlety. Roe was neither a lickspittle nor obsequious, and was possessed of an analytic eye. He saw immediately the essential rottenness of the vast Mogul Empire, seemingly so glorious and powerful.

'His greatness,' wrote Roe of the Emperor, 'substantially, is not in itself, but in the weakness of his neighbours, whom like an overgrown pike he feeds on as fry.'

But the English had no thought of an Empire, only of the peace to trade. The Portuguese, the first Europeans in India, had territory, the protection of which counterbalanced the profits of commerce. It was the same, also, with the Dutch. 'Let this be received as a rule that, if you will profit, seek it at sea, and in quiet trade; for without controversy it is an error to affect garrisons and land wars in India.'

But all was not well for the English; 'quiet trade' was hardly possible. Clashes with the waning power of Portugal and the ruthless Dutch finally drove the English to withdraw from the Spice Islands of Java and Sumatra where the original trade had

started, and for which India was to be merely a place to buy the
stuffs needed for commerce in those islands. The English were
to turn to the Indian mainland in their furious quest for trade,
and from then onwards, though sometimes in dire peril, the flag
followed trade.

In 1675, the ninth *guru* or teacher of the Sikhs, who under
Mogul persecution had become a military brotherhood, was
summoned to Delhi by the Emperor Aurangzeb and ordered to
accept conversion to Islam. On his refusal, he was thrown into
prison, and later executed. While imprisoned, he was accused by
the Emperor of staring in the direction of the Imperial harem. To
this the *guru* replied:

> I was not looking at thy private apartments, nor at thy queen's;
> I was looking in the direction of the Europeans who are coming
> from beyond the seas to tear down thy curtains, and destroy thy
> Empire.

Whether this was magnificent prescience, or merely the hind-
sight of the myth-maker matters little, for the English were on
the march again after a hibernation of many years. The Commonwealth had been and gone—King Charles had come into his own
again. Bombay, a malarial swamp, had been given by Portugal
as part of the dowry of Catherine of Braganza on her marriage
to Charles in 1662.

In 1611, a post had been founded at Masulipatan, on the east
coast of India, but soon the town of Madras, brought into existence by Fort St. George, was to become the headquarters of the
Company in South India, and the scene of the struggle with the
French. So, too, had a settlement been made in Bengal, but this
was to be of little importance until the building of Fort William
on the site of present-day Calcutta in 1690.

From 1660 to 1680, the Company reached its peak as a purely
trading body. Dividends averaged twenty-five per cent per
annum, and the value of stock steadily rose. Under Charles II the
Company was given the right to erect fortifications, to coin
money, to exercise jurisdiction over Englishmen in the East, to
declare war and make alliances. With this grew the idea of
dominion. The beginnings were loose and were never fully
formulated, but in the last days of the Mogul Empire, which had
at least given some political identity to India, the English were

having to fight for their very existence and the necessity of con-
trolling territory seemed inevitable. As Gerald Aungier, the
President of Surat, put it:

> The state of India . . . is much altered of what it was; that justice
> and respect wherewith strangers in general, and especially those of
> our native people, were wont to be treated with, is quite laid aside;
> the name of the honourable Company and the English nation
> through our long, patient suffering of wrong is become slighted;
> our complaints, remonstrances, paper protests and threatenings, are
> laughed at . . . in violent distempers, violent cures are only success-
> ful . . . *the times now require you to manage your general commerce
> with your sword in your hand!*

This advice found a receptive ear back in England at the Court
of Committees of the Honourable Company. In England, the
Company had fallen into ill-repute. What one modern historian
describes as 'a curious rebellion' organized by the commander of
the Royal Garrison in Bombay, took place in 1683-84. Captain
Richard Keigwin, the commander, seized the deputy-Governor,
Mr. Ward and members of the Council and issued a proclamation
annulling the authority of the Company and placing the island of
Bombay under the protection of the Crown. Attempts by commissioners of the Company to suppress the revolt were unsuccess-
ful, and though it ended with a settlement, and free pardon for
the ringleaders, this episode, and a rising on the island of St.
Helena, used as a revictualling station for the Company's marine,
brought allegations of tyranny against the Company.

The Court of Committees, in order to direct attention from
its supposed misrule, decided to throw caution aside and to
commence to exercise its sovereign will; to become, in effect, an
Indian power. In a despatch of the Committee, dated 12th
September 1687, can be seen the first conscious groping towards
English dominion in India. It was a grandiloquent gesture, made
without knowledge of what such a declaration would entail. The
Committee urged its representatives in India to

> establish such a Polity of civil and military power, and create and
> secure such a large Revenue . . . as may be the foundation of a
> large, well-grounded, sure English Dominion in India for all time
> to come.

So the Company declared war on the Emperor.
The extravagance of these claims was quickly demonstrated,

and the English were besieged in their trading posts. Only sea-power saved them, as it would save them from the French; and because of it a compromise was worked out with the Emperor.

Meanwhile, the Company's fortunes at home had been caught in a web of intrigue and carpet-bagging. The old Company had been a Tory enclave and, after the Revolution of 1688, it was subjected to the vitriol of the Whigs. The House of Commons decided, in 1694, that no Englishman could be denied trade in the Indies at the whim of the King, but only by the act of a sovereign Parliament. So a new East India Company was chartered in 1698 as a rival to the old royal company. But, strategically, the old Company was the stronger, being first in the field, and knowing most of the tricks of a difficult trade, and after lengthy negotiations, the two companies finally amalgamated in 1708, as the 'United Company of Merchants of England, trading to the East Indies'.

In India, the mutations that were to bring forth the Empire were beginning to be felt. On the death of Aurangzeb in 1707, the polity of the Mogul Empire started to disintegrate. With the coming of a weak ruler at the centre, the Empire was no longer the sum of its parts but a shadowy cliché contemptuously tolerated—almost a legal fiction.

But the English were tolerably ready to keep afloat in the coming anarchy. Their settlements had been fortified, and a certain degree of friendship, if only the friendship of trade, was between them and the successors, in the provinces, of the Mogul Empire. The English were beginning to acquire a sense of place. Firstly, trade. The original English settlements were merely emporia, bazaars, places of commerce, and no more. Then the element of security enters—the warehouses must be protected. The traders become *armed* traders. The next step is to employ soldiers to defend the settlement; then, to establish 'spheres of influence'. Slowly, the rhythm of Empire-building imposes itself on the simplicities of 'trade', and there was nothing that would halt it.

But the English are sticklers for the legal niceties. With some difficulty, *firmans* or signed privileges were obtained from the Mogul Emperor, granting land and other recognitions to the Company, making them, as Edmund Burke was later to point out, legally part of the Mogul Dominions, of an Empire coming apart at the seams. This legality meant nothing, and brought nothing, for the real enemy was a European one, and the battle would, essentially, be decided on the sea.

The French had originally established a 'factory' or settlement at Pondicherry, near Madras, in 1673, and at Chandernagore, near Calcutta, in 1670. Occasionally hostilities had broken out between the French and the English, but had meant really nothing until the Mogul Empire fell apart.

The country was in anarchy; the Mogul Empire, like the British Empire in its early years, was an administrative empire only. It existed in terms of revenue-collecting and the concentration of force at the centre. It imposed no unity on the country, only a discipline—there was no sense of nationhood, only a division of ruler and ruled. When the centre was strong, the parts were weak; when the centre was weak, the parts revolted, and revolt led to chaos.

Into this chaos came the French, consciously determined on building an empire. Knowing that their success would depend on sea-power, they had occupied the strategic islands of Mauritius and Réunion in the Indian Ocean, and all was ready for the great adventure that nearly ended in the French becoming the rulers of India.

In 1735, the Governor of Pondicherry started to intrigue in affairs in the Deccan. In 1740, the Marathas, the strongest and most ably led of the Mogul's legatees, invaded the Carnatic, a province which contained both Madras and Pondicherry, and the ruler was given protection by the French. For this the Governor of Pondicherry was created a *Nawab* or Prince, and because of it attained a greater measure of respect in Indian eyes than the English.

The French East India Company was not a trading corporation in the manner of the English. It was primarily an instrument of French foreign policy. It was strictly subordinate to its home governments, and had none of the enterprise or gambling instincts of the searchers after profit.

To it, in 1742, came a man of genius, irascible, imaginative and determined on creating an Empire, if only for his own greater glory. To do so, he decided to use Indian forms of government. Surrounding himself with great magnificence, he lived orientally and was recognized by other Indian rulers as one of themselves.

The quasi-independent princes aspiring to real independence were in many cases equally matched in strength and resources, and Dupleix, with his intimate knowledge of the country, realized that by throwing even the meagre weight at his disposal on one side or the other, would be decisive. He also established the fact that native troops, trained in European methods, and above all stiffened and led by Europeans, could, in only small numbers, defeat the irregular cavalry of the Indian rulers. This discovery was to be decisive for both the French and the English.

Unfortunately for Dupleix, he was bedevilled by the plans of the French Government, and by the great French sailor, La Bourdonnais, who had been sent to harass English ships in the Indian Ocean. Jealousy between the two, it has been said (though without historical foundation), lost France an empire. But in 1746, La Bourdonnais captured Madras, only to see it returned by the Treaty of Aix-la-Chapelle in 1749.

Out of this peculiar political rumba, there emerged one of the great names of British India—not a good name, not one to be unreservedly proud of or to emulate, but genuinely great. This name was to appear in a Company Minute on 2nd May 1747:

> Mr. Robert Clive, Writer in the Service, being of a Martial Disposition, and having acted as a Volunteer upon Our Late Engagement, we have granted him an Ensign's Commission upon his application for same.

Indian wars in the eighteenth century were remarkable for their lack of even the current expertize of the times. The number of troops engaged were derisive in their smallness, and they were essentially unprofessional, casual, and mercenary. To this un-military *mélange* came Major Stringer Lawrence, sometimes called the Father of the Indian Army, without whom it is unlikely we would ever have heard of Clive. Lawrence began to impose discipline on his tattered forces, and formed them into something militarily effective. The stage was set, and Clive took a leading role.

Clive has become, for the English, one of the few names remembered from the desperate cramming of the schoolboy; he is one of those shadowy beings, an Historical Hero. As a name, he is a convenient tag for a chapter in a not particularly perceptive history: *The Age of Clive*. It was the age of other names as well, but Clive has caught the desire for symbolic figures, those that symbolize their times, for he dominated them with that peculiar madness which was his substitute for genius.

Clive's seizure and his defence during the siege of the Fort of Arcot in 1751 was a turning-point in a petty war ostensibly between rival heirs in the Deccan and the Carnatic, but actually between the French and the English. Dupleix' schemes began to crumble and he was recalled to France in 1754. The French were no longer a danger, though they were to remain active in Southern India for some years. But in Bengal something took place that shifted attention to Calcutta. Another decisive period for the English was coming.

In Bengal, the English had neglected the fortifications of Fort William, and had not even bothered to organize a regular militia. They had, presumably because of the Company's victories in the South, become rather arrogant and lordly, and acted as if they were an independent and sovereign power. They attempted to operate in a way rather reminiscent of the Treaty Ports and Settlements in nineteenth- and twentieth-century China, with about as much justification and considerably less success. A contemporary, Captain Rennie, wrote:

> ... the injustice to the Moors [Indians] consists in that, being by their courtesy permitted to live here as merchants, to protect and judge what natives were our servants, and to trade custom-free, we under that pretence protected all the Nabob's [Governor of Bengal] servants that claimed our protection, though they were neither our servants nor our merchants, and gave our dustucks or passes to numbers of natives to trade custom-free, to the great prejudice of the Nabob's revenue; nay, more, we levied large duties upon goods brought into our districts from the very people that permitted us to trade custom-free, and by numbers of impositions (framed to raise the Company's, some of which were ruinous to ourselves)— such as taxes on marriages, provisions transferring land property, etc.—caused eternal clamour and complaints against us at Court.

Their arrogance was to lead them into considerable unpleasantness.

Siraj-ud-Daula, a weak youth who has had to bear the animus of the school-book historian, became ruler in Bengal in 1756.

He was a 'mean ruffian', wrote a modern historian, 'but we need not seek in original sin his reason for attacking the Com-

pany'. He had ample reason to fear the English. The lessons of
the South had not been lost on him, and when he saw the English
and French starting to fortify their settlements, he ordered them
to stop. The French were conciliatory, the English insulting.
The Nawab's answer was to march on Calcutta.

The Fort was taken by the Nawab after it had been deserted
by the Governor and many others. Left in command was Josiah
Holwell, who survived the notorious 'Black Hole' which is so
much a part of the martyrology of British India. The 'Black
Hole' was not the result of an act of policy or a display of meaningless cruelty but of negligence by subordinates; it was, however,
of inestimable value as a portable nightmare until the Mutiny
took its place.

When the news reached Madras, an expedition was fitted out
under the joint command of Clive and Admiral Watson. Calcutta
was captured without great difficulty in January 1757, and there
then followed a period of conspiracy and intrigue out of which
few of the principal characters emerge unsullied.

The Nawab was surrounded by a web of deceit and treachery,
and behind it were the English. They finally decided to replace
the Nawab by his General, Mir Jafar, and after the French had
been neutralized by the capture of their settlement at Chandana-
gore, fought the renowned but rather paltry Battle of Plassey on
the 23rd June 1757. This 'battle' consisted of two parts, an
artillery display in the morning, followed by severe monsoon
rain which put out of commission most of the Nawab's ammunition; then an attack by Major Kilpatrick which was foolhardy
and precipitate, but extremely successful. Clive's forces consisted
of eight hundred Europeans and two thousand native troops,
the Nawab's of some fifty thousand men. Casualties were ridi-
culous: twenty-three killed on the side of the English; about
five hundred on the Nawab's.

All the conspirators did rather well out of the Revolution in
Bengal.

The Company became *zemindar* (land-owner) of the twenty-four
Parganas, 880 square miles, mostly south of Calcutta, with rents
estimated at £150,000 (in practice they proved much less). Clive
received £234,000. This was the occasion when, in retrospect, he
was astonished by his moderation; but Clive was very easily
astonished in this regard. His conviction that whatever personal

3—T.N.H.

advantage he collected was somehow different from, and altogether holier than, gain seized by smaller men, was not quite sane in its cold firmness. Watts received £80,000, Walsh, £50,000, Scrafton, £20,000. Clive thought that altogether the Company and private persons netted three millions sterling. To engineer a revolution had been revealed as the most paying game in the world. A gold-lust unequalled since the hysteria that took hold of the Spaniards of Cortes' and Pizarro's age filled the English mind. Bengal in particular was not to know peace again until it had been bled white.

In the South, the French had again risen to contest the onward march of the English. Under the generalship of Lally, a brave attempt was made to seize the initiative, but after his defeat at Wandiwash the French finally dropped from the race, though intrigue and conspiracy continued, through agents and mercenaries at the courts of Indian princes.

In February 1760, Clive went back to England.

The position of the English after Clive's departure can best be described in the words of P. E. Roberts in his *History of British India*:

> A little body of Englishmen engaged in commercial pursuits had, within a few years, been raised from the control of a single town and some up-country stations to a real, though as yet unacknowledged, authority throughout a wide province. Theirs was the power of the sword that upheld the native rulers whose sway was acknowledged throughout Bengal, Bihar, and Orissa. This man, their tool and nominee, was himself in theory the deputy of the Mogul Emperor. The divorce of the *de facto* power from the *de jure* sovereignty was at this time the political fashion throughout India. . . . These political shams inevitably had a demoralising effect upon the trend of British policy. . . . For the British in Bengal to have accepted the native political claims at their face-value would have meant that the burden of the administration and of warlike operations would have fallen on their shoulders, while the profits of power would have been paid into the exchequer of worthless and helpless native rulers. The practice generally adopted by the British was to concede the native political claims as far as possible, at the same time taking care that their own services should not go unrewarded.

In Bengal, profitable 'revolutions' continued, three changes of ruler taking place during Clive's absence in England. During this period, one of the genuinely decisive battles in the history of

British-India took place at Buxar. In this battle, which was bloody and determined, were defeated the Mogul Emperor and his Prime Minister, and because of it the time was almost ripe for the East India Company to become, as one writer puts it, 'the most formidable commercial republic known in the world since the demolition of Carthage'. The battle at Buxar was the foundation-stone of the British-Indian Empire.

In 1765, Clive returned to Bengal for his second period of administration, and during it the first sovereign act of the Company took place. It 'stood forth as *diwani*', i.e., as the collector and administrator of the revenues of the province. This was an appointment granted by that dim figure, the Mogul Emperor, now practically a pensioner of the Company. Though the *diwani* meant that the entire civil administration was in the hands of the Company, Clive did not choose to exercise it directly. This was Clive's Dual System. Behind the façade of continuing native forms and administration, the Company exercised genuine authority without appearing to do so, and perhaps frightening others. Clive's political views were contained in a document dated 16th January 1767.

The first point of Politics which I offer to your consideration is the Form of Government. We are sensible that since the Acquisition of the Dewanni, the Power formerly belonging to the Soubah of these provinces is Totally, in Fact, vested in the East India Company. Nothing remains to him but the Name and Shadow of Authority. This Name, however, this Shadow, it is indispensably necessary we should seem to venerate; every Mark of Distinction and Respect must be shown him, and he himself encouraged to show his Resentment upon the least want of Respect from other Nations. Under the sanction of a Soubah, every encroachment that may be attempted by Foreign Powers can effectively be crushed without any apparent interposition of our own Authority; and all real grievances complained of then can, through the same channel be examined into and redressed. Be it therefore always remembered that there is a Soubah, that we have allotted him a Stipend, which must be regularly paid, in supporting his Dignity, and that though the Revenues belong to the Company, the territorial Jurisdiction must rest with the Chiefs of the Country, acting under him and this Presidency in Conjunction.

Behind this cloak, Clive rearranged the territory ostensibly ruled by his puppets, and overnight developed, as the product of

some immaculate conception, an attitude of high moral indigna-
tion. Calcutta became 'one of the most wicked places in the
Universe', and the Company's servants, 'beasts of prey'. He tried
to put down private trade by establishing a monopoly in salt to
the advantage of senior civil and military officers. He was only
successful in ensuring that the profits went to the right people.
'My grand object ... is that none under the rank of field officers
should have money to throw away!' In 1767, he returned to
England.

Much has been made of the character of Clive. His administration was rascally and immoral by standards imposed on him by
the Victorian coiners of 'improving' proverbs and 'moral' tales.
Some of his actions were bad by any standards, even those of his
own times. But empires are not constructed with kid-gloves, nor
made to the measurements of moral laws. When Clive had ended
his career, the East India Company found itself with, as Clive
himself pointed out,

> An empire more extensive than any kingdom in Europe, France
> and Russia excepted. They had acquired a revenue of four millions
> sterling, and trade in proportion.

He was an empire-builder without scruples, but he did not
practise dissimulation and deceit by pretending he was otherwise;
and, as Mountstuart Elphinstone wrote: 'In a life spent amid
scenes of blood and suffering, he has never been accused of a
single act of cruelty.' For this alone a great deal can be forgiven.

In 1773, in England, argument had been flowing about the
Company and the Crown. Clive had at one stage suggested that
the Crown should be the government of Bengal. It was first
thought that the Company need only pay a tribute to the Crown,
but disclosures made of the administration of Clive showed that
the Company was insolvent. Two Acts were passed by Parliament, one authorizing a loan to the Company; the other a Regu-
lating Act. This Act established the supremacy of Parliament over
the Company. It was the commencement of the decline of the
Company as a trading power.

The Act, apart from reorganizing the constitution of the Company, called for the appointment of a royal Governor-General.
The first appointment was Warren Hastings, who was to become

for both his own times, and for later historians as controversial a figure as Robert Clive.

The highlights of Hastings' life are well known. Most people have heard of his impeachment by the House of Commons. He was, undoubtedly, one of the greatest men the English ever sent to the East.

Under his administration, the outlines of British-India were formed. He attempted for the first time to establish the concept of a central authority: to introduce a system based not upon the necessity of the moment but on organization and policy. Above all, he was the first to suggest that India was not merely 'the Investment' of shareholders on a remote island off the coast of Europe, but an obligation requiring sympathy and understanding, the essence of good government. In his own age and that of the later Victorians, he has been the subject of much criticism, both vicious and puling. In the twentieth century, the wheel has turned full circle—to adulation.

His experiences with his Council, in which he was in a minority, were, to say the least, difficult and were aggravated by the pettiness and personal spite of one member, Sir Philip Francis, the supposed author of *The Letters of Junius*. Hastings' administrative reforms were carried through like a battle at sea, in a continuous running fight, until the death of a member of Council put him in a majority of one. The most unpleasant act of his administration, and the one which has excited historians and propagandists to the point of combustion, was the execution of Nandakumar, who was hanged for forgery, while investigations were pending of charges, encouraged by Francis and others, which he had made against the Governor-General.

The execution was believed to have been, not for forgery, but for criticism of Hastings. That this was actually a judicial murder cannot be proved. Nandakumar was a casualty in the establishment of Western law and method in India, and in fact the English law, making forgery a capital offence, was not applicable in India until some years after Nandakumar's conviction. It was one of the first examples of the error of imposing Western judicial ideas upon an alien consciousness of right and wrong.

Hastings was not without difficulties outside those of administration. In South India, a French fleet under the command of de Suffren, had fought several engagements with the British, and

France had found a land ally in the Sultan of Mysore: Haidar Ali. This brilliant monster had enlisted as an officer under the Raja of Mysore in 1749, but had usurped the throne in 1761. In 1769, he found himself strong enough to intimidate the English at Madras into making a very favourable treaty with him. In 1778 the Council of Madras drifted into war against him. Haidar Ali descended upon them with an army of ninety thousand men and a hundred guns, burning and pillaging up to the gates of Fort St. George. The Council appealed to Hastings for help after a force under Colonel Baillie sent out against Haidar had been destroyed.

Hastings responded with men, money, and the services of Sir Eyre Coote, who defeated Haidar Ali at Porto Novo. Haidar Ali died in 1782 and was succeeded by his son, Tippu Sultan, who signed a treaty with the British after the French could no longer assist him. Haidar Ali was one of the first to recognize that the essential element in the conquests of the English was that of sea-power. 'The defeats of many Braithwaites and Baillies,' he said, 'will not destroy them. I can ruin their resources by land, but I cannot dry up the sea!'

In Central India, the warlike nations of the Marathas were again on the march, and after adventurous feats of arms and immense travels across hostile territories by small bands of British troops, a peace was signed in 1782 which was to be preserved for the next twenty years.

On the passage of Pitt's India Bill of 1784, Hastings returned to England, there to become the centre of controversy, and to suffer impeachment. Hastings was finally acquitted on every charge.

So the Indian Empire began. Unformed, casual but hardly accidental. Constructed with mixed motives, vitiated by a passionate preoccupation with personal profit. If there was a logic behind it, it was the hero's logic that action is a one-way street; that there is only one direction and that is forward. It was an immense adventure, played out against a background of incredible bizarrerie, like a thriller at Grand Guignol. Life was lived at an immense speed, a race against disease and circumstance. It was not a 'respectable' period, but it was rich and vigorous. Empires are not made in a sterilizer, and the Indian Empire was no exception. From this frequently unpleasant and often dangerous parturition was to emerge an entirely different concept of India which was to remain unbroken until the Mutiny of 1857.

CLEANING THE AUGEAN STABLES

So THE disorganized, the almost casual period of British rule in India, the old days of corruption and nepotism were coming to an end. A new India was in the making and the first sound of it was Pitt's India Bill of 1784.

The Bill set up a Board of Control consisting of allegedly impartial persons of note. A royal Governor-General was now to have the authority to over-rule his Council and the Governors of Madras and Bombay. The Directors were left with only one powerful weapon, that of patronage.

Hastings was succeeded by Sir John Macpherson, whose rule was described by the next Governor-General as 'a system of the dirtiest jobbing'. This criticism is just but mild.

In 1786 Lord Cornwallis, whose reputation had apparently not suffered by his surrender to Washington at Yorktown, was appointed Governor-General. He was a new kind of ruler for India: courteous and incorruptible. Quick, too, to smell corruption, he was decisive in suppressing it at every level. He suffered from two centres of organized corruption. 'The Augean stables of Benares and Lucknow', as he described them in a letter of 1786. In Benares the Resident, 'although not regularly vested with any power, enjoyed the almost absolute government of the country without control' and his income from dishonest practices was some four hundred times his official income.

Cornwallis soon set himself to the task of cleaning the stables. Under his rule, the Civil Service was divided into the executive and judicial branches, and salaries were increased, making private trading unnecessary in theory, though in practice various devices were used to perpetuate it. 'I am sorry to say,' wrote Cornwallis, 'that I have every reason to believe that at present almost all the collectors are, under the name of some relation or friend, deeply engaged in commerce, and by their influence as collectors and judges of Adalat become the most dangerous enemies of the Company's interest.'

Cornwallis's name will always be associated in the history of

British India with what is known as the Permanent Settlement. This was a revenue act much needed but misguided. Its intention was to fix the amount of land-tax to be paid. This had previously been arbitrary, assessments being made on the principle of maximum squeeze. It broke up the whole Indian concept of land-rights by guaranteeing freeholds. It has been the subject of much controversy, and acres of learned dissertation. The effects (both of the Settlement and of the criticism) are still being felt.

Though Pitt's India Act aimed at discouraging the expansion of British India, Cornwallis was forced by the anarchy of the native states by which he was surrounded, and by military adventurers as legally respectable as himself, to go to war.

Cornwallis, on his retirement in 1793, was succeeded after an interregnum by Lord Wellesley, who brought with him his brother Arthur, later Duke of Wellington. With the Napoleonic Wars, French agents were active at native courts. Tippu Sultan, who still reigned in Mysore, had been hailed in France as 'Citizen' Tippu, and when the news came of Bonaparte's landing in Egypt, Wellesley declared war on Tippu. In 1798 the fortress of Seringapatam was captured and Tippu killed. The *Pax Britannica* spread a little further.

The Marathas, still a power in Central India, were divided amongst themselves. They were defeated in two battles by Arthur Wellesley, and Delhi was occupied by Lake, another competent general whom Wellesley was fortunate to have with him. The harsh interpretations of the peace treaty by Wellesley forced another Maratha chief to revolt, and he defeated the British at Bharatpur.

Wellesley was ambitious. He wished, openly, to extend British dominion in India. But his very ambitions were his undoing. The Directors of the East India Company deemed annexation bad for trade, and he was recalled in 1805, to be succeeded by Lord Cornwallis, whose second administration was terminated a few months later by death. Cornwallis's second term of office was a failure, but his epitaph is in the words of that great administrator Sir John Malcolm:

> However questionable the policy of some of the last acts of this nobleman may be to many, or whatever may be their speculations upon the causes which produced such an apparent deviation from the high and unyielding spirit of his former administration, no man

can doubt the exalted purity of the motive that led him to revisit that country. Loaded with years, as he was with honour, he desired that his life should terminate as it had commenced; and he died as he had lived in the active service of his country.

In 1806, a mutiny broke out amongst the sepoys at a town called Vellore in the Madras presidency. Regulations had been introduced forbidding caste-marks, and introducing a special type of turban. These were judged by the sepoys to be an attack on their religion. Sir Thomas Munro, writing to the Governor of Madras, said: 'However strange it may appear to Europeans, I know that the general opinion of the most intelligent natives in this part of the country is that it was intended to make the sepoys Christians.' These senseless regulations were the shadow of the causes of the great mutiny of 1857. The mutiny at Vellore followed, on a smaller scale, the pattern of the later and more terrible outbreak. The mutiny was suppressed and followed by executions. The regulations were made without intent, and demonstrate only a criminal lack of understanding of native prejudices, which were to become more and more irrelevant to the rulers as administrative techniques were perfected and the British became conscious of their 'mission' in India.

Under the Governor-Generalship of Lord Minto (1807–13), a significant change came over the administration. He found the Company's possessions, as one writer puts it, ruled by 'a government militarized and still mediæval' and left it with the 'amenities of a civilized administration'. During his period of office, Sir Stamford Raffles occupied Java, and the French were finally disposed of by the taking of the islands of Bourbon and Mauritius. Under Minto, the last great native power in India rose in the Punjab under the leadership of Ranjit Singh, of which more will be heard later.

Minto was not a 'great Pro-consul'; he was without pretence, and was very conscious of the humour of the pomp and ceremony which had come to surround the Governor-General. He wrote in his 'log kept for the benefit of the family-circle at home':

The first night I went to bed at Calcutta, I was followed by four-teen persons in white muslin gowns into the dressing-room. One might have hoped that some of these were ladies, but on finding there were as many turbans and black beards as gowns, I was very desirous that these bearded handmaids should leave me ... which, with some trouble and perseverance I accomplished; and in that one room I enjoy a degree of privacy, but far from perfect. The doors are open, the partitions are open—or transparent—also, and it is the business of a certain number to keep an eye upon me, and see if I want the particular service which each is allowed by his cast to render me. It is the same in bed; a set of these black men sleep and watch all night on the floor of the passage, and an orderly man of the bodyguard mounts guard at the door with sepoys in almost all the rooms, and at all the stair-cases. These give you a regular military salute every time you stir out of your room or go up or down stairs, besides four or five with maces running before you.

The trappings of Empire, the pomp and the splendour, were slowly being assembled.

In Lord Hastings, who became Governor-General in 1813, the British again found a supporter of expansion. His rule saw wars with Nepal, the real value of which was to enrich the Indian Army with Gurkhas. So, too, a vast campaign was launched against the Pindaris, marauding bands of robbers. This led to the third war with the Marathas, as the Pindaris claimed to be in alliance with the great Maratha Chief, Holkar. After two years (1816–18), they were defeated and the whole of Central India came under the control of the British.

In the meanwhile, at home the East India Company's charter had come up for renewal in 1813. The result was the abolition of the Company's trading monopoly, except that with China, but the Company was to remain the ruler of India for another twenty years until the charter again came up for renewal.

Under Hastings' administration flourished some of the greatest men the British had ever exported to India. Men who knew not so much the India which is nothing more than a geographical fiction, but Indians. There was Mountstuart Elphinstone in the Deccan, Colonel Tod in the Rajputana, and Thomas Munro in Madras. These men felt a genuine responsibility for those they governed. Munro, in a letter of 1821, expressed views that were not uncommon at the time, and represent one contribution to the paradox of British imperialism.

Our present system of government, by excluding all natives from power, and trust, and emolument, is much more efficacious in depressing than all our law and school-books can do in elevating their character. We are working against our own designs and we can expect no progress while we work with a feeble instrument to improve, and a powerful one to deteriorate. The improvement of the character of a people, and the keeping of them, at the same time, in the lowest state of dependence on foreign rulers, to which they can be reduced by conquest, are matters quite incompatible with each other. There can be no hope of any great zeal for improvement when the highest acquirements can lead to nothing beyond some petty office, and can confer neither wealth nor office.

But these sentiments were commendable rather than immediately practicable, for the many things wrong with Indian manners and morals needed the hand and ruthlessness of an alien autocrat to correct them.

Hastings commenced many of the reforms that have come to be associated with other and later names. He established the earliest vernacular schools near Calcutta. Canals and other public works were started, and legal measures to protect the peasant from the landlord were enacted.

Hastings was followed by Lord Amherst, the first war against Burma, and another mutiny, this time at Barrackpore, near Calcutta. The native soldiers feared to lose caste by crossing the Bay of Bengal. They also had a sound financial grievance. It was another rehearsal for the great Mutiny of 1857.

THE GREAT INDIAN LOTTERY

So MUCH for the political climate, the great names, and the calendars of events. History is not merely the sum of battles and legislation. What of flesh and blood?

Someone had described life in India in the eighteenth century as a lottery which paid off in Life. Simply in winning back to England preferably with the price of a rotten borough in the pocket and not too much fever in the blood. But the risks were high. From disease and from their mode of living, many found in an early grave a 'blank in the great Indian lottery'.

Much has been written about life in India during the period we are observing. Memoirs, letters, diaries, even Parliamentary Reports give some feeling of the closed room of English society in India. But for our excursion behind the screens we will not follow the carefully calculated footsteps of the memoir-writers and special pleaders but, and this is the time for the academic historians to lock themselves in the muniment room, we will use —a novel!

There is always a conscious mystique of memoir-writing, especially about an Empire—the flag is continually at the top of the flagstaff. Even the letter to Mother is a censored thing. But the 'let's pretend' of fiction is an adequate alibi and in many of the novels of 'Anglo-India', Truth, not too heavily disguised as Fiction, is there for the taking.

One of the liveliest descriptions of a young man's life in India in the eighteen-thirties can be found in *Peregrine Pultuney* or *Life in India*, published anonymously in 1844. Its author was John William Kaye, later to become a hagiographer of Indian heroes and historian of the Mutiny of 1857.

The story is simple. The author, like many another, hangs his tale on the adventures of the innocent eye. Peregrine Pultuney, our hero, is to go out to India. His background is that middle-class which made the Empire and sustains it.

Mr. Pultuney Senior, it seems, is a younger brother and Peregrine, a younger son. And this is seemly as the pages of British-India are a sort of dynastic history of the younger son. Peregrine, like many a real boy must be provided for and an appointment in India is the inevitable answer.

Peregrine is just fourteen years of age but India is a young man's country and, of course, he is not to set out right away. A year more at school and then to Addiscombe, the East India Company's military establishment. But first patronage must be invoked.

'Mr. Pultuney went up to London, called on his friend the director, stated his wish, which was instantly complied with, and dined with the "tea-dealer" in the evening. A cadetship was promised, with a nomination to Addiscombe at the commencement of the ensuing term, and Mr. Pultuney was exhorted to prepare his son in vulgar and decimal fractions, and Caesar; such being the full extent of the ordeal, these embryo soldiers have to pass—yet, incredible as it may appear, a vast number of aspiring heroes are "remanded for future examination" as the police reports say, every year!'

So Peregrine becomes a cadet.

Life at Addiscombe permits Peregrine to indulge in the manly virtues: to stand up for the weak, to take a little discipline and to make a friend who will act as a foil for his explanatory character. He has his necessary tussles with rather stupid authority, indulges in the customary criminalities of public school life and receives his punishments.

'Yet, in spite of all this, Peregrine Pultuney got through Addiscombe in a creditable manner. He had very few extra drills, he was the best fugleman, the best cricketer, the best classic in the seminary, and popular opinion went far enough to say that he was the best fellow to boot. No one, from the lieutenant-governor down to the small abortion of a boy who played on a thing called a triangle disliked him, and finally he gained three or four prizes, and a commission in the Artillery of Bengal.'

But before Peregrine can get to India much is to be done. He has to be sworn at India House.

'He was marched into a room, where some half dozen old gentlemen were sitting at a long table and looking as solemn and dignified as such people can possibly be. There a book was put in his hand, and he was told to repeat a few sentences beginning

with "I, Peregrine Pultuney" and ending with something or
other about the East India Company and the articles of war,
having done which he received an exhortation from a little man
with a cream-coloured face to conduct himself like a gentleman
and not kill more natives than he can help.'

There are letters of introduction to be obtained, 'Old Indians'
to be seen and asked for their invaluable advice.

Finally, all is ready for the journey to India. A servant, Peer
Khan, is acquired by a little chivalry when he is being baited by
an English crowd in King Street, Covent Garden, and turns out
to be quite indispensable on board the East Indiaman that is to
take them both to Calcutta.

After a journey conveniently long enough to fill up the first
volume, Peregrine's vessel arrives off Calcutta. The journey has
had its usual highlights: flirtations, enmities, amateur theatricals,
and a bully defeated. His companions have been Julian Jenks
and Cadet Doleton who, a poor weak youth, is returning to his
parents in India, and will be used to show the tragedy of separation. But now, after negotiating the tedious stream of Hooghly,
they have arrived.

The friendly young ladies of the voyage are met and disappear
for a while. Cadet Doleton is claimed by his father and Peregrine
and Julian make for Spence's Hotel.

'And thus, having located our hero in Calcutta, it would be
but proper, we think, to describe what sort of a place Calcutta
really is. We have nothing to do with what it ought to be—we
leave all that to the fertile imaginations of panorama-makers and
writers of travels. In these volumes we have confined ourselves
exclusively to the *real*, and intending to do so throughout, we are
afraid that we cannot embellish our picture of Calcutta with any
very gorgeous assemblages of caparisoned elephants and Indian
princes, glittering with jewels and gold. Troops of mounted
Mamelukes, on capering Arabs, with long spears resting on the
toes of their upcurling slippers, we cannot admit into our sketch;
and although there is a great plain in the front of the city, and
plenty of green pasturage, we are sorry to say, that "browsing
camels" with their "tinkling bells" have no legitimate place in
the picture we intend to offer of the City of Palaces, "as it
is".'

Our two friends have settled into their hotel, been astounded

THE GREAT INDIAN LOTTERY 25

at the commonplaces of Anglo-Indian life—hard mattresses, punkahs, and peculiar servants, and signed themselves in at Fort William. They are now ready to tackle Chowringhee, then a street of fine houses, in order to call on Peregrine's aunt, Mrs. Poggleton. After some encounters with ignorant servants without a word of English between them, Peregrine is finally admitted—to the wrong house.

'It was a fine house in one of the best Chowringhee roads (but not in *the* Chowringhee road) that Peregrine Pultuney now found himself entering. Like all Calcutta houses in the rains, it had a somewhat desolate aspect of uninhabited grandeur; for the walls and the pillars were black and weather-stained, large patches of green damp were visible about the base, and down the sides of the house you might trace the course of the water, that had been, almost incessantly for the last two months, streaming down from the conduits on the roof. The house, too, was shut up; between the pillars of the spacious verandah (a distinguishing mark, by the way, of a good Indian residence), large green blinds, made of thin pieces of split and painted bamboo, were let down to exclude the glare.'

After being ushered upstairs, 'Peregrine entered a large drawing-room; they were all open, so as to give free circulation to the little air that might chance to struggle into the house, but, as in a dwelling where there are no passages between the rooms this open system must have its inconveniences, a kind of half-door made of toon-wood and crimson silk, which neither reached nearly to the top nor the bottom of the aperture, had been contrived so as to answer tolerably well for all purposes of concealment; though Peregrine Pultuney did think that he saw something like the feet of a bedstead beneath one of them.

'The prints were principally large mezzotinto ones, from the paintings of Cooper, Marten, and Danby, and with the exception of one from Lawrence's picture of that angel-boy, young Lambton, Peregrine thought that they were all monstrosities, and it is very probable that he was right. Besides the doors and the pictures, which relieved the dead white expanse of the walls, our hero observed every here and there what to him were branch-candle-sticks, bracketted on to the walls, with great large glasses, in shape like large inverted sugar-loaves, to keep the candles, when they were lit, from blowing out; these things which Peregrine afterwards found were called wall-shades, being set off by a number of glass "drops", and a great deal of gold leaf about the bracketts, had a somewhat theatrical effect, and Peregrine thought, wisely enough, that if they were all of them, for he counted about thirty sugar-loaf glasses, set alight at the same time, the quantum of caloric they would produce, on a moderate calculation, would be equal to that of an ordinary-sized kitchen fire on the day that a young marquis comes of age.'

Peregrine completes his survey of the room by sitting down on a sofa, 'and thinking to beguile the time that might happen to intervene before his respectable aunt made her appearance, he took from off the mahogany table a magazine-looking book, which upon observation he discovered to be a number of the *Calcutta Christian Observer*—a discovery which would have given him a very favourable impression of the religious character of the lady of the house, if, most unfortunately, the volume, though nearly a month old, did not bear most unequivocal symptoms of having been unread, which symptoms were none other than the staggering fact, that the leaves of the book were *uncut*.'

In the meanwhile Julian Jenks had discovered that his bankers, Messrs. Cutanrun, have failed, and his letter of credit, consequently, valueless. Undismayed he visits Fort William and hears of a dying friend who will give the author the opportunity of describing his rooms and reflecting on the cheapness of life in India.

'The room was of the same dimensions and quite as uncomfortable as that they had just quitted. Indeed, its aspect was still more wretched, for it was dirtier and more disordered, and in one corner of the room was a heap of dirty linen, the chief part of which was stained and stiffened with blood. On the table were two or three bottles of physic, a pill-box, and a number of blue powder-papers, a wine-glass with the remains of a draft at the bottom and clinging to the sides, a few scraps of lime, a tea-spoon, which looked as though it had held a powder, and lastly a plate full of salt and blood, in which evidently a dozen leeches or so had lately been disgorging the sanguinary meal they had made. Besides these paraphernalia, which adorned the table, there were a number of sodawater bottles, some full and some empty, in the corner of the room opposite the linen, and scattered about the floor were several large locks of beautiful soft yellow hair, which you might have taken for a woman's, so fine and luxuriant did they look.

'Beneath a punkah, which a bearer more than nine-tenths asleep was drowsily pretending to pull, was just such a camp-bed as Julian Jenks had seen in Mr. Phillimore's quarter, and on this bed, which was surely never designed for an invalid, lay the unfortunate, fever-stricken patient, his head shaven close to the scalp, his left arm bandaged and blood-stained, and his brows bearing evident symptoms of having lately worn a garland of leeches. Tossing about restlessly, as though seeking in vain for an easy position, and groaning like a person with a weight upon his chest, he presented to Julian Jenks and Mr. Phillimore, as they entered, an aspect to the last degree pitiable; and Julian felt his heart sink within him, as he contemplated the pale sunken cheeks, the emaciated limbs, and the distorted features of one who a few months before he had seen in all the fulness of youth and health and boundless animal spirits, with a face and figure that might have served as a model for the painter or the sculptor, who would body forth a Ganymede or an Antinous.'

Peregrine, still in the wrong house but met by some chance with his aunt, is fortunately there at the opportune moment. A circular, send by the undertaker, announces the death of a certain Mr. Collingwood.

'Mr. Collingwood,' returned Mrs. Parkinson; 'it really is quite shocking; he dined with us the day before yesterday— cholera, I suppose—dreadful!' and Mrs. Parkinson endeavoured to look quite overcome, but was not particularly successful.

But Mrs. Poggleton pretended nothing at all: she leant forward, held out her hand for the undertaker's circular, looked rather pleased than otherwise, and said, 'Dear me! if it is not the gentleman with that pretty carriage, I declare!'

'Small use to him a pretty carriage now,' said Mrs. Parkinson, 'the only carriage that he needs is a hearse.'

'Oh! but,' exclaimed Mrs. Poggleton, with more eagerness than she had manifested throughout the conversation, 'I have been dying a long time for that carriage, and now I shall be able to get it. What a nice thing to be sure!'

Upon this Mrs. Parkinson lifted up her hands, and pretended to be immeasurably shocked, muttering to herself, but quite loud enough for everybody to hear, that life was a span, and death hanging over us, and that the world might be destroyed tomorrow, for anything she knew to the contrary, with sundry other moral reflections of this kind, equally original, and expressive of virtuous emotion.

Immediately, the contrast is pointed. The author is no longer satirist but moralist. Peregrine hurrying to his dying friend moves from the flippancy and heartlessness of the drawing-room to the tragic pathos of the ill-fitted room at the barracks, of the young dying young with nobody caring unless the dead man is important enough for someone to covet his appointment.

In the closed society of the British in Calcutta, women domi-nated its little world with their boredoms. They had nothing to occupy their hands with but a little embroidery and less to occupy their minds. An aristocratic society is a letter-writing society, a community of gossips and scandal-mongers, it invents slanders and circulates them, watching them as they grow and change, produce their enmities and burst into flame.

Julia Poggleton, Peregrine's cousin, in answer to the question about what she thought of Calcutta society, replies:

'I don't quite know what to tell you. It is not to my taste certainly, but then to be sure, I am no judge. I saw a little of English society before I came out, quite enough to perceive the contrast.'

'Then you *are* a judge,' interrupted Peregrine.

'Oh! no; I don't profess to be that—you are welcome to my opinions, though they are not worth very much. They are a strange set of people here, and do nothing all the day but write chits and abuse one another.'

'Why; that they do in all places,' said Peregrine.

'What?—abuse one another—so they do; but of all places that I ever visited Calcutta is the most scandalous. In other parts of the world they talk about things, here they talk about people. The conversation is all personal, and, as such, you may be sure tolerably abusive.'

'But what,' asked Peregrine, 'do the people find to say about one another?'

'Oh!' returned Miss Poggleton; 'the veriest trifles in the world. Nothing is so insignificant as the staple of Calcutta conversation. What Mr. This said to Miss That, and what Miss That did to Mr. This; and then all the interminable gossip about marriages and no-marriages, and will-be marriages and ought-to-be marriages, and gentlemen's attention and ladies' flirtings, dress, reunions, and the last *burra-Khana*——'

'Pictures, taste, Shakespeare, and the musical glasses,' suggested Peregrine, with a smile.

'Oh! dear no, nothing half as good as that,' returned Julia Poggleton; 'the only Shakespeare known in Calcutta is a high civilian of that name—a *Sudder* judge, or something of that sort. As for "taste" I'm afraid there is none in Calcutta, and the only pictures we know anything about are annual prints and our own portraits, which we sometimes send to Europe to show our friends what kind of an animal an old Indian is. I say "we" for I think myself one of the genus, having been born and partly bred here. I feel myself thoroughly *qui hi*, and am getting as bad as the worst of them.'

If chit writing is the private occupation of women, the 'big-dinner' is the ritual of the outer life.

'You cannot conceive how tired one gets of the hams, and turkeys, and limp jellies. A turkey and a ham are as necessary to a Calcutta dinner as a table-cloth and chairs; and such a profusion too always!—a very hetacomb under a punkah—every thing too *so* cold.'

'Cold!' exclaimed Peregrine; 'that is a fault I should scarcely have expected to hear mentioned.'

'Oh! but I am right I assure you. It may seem strange, but though a dinner party is a very hot thing, the dinner is sure to be cold. In the first place the kitchens, or cook-rooms as we call them here, are often a long way from the house—at the further end of the compound—and then if the passage through the open air does not cool the dishes thoroughly, the air from the punkah does.

'There is no theatre, no opera to talk about; not that I admire such subjects as these, but they are fifty times better than Indian subjects. I was asked two or three hundred times at least during my first fortnight, "how I like India". I was so tired of answering that I was "scarcely qualified to form an opinion". I would have given the world for a fresh answer. And then we young ladies, to say the least of it, are in a very disagreeable situation here—our position is constrained and artificial—I dare say you know what I mean. It is the vulgar opinion that every unmarried female in

India has but one wish burning in her heart, the wish to make a good marriage; and we can scarcely move, speak, or act, according to the natural impulses of our hearts, for fear it should be said of us that we are laying traps, or making overtures, or something of this kind. And the consequence is, I can assure you, distressing in the extreme.'

But this is the life of the upper-crust. Society in India was not a solidarity of white-skins but a hierarchy. The Civil and Military Lists were its Debrett and Burke. Society was a series of rooms, entered by promotion, each carefully sealed against the outsider. At the centre were the Civilians, well-paid and important. On the outer fringes, the lesser Military.

Peregrine and Julian have been posted to Dum-Dum, some distance from Calcutta and there, through the mouth of Lieutenant Clay, the Army will be given its chance to complain.

'When you have been here—I mean India—a little time, you will be very unpleasantly made sensible of the fact, that our honourable master, the Company, pay their different servants after a very different fashion indeed; and that their worst paid servants of all are those who are called upon occasionally to "come and be killed", like Mrs. Bond's dillies. They get men cheap enough to stand up and be shot; but they pay a good price for their quill-drivers. Captain Sword fares but poorly, whilst Captain Pen lives in clover.'

The financial ill-treatment of those who stayed with their regiments drove the younger men into civil employment. Promotion in the Company's army was slow. A death higher up the scale or a retirement through ill-health and not merit were the means. Because of a flight of talent to the civil administration the Indian Army weakened until its aged commanders and its undermanned regiments were to be caught and shattered by the wind of the 'Mutiny'.

Peregrine Pultuney shows something of the hates and the trivialities and the unsung tragedies of 'Anglo-Indian' life. They all have their place in the pattern of British rule in India in the nineteenth century. Calcutta society was only the society of the up-country Station writ large. In going out to the District, the English took their England with them but it was the false England of Calcutta. Each Station was a little world insulated as best it could from the great black sea of India. The trivialities of life were a refuge, the elevation of the ephemeral a sort of reflex to the fragility of more noble things. Because there was no stability in life, nothing must be of eternal importance. Because life itself was brittle, a sort of card-game, men must laugh at the things that were not funny in case they should spend their time in tears for the things that were sad and hateful. Like the pre-revolutionary aristocracy in France, 'Anglo-Indian' society cut itself away from the surrounding world and fortified itself with a sense of its own superiority and the strength of its laughter.

But it is the false laughter of the frightened man in the dark of a haunted house. The dead were hurried to the grave not only for sanitary reasons but to abolish memory the easier—to pretend they had never really been there.

'The great world is full of changes,' writes the author of *Peregrine Pultuney*, 'but the Calcutta world is far more changeable than any of the lesser ones it contains in its vast cycle. Society, in these parts, is a sort of ever-moving procession, and the same characters are seldom to be seen upon the stage many months together. If our work has been somewhat desultory this must be our excuse—Life in India is always desultory.'

There emerges from the sly humour of *Peregrine Pultuney* a picture of the real life of the British in India. We are able to grasp the pettiness, insecurity, stupidity, and quiet heroism that they practised and felt. The Empire was constructed out of individual sacrifice, not the incandescent sacrifice of the battlefield, nor the conscious hand-on-heart, all-for-England sacrifice of the comfortable propagandists back Home, but the commonplace, almost casual acceptance of discomfort, boredom, and death. It is easy, almost inevitable, to dislike the great-names of British India, to be revolted at their cruelties, their indifference, and their shallow minds. But for those unknowns who really made the Empire, the soldiers, the clerks, and the women who lived and died and were forgotten, it is possible only to feel pity. They were no Empire-builders heavy with plans for expanding frontiers, but wishing only to stay within the confines of the little Englands they brought with them. Their arrogance was actually fear and their preoccupation with precedence only the ordering of a closed society in which a sense of one's place seemed to give stability to the flux of life.

'Anglo-Indian' society, based upon so little of value, pleasure-seeking, superficial and deadly dull, cannot be dismissed as irrelevant to the history of British India. If the influence of its emptiness can be overstated, it cannot be dismissed, for out of the social formalities of 'Anglo-India' emerged the shibboleths of 'official' thought and action if not upon the highest planes of policy at least at the levels of administrative immediacy. However close the more enlightened men came to recognizing the sources of Indian behaviour they were never committed to accepting them.

They were always drawn as by some centripetal force to the empty centre of 'Anglo-Indian' society and hurried back from the real world of the District to the sham of Calcutta or some other station. The arbiters of this society were the women. Life in Calcutta and elsewhere revolved around them, they made its laws and supervised their enforcement by a variety of blackmail. Consideration for their tender feelings may have influenced the reforms in Hindu religious practice more than the ideas of Wilberforce, and their boredoms produced the quick hates and shallow judgements which influenced their men-folk.

We can now see some of the picture, but to complete it we must know a little about the Indians themselves, and their relations with Europeans, for we cannot hope to understand the tensions that produced the Indian Mutiny without knowing their source.

VULGAR, IGNORANT, RUDE, FAMILIAR AND STUPID

WHEN the English in India were feeling their way to dominion and power, contact with Indians was a necessary part of their life. It takes two sides to make a bargain, and the English were primarily traders. Intercourse between European and native was unselfconscious, even to manner of dress. The English wore a variety of native clothes, loose coats and 'Moormen's' trousers. But with growing power and increasing numbers the Englishman acquired a patriotic contempt for an 'inferior' civilization and abandoned its mannerisms, though retaining, incidentally, the ubiquitous pyjama.

The great men of the Golden Age of the late eighteenth century had more than a passing interest in the language and literature of those they ruled. Hastings, William Jones, the translator from Sanskrit, and many others through their tastes made close friendships with Princes who were also scholars.

But a new generation brought with it the arrogance of power. Cornwallis and his attitude to Indian officials was merely a symptom. Wellesley, that posturing empire-builder, summed an attitude in a phrase, Indians were 'vulgar, ignorant, rude, familiar and stupid'.

Yet, digging deeper, we find the source of this attitude in fear. The increasing number of women in the European settlements brought with them the materials of a closed society—totems and taboos. The zenanas and their 'sleeping dictionaries' disappeared. Surrounded by the black sea of India the English turned away in panic to the careful ordering of position and preferment. The Indians threatened their security in an irrational and frightening way. It was best to keep away from them. This sense of siege is the explanation of much of the wilful cruelty of the Mutiny.

One anonymous contemporary has described the attitude of the new administrators.

> Every youth who is able to maintain a wife, marries. The conjugal pair become a bundle of English prejudices and hate the

country, the natives and everything belonging to them. If the man has, by chance, a share of philosophy and reflection, the woman is sure to have none. The 'odious blacks', the 'nasty heathen wretches', the 'filthy creatures' are the shrill echoes of the 'black brutes', the 'black vermin' of the husband. . . . Not that the English generally behave with cruelty, but they make no scruple of expressing their anger and contempt by the most opprobrious epithets that the language affords.

India settled to a period of racial segregation which was never entirely destroyed.

Lord William Bentinck who became Governor-General in 1828 attempted to break this dangerous estrangement of the races, but this was only a passing improvement for the administration of India was soon to fall from the 'saddle-rulers', men who moved amongst the governed in preference to the hot-house of the council chamber. The ideologue was turning the corner and soon would be recognized as—Thomas Babington Macaulay.

With him the belief in a better civilization, religion, and culture took on a legal structure. But Macaulay's Minute on Education was not merely a symbol of racial prejudice, for he saw in the use of English as a medium of education an instrument of rule. 'It is impossible,' he wrote, 'for us with our limited means, to educate the body of the people. We must do our best to form a class who may be interpreters between us and the millions whom we govern; a class of persons, Indian in blood and colour, but English in taste, in opinions, in morals and in intellect.' And though he went on to add that these middle-men would carry the boons of Western science and know-how to the ignorant peasantry, his action was to place yet another fortification between the English and the Indians.

The old free and easy life of the English in India was almost over. The dry-wind of conscious imperialism parched the field of mutual respect into a desert. But some still created little oases of friendliness and tolerance. One was Henry Lawrence.

But we must answer Private Mulvaney's question: The English came to trade and stayed to rule. What that rule was like it is the purpose of this book to answer. But first we must meet two of our actors. It is time for John and Henry Lawrence to make their appearance.

II

THE PLANTING OF
THE TREES

Plant trees but don't let them touch
Punjabi Proverb

CATHERINE, STAND ASIDE!

BEFORE we can allow the Lawrences to explain the India they lived in to us, we must know something of their background and childhood. Without doubt the Child is Father to the Man, none will cavil at that, but the number of times a child wetted the bed, and the rest of some biographers' 'explanations' of later action, will find no place here.

It can be said of the British-Indian Empire that it was conquered by the Irish and Scots, ruled by the English and destroyed by the Labour Party, an explanation good enough for any cocktail party or the hustings. But the position of the Northern Protestant Irish in the establishment of the Empire is interesting and unique. The father of John and Henry Lawrence came from that tradition and stock and his story is not without the pathos and rather tarnished glory of so many of those who painted the map red with their own blood.

Alexander Lawrence spent some twenty-five years in India, mainly in the south against Mysore, and in Ceylon, distinguishing himself in the final attack on Seringapatam in 1799, the story of which he wrote himself in memorials to the Duke of York and the East India Company's Directors.

> On the 4th of May he was the senior subaltern of four who volunteered the command of the covering parties for the Forlorn Hopes. The other three officers were killed. He received a severe wound in the right hand. Just at that moment his party was brought up on the top of the glacis where Sergeant Graham's storming party had formed and commenced a fire (instead of carrying on). He ran from right to left hurrahing to them to move on, but at last was obliged to run through the files to the front, calling out 'Now is the time for the breach.' This had the desired effect. At the foot of the breach he received a ball in his left arm where it still remains. He did not then give it up, until he saw the few remaining men gain the breach, then fainting from the loss of blood he was removed to a less exposed place.

This episode was soon followed by a shipwreck off the coast near Cannanore.

Alexander Lawrence in 1798 had married Letitia Catherine Knox, and six of their twelve children, including Henry in 1806, were born in Ceylon.

The remainder of his life though not so colourful was just as wearing. He became Major in the 19th Foot stationed at Richmond in Yorkshire; Lieutenant-Colonel of the 4th Garrison Battalion in 1812 serving in Guernsey and Ostend. In the year of Waterloo he almost perished from a bursting abscess of the liver in the midst of a gale on his way to Ireland. His conduct at the time is the index of his character. Let Herbert Edwardes describe it for us.

> ... on the way back with his regiment to Ireland, in a dreadful gale off Torbay, on 6th January 1816, an abscess burst in his liver, and it was thought he could not survive the night. His naturally hardy constitution, however, still bore him up, and with great difficulty the ship stood in for Dartmouth, and put him on shore. The surgeon had prepared everything for carrying the sick man to the ship's side, but it is still remembered how he refused to be carried, gathered his cloak around him, bade his wife 'Catherine, stand aside!' and grasping his favourite stick 'Sweet-lips' in his hand, marched firmly to the boat.

He was finally promoted to the Governship of Upnor Castle in Kent. There, broken in body and troubled in mind, he petitioned the East India Company for a pension, ending his appeal with these pathetic words:

> To whom can he apply, having no interest, and nothing to produce but wounds and loss of health. His left arm is considerably wasted away by a ball being in it since the siege of Seringapatam, it often giving him excessive pain; his right hand dreadfully mangled; his health so bad as to be always in the doctor's hand.

His appeal was answered and he retired to Cheltenham and finally to Clifton.

His two sons inherited his physical strength and energy and to a certain extent his example, as one was to write:

> I should say that on the whole we derived most of our metal from our father. Both my father and mother possessed much character. She had great administrative qualities. She kept the family together, and brought us all up on very slender means. She kept the purse and managed all domestic matters. My father was a very remarkable man. He had left home at fourteen years of age, and had to struggle

with the world from the beginning to the end. But he possessed great natural powers; ever foremost in the field, and somewhat restless in times of peace. He was a fine, stout, soldier-like-looking fellow, a capital rider, a good sportsman, and an excellent runner. I have heard old military men, when I was a boy, say that he was one of the hardiest and best officers they ever met, and that he only wanted the opportunity which rank gives to have done great things. ... I fancy he was rather headstrong and wayward, and though much liked by his equals and inferiors, not disposed to submit readily to imbecility and incompetence in high places. When I was coming out to India, my poor old mother made me a speech somewhat to the following effect: 'I know you don't like advice, so I will not give you much. But pray recollect two things. Don't marry a woman who had not a *good* mother; and don't be too ready to speak your mind. It was the rock on which your father shipwrecked his prospects.'

NOT A CHRISTIAN TO SPEAK TO

HENRY, who was born on 28th June 1806, arrived in England with his father and mother in 1808. At the beginning he and his brothers, Alexander and George, went to their uncle's school in Londonderry. From Foyle's School Henry received little teaching, for though not a Dotheboys the establishment offered 'vigorous training' and no doubt the usual rigours of boarding-school life in the early nineteenth century.

Henry, though hot-tempered, had no love for games and seems to have been somewhat of a prig in the Washington manner, though his first biographer, Herbert Edwardes, naturally ascribes this episode as emerging from 'moral strength'!

The 'Sweetness and gentleness of his disposition is the trait by which this schoolfellow best remembers him; but there is one anecdote of the same days at Foyle treasured up by his eldest sister, which reveals the moral strength which lay beneath. The boys had been breaking windows (their "custom always in the afternoon"), and Henry Lawrence had not joined. At last they enticed him to aim at a mark upon the wall, missing which (as the young rogues expected) he smashed a pane of glass. Without a remark, and doubtless amidst roars of laughter, he left the playground, knocked at the awful "library" door and, presenting himself before his uncle, said, "I have come to say, sir, that I have broken a window!" His sister adds, "I cannot recall his ever telling an untruth." Reader, of how many of us could the same be said, even by a dear sister?'

Henry joined the East India Company's Military College at Addiscombe in 1820 and a fellow pupil has left a revealing description of his life there.

On joining Addiscombe as a cadet on the 2nd of February 1821, I found Henry Lawrence there, and in the third class, having joined the College in the previous term. I was of course in the fourth or junior class, and therefore not in the same study with him at first. In the course of the term, however, Mr. Andrews, the principal of the College, promoted the first six of the fourth class into the third;

and as I was one of the number I found myself in the same study with Lawrence. He was well up in his class at the time, being about the third or fourth from the top, and, though evincing no marked talents, yet he was quick, intelligent, and, on the whole, industrious at his studies. At the end of the term the senior or first class was examined and sent out to India, so that, on our assembling after the vacation, we found ourselves the second class at the College, the second of the previous term having become the first. Several of the cadets of this class had left College, thus leaving it weak in numbers. Dr. Andrews determined therefore to complete it to the full number, as officers were so much wanted for Artillery and Engineers. He accordingly selected the first eight in the second class for examination. Among these eight was Henry Lawrence, who must therefore have stood near the head of the class at the time, and his general conduct must have been good, for this was an indispensable with the Doctor. The cadets of the class we now entered had been at the College a whole term before Lawrence, and therefore had advanced considerably in mathematics, Hindustani, fortification, military drawing especially. Therefore it was not to be wondered at that Lawrence never rose higher than the middle of the class. Even to do this was highly creditable to him, and showed either great application or considerable ability. It was during this term that he acquired a knowledge of military surveying, and no one more thoroughly enjoyed the excursions over the country in carrying on his surveys. I was constantly told of Lawrence's 'spouting Scott', as the boys called it, at such length as almost to weary his companions. He had just had lent him *The Lady of the Lake*, and so charmed was he with it that he possessed himself of whole cantos, and would recite page after page with the utmost enthusiasm.... He was a quiet and thoughtful youth, preferring walking with some companion to joining in the games of cricket, football, hockey, etc., but all of us knew there was no lack of spirit in Pat Lawrence.... He was no doubt very passionate, and anything mean or shabby always roused his ire, and then the curl of his lip and the look of scorn he could put on were the most bitter and intense that I ever witnessed. His heart, too, was very warm, and he was always ready to take the part of the weak, and sometimes got into trouble by doing so. His attachment to his family was remarkable, and thoughtless as boys generally are to any great display of this kind, yet Pat Lawrence was known to us all as a devoted son and brother. His course at Addiscombe was one of steady application and good conduct. I do not remember his ever being sent to the black hole, or getting into any serious scrape. He seemed even then to have organized a course for himself, and was neither to be

coaxed nor driven out of it. I can speak of his being a most generous
rival. We stood next each other in the class for several months, our
numbers being so nearly equal that one month's report would put
him before me, and the next below me, in the class. As rank in
India depends upon the place held by the cadet in the class in the
last month's report before leaving the college, many were anxious,
when we knew that the report was prepared, to see how they stood,
and who was to be senior. One of the cadets volunteered to get into
the window of the Masters' Room where the report book was kept,
and we thus ascertained before it was legitimately made known. I
was told that Lawrence was above me. When I told him this, he said,
with one of his pleasing smiles, 'I am sorry you are disappointed,
and would just as soon you had been first.' He passed a creditable
examination, but, not standing very high in either mathematics or
fortification, he was not called upon to do much at the public
examination.

So ended Henry Lawrence's 'school-days' in May 1822. Three
months later he sailed for India.

We cannot leave his early life without quoting a significant
passage, for it represents very clearly two fundamental characteristics of Henry, the man. Again the source is Herbert Edwardes.

To what are called 'amusements' in the bigger world of society,
Henry Lawrence was no doubt indifferent even as a boy. Coming
home one night from a ball to which he had gone with Alexander,
George and Letitia he said to his sister, 'What a wretched unprofit-
able evening! Not a Christian to speak to. All the women decked
out with flowers on their heads, and their bodies half-naked.'
Simple, earnest and modest, he shrank even then from frivolity;
and in later years, in India, he never could see English ladies dancing in the presence of native servants or guests, without being
thoroughly wretched.

But was there something deeper and more dangerous than
simplicity, earnestness, and modesty, innocuous qualities however
boring they may be? Was it in reality the matrix of the Puritan,
a forecast of the iron-heart in the Ironside?

Henry Lawrence's first tour in India we must dispose of
briefly, for it is our purpose to see the brothers on stage *together*;
to watch them play out their own tragedy and that of the Indian
Empire.

Henry, arriving in India in February 1823, was posted to the

John Lawrence as Viceroy

Calcutta

Headquarters of the Bengal Cavalry at Dum-Dum a few miles from Calcutta. Two letters addressed to his sister Letitia give some idea of his life there. The first is dated 2nd August 1823:

I had been long looking out for an English letter, when yours of January made its appearance two days ago. You may suppose it put me into a state when I found it had gone up to Benares (600 miles off), to a Lieutenant Henry Lawrence, 19th N.I. . . . Mr. L. opened it, but on finding his mistake, immediately sent it to me with a very polite note, which of course prevented me from challenging him with 18-pounders! . . . Alexander is now behaving nobly, and I highly commend him for offering the overplus of his pay to his parents, who really require it, instead of idly squandering it in vice and folly, as is generally the custom in this part of the world. . . . The proximity of Calcutta is a great incentive to spending money. I know one or two lads who have not been above two years in the country that owe 8,000 or 9,000 rupees. I owe 250, but I hope to be clear of the world in three or four months. . . . I have written by almost every ship to you, mamma, and the rest of the family. I am very glad to hear that papa's health is improved. . . . I am now doing duty in Fort William for one week, and it has been rather a busy one. I have been afraid to move out of the fort, lest Lord Amherst should come up, and I not be ready to receive him. At last he made his appearance on the 1st ultimo, about half-past five in the morning, and passed my battery in the Company's yacht, when I gave him a salute of nineteen guns. In about two hours he landed at a ghaut about half a mile from the fort, under another salute. He then walked up to the Government House, and took his oath, when I gave him another nineteen. Now, ought he not to give me an appointment for receiving him so politely? He is to be proclaimed in garrison to-morrow morning, when I am to give another and final salute, and immediately after I shall be relieved and return to Dum-Dum. . . . I almost despair of the Horse Artillery. By all accounts it is a noble service. . . . It is the rainy season here, and the whole country is one large mass of water. I might almost go to Dum-Dum to-morrow by water. . . . In all the King's regiments, I meet with some officer or officers who have known papa. . . . My poor chum Edwards has been obliged to go to Penang and China for his health, which has been very bad ever since he arrived, but I hope to see him in six months quite brisk. He is a good fellow, and we get on very well. On his departure, I took up my quarters with a lad of the name of Ackers, who has been a couple of years out, and he has been dreadfully ill, and is obliged to go home, and, I am afraid, not to come back. . . . For my part, I feel as well as ever I was in my life, and only require plenty of English letters to make me as happy as I can be at such a distance from my friends. I used foolishly to think it would be very fine to be my own master; but now what would I give to have some kind friend to look after me.

And on 8th October:

I can get so many excellent works at the mess library that I am never in want of a book to read. At present I am *wading* through Gibbon's *Decline and Fall of the Roman Empire*. Books are sometimes to be had in Calcutta for mere nothing. I bought Shakespeare lately for *two rupees*—certainly not so elegant an edition as yours. ...In my last I mentioned my wish to get exchanged into the cavalry, and I also gave you my reasons. If Mr. H(udleston) could do it I shall be infinitely obliged. If you remember, when we were in Monmouthshire he told you to tell me that if I preferred the cavalry he would send an appointment after me to India; which I am sorry I at that time declined, as if even I do get it now, I shall lose many steps. George's regiment goes to Mhow some time this month; I shall take care that your picture, when it arrives, is safely sent up to him. ... Lewin has turned an excellent religious young fellow; indeed, I am quite surprised at the change; his whole care seems to be what good he can do. And of course he is designated a 'Methodist', but I wish we had a few more such *Methodists*. I often think, my darling Lettice, that when I was at home I might have made myself so much more agreeable than I did. Oh, what would I not give to spend a few months at home, was it but to show how much I love you all! Indeed, it quite sickens me when I think that I am here, left entirely to myself, without any kind friend to guide me or tell me what is and what is not right. ... Give my kind regards to Miss Slack, and tell her I shall never forget the delightful week we spent together. People in England may talk of *India* and the *City of Palaces*, but where will we find such scenery as along the banks of the Wye? ...I wish you could take a peep into my bungalow at Dum-Dum. I am as comfortable as an old bachelor of forty. I am in a very friendly neighbourhood (that is, I *believe* I am welcome at all hours at the houses of my married neighbours), but there is still something wanting—*a mamma or a sister*—in fact, a kind friend to whom I could open the recesses of my heart, and whose hopes and wishes would be entirely in unison with my own. ... (Nine o'clock at night.) There is a play here to-night, but, as I did not feel inclined to go, I took tea with Lewin, and am just returned home. It is really wonderful to me the conversation of Lewin, having known him as a wordly-minded lad. His whole thoughts seem *now* to be of what good he can do. I only wish I was like him.

But to counter his loneliness and incidentally to give definition to his 'moral picture' there was—Fairy Hall. This was a large house in which George Craufurd, assistant chaplain of the Old Church in Calcutta, had brought together a group of evangelical officers. 'I met a clergyman,' wrote one of these men, 'of the name of Craufurd who taught me that the paths of sin are unhappiness and misery and that the paths of righteousness are happiness.'

But Henry was rather poor material for these early Oxford Groupists. His religion was unemotional, though serious. His Christianity was of a muscular, practical sort, almost Cromwellian. 'What I want to be assured of,' he said to Craufurd, 'is that this Book is God's: because when I know that, I have nothing left but to obey it.'

Soon the almost meditative gloom was to be broken by the first Burmese War of 1824-6. The Burmese Empire was now on the north-east frontier of Bengal and the King of Burma, grossly unaware of the strength of the East India Company, raided territory under its control. The Governor-General, Lord Amherst, declared war.

It was to be yet another of those terribly successful empire-expanding wars which were won by the Company's forces mainly because of the greater incompetence of the generals on the other side. Fever, bad generalship, and a muddling commissariat did not, however, prevent a Burmese defeat and the annexation of the Arakan.

Henry kept a journal and in it records an episode typical of Indian campaigns in the nineteenth century:

When the bugle sounded to strike the tents the scene was really amusing. We were just going to our mess, so we hastily crammed something down our throats, and returned to our tents to get our troops off the ground. The whole encampment was now one continued blaze; for the servants, as soon as the order is given to march, set fire to all the straw to warm themselves, as well as to serve for a light while packing up. Stray bullocks, frightened by the flames and noise, rushing up and down the camp; soldiers and camp-followers rushing here and there about their several duties, and our own servants yelling to each other, formed a scene I was quite unaccustomed to, and worthy of a more practised pen. We commenced moving about 8 p.m., already fatigued with our day's work, and what with the darkness of the night, the badness of the road, the bullock-drivers falling asleep, and many of them being *unable to see at night*, we were obliged to stop almost every hundred yards, either to get the guns out of a ditch, or to bring up fresh bullocks. In fact, so tedious was this march, that we did not reach the encamping-ground till past three o'clock in the morning, having been seven hours in accomplishing little more than nine miles.

Being obliged to make another march that morning, Lieutenant-Colonel Lindsay, our commanding officer, thought it useless pitching the tents, so the bullocks being unyoked, every man passed his time (on the high-road) as he liked. Some of the men managed to light a fire, others sat on their guns and whiled away the time with conversation. Most of the officers seated themselves under a large tree, and some fell asleep, while others smoked cheroots; but I was so fatigued that I quickly lay down on the road, rolled up in my boat-cloak.

The bullock-drivers taking compassion on me, brought an old greasy cloth for me to lie on, so to improve my situation still more I moved it under a gun, and there lay, getting the benefit of the men's conversation, who were sitting above me, till I fell asleep, but had scarcely dozed half-an-hour before a sergeant called me, saying that the bugle had sounded to march; so we got under weigh again, having *rested* about two hours, which, in my opinion, did us more harm than if we had marched straight on, for many of the poor fellows lay down on the damp ground, under a heavy dew, without any covering. Having less difficulties as soon as we got day-light, we managed to arrive on our ground, at Maha Sing, by ten o'clock. I walked the most of this last march, and, on reaching the encampment, found myself quite sick from fatigue and (I think as much as anything else) from having frequently drank cold water during the night. Fortunately our tents were up a short time before us, so I soon got under cover and into bed, went without my breakfast, and was quite well and hearty by dinner-time.

And later a final comment which though slightly nauseating to us shows that combination of arrogance and humanity which was as much a part of the Indian Empire as it was of those like Henry Lawrence who made it so.

Imagine from the chain of masonry works of very ancient date that this has been a connected line of hill forts. . . . On the first *rear* hill was a very ancient pagoda, entirely in ruins, and from it, to the rear, was the most beautiful prospect I had ever seen; and Greene and I sat nearly half-an-hour, admiring the noble works of nature and man around us. To our left were most romantic hills with verdant plains, intersected with lakes, in several of which were little islands with a few huts on them; and close on the right we had a full view of Arracan emerging from behind the range of fortified hills on which we stood. Never did it appear to so much advantage, for here we had a full view of all its beauties, its numberless pagodas, its peculiar houses, and the river running through the town, without being offended by its unwholesome odour. This town, we thought, had but one short month ago been thronged with numerous inhabitants. Now what a difference! Desolation! Not a native to be seen. None but a hired soldiery and a set of rapacious camp-followers. But they deserved it, for they are a barbarous race. Our camp from these hills seemed a mere nothing, and the Burmahs, no doubt, thought so too, and looked on us as a mere handful given over to destruction. Oh! I shall never forget their shouts and their horrid yells of defiance on the 29th. They went to my heart then, and I think I still hear them. . . . On coming back through the pass, we saw a poor Light Infantry Sepoy (a Brahmin) heaping up the dry wood over what we took for a grave. On being asked, he said it was his brother. I felt for him.

The 'Arracan fever' (a particularly virulent malaria) and other diseases claimed the real victory, for in five months alone 259 Europeans out of 1,500 and 900 out of 1,000 Indians died and in the month of September 1825, 400 Europeans and 3,600 Indians were in hospital. In November Henry Lawrence was also attacked and left for Calcutta to recuperate, but though he returned to the Arakan he was ordered home on sick-leave and sailed on 6th August 1826.

A SOLDIER I WAS BORN AND A SOLDIER
I WILL BE!

BUT what of John Lawrence? John Laird Mair Lawrence was born at Richmond, Yorkshire, on 4th March 1811. In 1819 when his elder brothers left Foyle College he spent a short time at school in Bristol with brother Henry. The school at College Green seems to have sat firmly in the 'hot-bottom' tradition of its type, for when, as Lord Lawrence, John was asked if the birch was used often at his school, he replied: 'I was flogged every day of my life at school except one, and then I was flogged twice.' In 1823 he left for the milder regimen of Foyle College.

1825 saw John away from Foyle and completing his education at Wraxall Hall in Wiltshire and a contemporary has left a description of him there.

> John Lawrence was tall and overgrown; I was much struck by the angular formation of his face. He was rough but kindly; hot-tempered but good-natured withal. We had a rough enough life of it at school; our bedrooms were so cold that the water used to freeze hard in the basins, and the doctor used to remark that it was no wonder that we were all in such good health, for every room had a draught in it. This was true enough. The window-frames of our bedroom were of stone, and an iron bar across the centre was supposed to prevent ingress or egress. Lawrence managed to loosen it so that it could be taken out and replaced without attracting observation, and when the nights were hot he would creep through it in his nightshirt and, reaching the ground by the help of a pear-tree which grew against the wall, would go and bathe in the neighbouring stream. We were fast friends, and in the kindness of his heart he would have done anything for me. I was very fond of bird-nesting. A swallow had built its nest at the top of our chimney, and I expressed a wish to get at it. 'I'll get the eggs for you,' said John, and went straight to the chimney, and began to climb up it inside. It soon became too narrow for his burly frame. 'Never mind, I'll get them yet,' he said, and at once went to the window. I and my brother followed him through it, and, climbing a wall twelve feet high, which came out from one end of the house and formed one

side of the court, pushed him up from its summit as far as we could reach towards the roof. He was in his nightshirt, with bare feet and legs; but, availing himself of any coign of vantage that he could find, he actually managed to climb up the wall of the house by himself. When he reached the roof, he crawled up the coping stones at the side on his knees, and then began to make his way along the ridge towards the chimney; but the pain by this time became too great for human endurance: 'Hang it all,' he cried, 'I can't go on!' and he had to give it up.

But a turning-point in John's career was to come in 1827. Then John Hudleston, a friend of the family who had the good fortune to be a director of East India Company and a Member of Parliament and had used his patronage to get Alexander, George, and Henry Lawrence cadetships in the Company's army in India, offered John an appointment in the Bengal Civil Service.

But this was by no means the appointment John Lawrence felt his due—a *civilian*, what an idea!—for his aspirations were entirely military. Even Henry, disgusted with his experiences in the Burma campaign, failed to dissuade him. There was, however, a stronger will than his in the Lawrence family, their elder sister Letitia.

An eyewitness has described the 'persuasion' with all the delicious overtones which we associate with a Victorian 'improving' tale. The elder sister doing her bit for the greater glory, the weak, white hands that make a hero.

John Lawrence's eldest sister was an extraordinary woman: strong of mind and of will, quick in apprehension, yet sound and sober in judgement, refined and cultured, with a passionate enthusiasm for all that was 'pure and lovely, and of good report'. In a word, hers was a nature possessed by the highest qualities of her soldier brothers, in combination with feminine gentleness and goodness. She had enjoyed varied advantages in the society in which her lot was occasionally cast. At the house of Mr. Hudlestone, among other distinguished men, she had often met Wilberforce and the Thorntons, and had quietly drunk in their wit and conversation from the sofa to which, as an invalid, she was long confined. Perhaps her brother Henry, who more nearly resembled her in character and disposition, was most amenable to her influence; but John, too, though the greater independence of character manifested in his after life was early developed, cherished what might be called without exaggeration a boundless reverence for all she said and thought.

In the present stern conflict between duty and inclination the family 'oracle' was lovingly resorted to. The scene in Letitia's room can never be forgotten by those who witnessed it. It may have been the crisis in John's life. He was seated at the foot of the invalid's couch in earnest debate about the perplexing gift. With all the vehemence of his ardent boy nature, as if to leave no doubt as to his own decided prepossessions, and perhaps with a bold effort to win the assent which he felt to be indispensable, he exclaimed, 'A soldier I was born, and a soldier I will be!' The prudent counsellor, however, advised differently. She urged him without hesitation to accept the boon, as affording in every way advantages unknown to the military life. Other influences no doubt conspired with hers to induce him to make what was to his own personal feelings and aspirations a great self-sacrifice, but it was to Letitia's calm advice and good judgement that he reluctantly but bravely yielded. She may be said indeed to have turned the scales, and thus in a measure determined an illustrious future.

To the East India Company's college of Haileybury went John Lawrence, and his contemporaries read like a hagiography of Empire, if we could bother to remember them. A friend of Lawrence has left for us a description of John's life at Haileybury which again catches the Victorian bathos of the 'bad' boy at school who 'made an Empire'.

John Lawrence was in appearance rugged and uncouth, but his tall gaunt figure was sufficiently set off by an intelligent face and by his high good humour. He did not much affect general society; and though, like others, he sometimes 'rode in the dilly' to Ware or Hertford, he on the whole preferred mooning about the quadrangle and the reading-room, or wandering over the wild neighbouring heath, not uncommonly varying the game of fives at the college racquet-court by one of skittles or bowls or quoits behind the 'College Arms', and the bad beer procured at this and neighbouring hostels was often recalled, not without regret, in after life by the exiles of Bengal, Madras, and Bombay. Lawrence at that time displayed a good deal of the Irish element, and he with his intimate friend Charles Todd—who died after a short career in India—first initiated me into the mysteries sacred to St. Patrick's Day, Hallowee'n, the glorious, pious, and immortal memory of King William, the 'prentice-boys of Derry, etc. By a stupid and inexcusable failure in Bengali, I managed to come out only sixth in my last term, while Lawrence was third. But it was a failure which enables me to record a characteristic anecdote. On that great final day of our Collegiate career, the 28th of May, 1829, my father, the Principal, was in high good humour, for in spite of the disaster just described, I had delivered before a rather brilliant audience in the Hall a prize essay on 'The Power of the Romans in the West compared with the British in the East'; and going up with pretended anger to John Lawrence, he said good humouredly, 'Oh, you rascal, you have got out ahead of my son'; to which with ready wit Lawrence replied, 'Ah, Dr. Batten, you see it's all *conduct*; I fear Hallet has not been quite so steady as I'; thus turning the tables on the Principal, who, to Lawrence's knowledge, had more than once remonstrated on my 'loafing about with that tall Irishman'.

This brings me to another anecdote. When I was at home on furlough during what turned out to be the Mutiny year (1857), I went to Brighton to pay my respects to Mr. Le Bas, who had long since retired from the Haileybury Principalship, in which he succeeded my father. Those who knew the man, with his sharp peculiar voice, and his hand to his ear, can easily imagine the scene. He called out to me, 'Hallet, who is this John Lawrence of whom I hear so much?' to which I replied, 'Don't you remember a tall, thin Irishman with whom I much consorted, who once kept an Irish revel of bonfires on the grass plot opposite to Letter C; and whom you forgave on account of his Orange zeal and his fun?' 'Aha!' said the old dean, 'I remember the man; not a bad sort of fellow;' and then he burst into one of his fits of laughter, ending with the dry remark, 'But what has become of all our *good* students?'

John Lawrence left Haileybury in May 1829 and stayed some four months in England so that he might 'have the benefit of his brother Henry's society on his voyage out'.

The two brothers, accompanied by their sister Honoria, left Portsmouth on 2nd September 1829, and reached Calcutta by the long voyage round the Cape on 9th February 1830. The great stage of India was awaiting them.

JAN LARENS SUB JANTA

JOHN LAWRENCE was fortunate to spend only a little time in Calcutta. The 'City of Palaces' it may have been but the soft colours of the aquatint hide the brutality of truth. Cholera was endemic. The water-supply, two open tanks. The river, a continuous perambulation of half-burned corpses that stuck in the anchor-chains of ships and filled the air with the cloying sweetness of death. Sewage in open drains bubbled in the strength of the sun like an organized swamp. The cemeteries of the city quietly extended their grip on the land.

> Here lies Mr. Wandermere
> Who was to have gone home next year.

Calcutta had the English by the throat. John Lawrence lived in a sick hate. In later years he was often to say that the offer of a hundred pounds a year in England in those tortured months would have sent him straight home—without regret.

But release came at the end of 1830 when he passed his language examinations and was, at his own request, appointed to the Delhi Territory.

He was in such a hurry to leave Calcutta that he travelled by palanquin the distance of nine hundred miles to Delhi in eighteen days. Dislike of the capital spurred him on. He never forgot his hatred of Calcutta.

We must here take a little time in getting acquainted with the city of Delhi, and its peculiar position in the structure of the Company's India.

The Delhi Territory had come into British possession at the collapse of the Maratha Confederacy in 1803. The old Emperor Shah Alam was rescued and restored to his throne and, in exchange for conferring on the new conquerors the territories they had acquired, received an allowance of some £120,000 a year. The city of Delhi and the lands that produced his allowance were left sovereign to the King and a British Resident administered justice and collected revenue in his name. The King and his court existed in a make-believe of power, surrounded as one historian has put it 'with all the paraphernalia of imperial dignity, he received from his protectors the symbols of an allegiance they did not pay, and affected to dispense an authority he no longer possessed'. This romantic nonsense was to pay off in blood. The shadow of Mogul greatness fascinated the people of India and the Emperor remained the potential axis of revolt; his tattered glory, a rallying point of disaffection.

Reginald Heber, Bishop of Calcutta, was received in audience by Bahadur Shah, destined to be the last King of Delhi, in 1825, and his description shows that mixture of the squalid and the dignified which was characteristic of the Court, as well as the mixture of romance and business that was the Company's attitude to the King.

The 31st December was fixed for my presentation to the Emperor, which was appointed for half-past eight in the morning. Lushington and a Captain Wade also chose to take the same opportunity. At eight I went, accompanied by Mr. Elliot, with nearly the same formalities as at Lucknow, except that we were on elephants instead of in palanquins, and that the procession was, perhaps, less splendid, and the beggars both less numerous and far less vociferous and importunate. We were received with presented arms by the troops of the palace drawn up within the barbican, and proceeded, still on our elephants, through the noblest gateway and vestibule which I ever saw. It consists, not merely of a splendid gothic arch in the centre of the great gate-tower—but, after that, of a long vaulted aisle, like that of a gothic cathedral, with a small, open, octagonal court in its centre, all of granite, and all finely carved with inscriptions from the Koran, and with flowers. This ended in a ruinous and exceedingly dirty stable-yard! where we were received by Captain Grant, as the Mogul's officer on guard, and by a number of elderly men with large gold-headed canes, the usual ensign of office here, and one of which Mr. Elliot also carried. We were now told to dismount and proceed on foot, a task which the late rain made inconvenient to my gown and cassock, and thin shoes, and during which we were pestered by a fresh swarm of miserable beggars, the wives and children of the stable servants. After this we passed another richly-carved, but ruinous and dirty gateway, where our guides, withdrawing a canvas screen, called out, in a sort of harsh chaunt, 'Lo, the ornament of the world! Lo, the asylum of the nations! King of Kings! The Emperor Acbar Shah! Just, fortunate, victorious!' We saw, in fact, a very handsome and striking court, about as big as that at All Souls, with low, but richly-ornamented buildings. Opposite to us was a beautiful open pavilion of white marble, richly carved, flanked by rose-bushes and fountains, and some tapestry and striped curtains hanging in festoons about it, within which was a crowd of people, and the poor old descendant of Tamerlane seated in the midst of them. Mr. Elliot here bowed three times very low, in which we followed his example. This ceremony was repeated twice as we advanced up the steps of the pavilion, the heralds each time repeating the same expressions about their master's greatness. We then stood in a row on the right-hand side of the throne, which is a sort of marble bedstead richly ornamented with gilding, and raised on two or three steps. Mr. Elliot then stepped forwards, and, with joined hands, in the usual eastern way, announced, in a low voice, to the Emperor, who I was. I then advanced, bowed three times again, and offered a nuzzur of fifty-one gold mohurs in an embroidered purse, laid on my handkerchief, in the way practised by the Baboos in Calcutta. This was received and laid on one side, and I remained standing for a few minutes, while the usual court questions about my health, my travels, when I left Calcutta, etc. were asked. I had thus an opportunity of seeing the old gentleman more plainly. He has a pale, thin, but handsome face, with an aquiline nose, and a long white beard. His complexion is little if at all darker than that of a European. His hands are very fair and delicate, and he had some valuable-looking rings on them. His hands and face were all I saw of him, for the morning being cold, he was so wrapped up in shawls, that he reminded me extremely of the Druid's head on a Welch halfpenny. I then stepped back to my former place, and returned again with five more mohurs to make my offering to the heir apparent, who stood at his father's left hand, the right being occupied by the Resident. Next, my two companions were introduced with nearly the same forms, except that their offerings were less, and that the Emperor did not speak to them.

The Emperor then beckoned to me to come forwards, and Mr. Elliot told me to take off my hat, which had till now remained on my head, on which the Emperor tied a flimsy turban of brocade round my head with his own hands, for which, however, I paid four gold mohurs more. We were then directed to retire to receive the 'Khelats' (honourary dresses) which the bounty of 'the Asylum of the World' had provided for us. I was accordingly taken into a small private room, adjoining the Zennanah, where I found a handsome flowered caftan edged with fur, and a pair of common-looking shawls, which my servants, who had the delight of witnessing all this fine show, put on instead of my gown, my cassock remaining as before. In this strange dress I had to walk back again, having my name announced by the criers (something in the same way that Lord Marmion's was) as 'Bahadur, Boozoony, Dowlut-mund', &c. to the presence, where I found my two companions who had not been honoured by a private dressing-room, but had their Khelats put on them in the gateway of the court. They were, I apprehend, still queerer figures than I was, having their hats wrapped with scarfs of flowered gauze, and a strange garment of gauze, tinsel, and faded ribbands flung over their shoulders above their coats. I now again came forward and offered my third present to the Emperor, being a copy of the Arabic Bible and the Hindoostanee Common Prayer, handsomely bound in blue velvet laced with gold, and wrapped up in a piece of brocade. He then motioned to me to stoop, and put a string of pearls round my neck, and two glittering but not costly ornaments in the front of my turban, for which I again offered five gold mohurs. It was, lastly, announced that a horse was waiting for my acceptance, at which fresh instance of imperial munificence the heralds again made a proclamation of largesse, and I again paid five gold mohurs. It ended by my taking my leave with three times three salams, making up, I think, the sum of about threescore, and I retired with Mr. Elliot to my dressing-room, whence I sent to her Majesty the Queen, as she is generally called, though Empress would be the ancient and more proper title, a present of five mohurs more, and the Emperor's *chobdars* came eagerly up to know when they should attend to receive their *buk-shish*. It must not, however, be supposed that this interchange of civilities was very expensive either to his Majesty or to me. All the presents which he gave, the horse included, though really the handsomest which had been seen at the court of Delhi for many years, and though the old gentleman evidently intended to be extremely civil, were not worth much more than 300s. rupees, so that he and his family gained at least 800s. rupees by the morning's work, besides what he received from my two companions, which was all clear gain, since the Khelats which they got in return were only fit for May-day, and made up, I fancy, from the cast-off finery of the Begum. On the other hand, since the Company have wisely ordered that all the presents given by Native Princes to Europeans should be disposed of on the Government account, they have liberally, at the same time, taken on themselves the expense of paying the usual money nuzzurs made by public men on these occasions. In consequence none of my offerings were at my own charge, except the professional and private one of the two books, with which, as they were unexpected, the Emperor, as I was told, was very much pleased. I had, of course, several *bukshishes* to give afterwards to his servants, but these fell considerably short of my expenses at Lucknow. To return to the hall of audience. While in the small apartment where I got rid of my shining garments, I was struck with its beautiful ornaments. It was entirely lined with white marble, inlaid with flowers and leaves of green serpentine, lapis lazuli, and blue and red porphyry; the flowers were of the best Italian style of workmanship, and evidently the labour of an artist of that country. All, however, was dirty, desolate, and forlorn. Half the flowers and leaves had been picked out or otherwise defaced, and the doors and windows were in a state of dilapidation, while a quantity of old furniture was piled in one corner, and a torn hanging of faded tapestry hung over an archway which led to the interior apartments. 'Such,' Mr. Elliot said, 'is the general style in which this palace is kept up and furnished. It is not absolute poverty which produces this, but these people have no idea of cleaning or mending any thing.' For my own part I thought of the famous Persian line, 'The spider hangs her tapestry in the palace of the Cæsars'; and felt a melancholy interest in comparing the present state of this poor family with what it was 200 years ago, when Bernier visited Delhi, or as we read its palace described in the tale of Madame de Genlis.

After putting on my usual dress, we waited a little, till word was brought us that the 'King of Kings', 'Shah-in-Shah', had retired to his Zennanah; we then went to the hall of audience, which I had previously seen but imperfectly, from the crowd of people and the necessity of attending to the forms which I had to go through. It is a very beautiful pavilion of white marble, open on one side to the court of the palace, and on the other to a large garden. Its pillars and arches are exquisitely carved and ornamented with gilt and inlaid flowers, and inscriptions in the most elaborate Persian character. Round the frieze is the motto, recorded, I believe, in Lalla Rukh,

> 'If there be an Elysium on Earth,
> It is this, it is this!'

The marble floor, where not covered by carpets, is all inlaid in the same beautiful manner with the little dressing-room, which I had quitted.

The gardens, which we next visited, are not large, but, in their way, must have been extremely rich and beautiful. They are full of very old orange and other fruit trees, with terraces and parterres, on which many rose-bushes were growing, and, even now, a few jonquils in flower. A channel of white marble for water, with little fountain-pipes of the same material, carved like roses, is carried here and there among these parterres, and at the end of the terrace is a beautiful octagonal pavilion, also of marble, lined with the same Mosaic flowers as in the room which I first saw, with a marble fountain in its centre, and a beautiful bath in a recess on one of its sides. The windows of this pavilion, which is raised to the height of the city wall, command a good view of Delhi and its neighbourhood. But all was, when we saw it, dirty, lonely, and wretched: the bath and fountain dry: the inlaid pavement hid with lumber and gardener's sweepings, and the walls stained with the dung of birds and bats.

We were then taken to the private mosque of the palace, an elegant little building, also of white marble and exquisitely carved, but in the same state of neglect and dilapidation, with peepuls allowed to spring from its walls, the exterior gilding partially torn from its dome, and some of its doors coarsely blocked up with unplastered brick and mortar.

We went last to the *Dewani aum*, or hall of public audience, which is in the outer court, and where on certain occasions the Great Mogul sat in state, to receive the compliments or petitions of his subjects. This also is a splendid pavilion of marble, not unlike the other hall of audience in form, but considerably larger and open on three sides only; on the fourth is a black wall, covered with the same Mosaic work of flowers and leaves as I have described, and in the centre a throne raised about ten feet from the ground, with a small platform of marble in front, where the vizier used to stand to hand up petitions to his master. Behind this throne are Mosaic paintings of birds, animals, and flowers, and in the centre, what decides the point of their being the work of Italian, or at least European artists, a small group of Orpheus playing to the beasts. This hall, when we saw it, was full of lumber of all descriptions, broken palanquins and empty boxes, and the throne so covered with pigeon's dung, that its ornaments were hardly discernible. How little did Shahjahan, the founder of these fine buildings, foresee what would be the fate of his descendants, or what his own would be! 'Vanity of vanities!' was surely never written in more legible characters than on the dilapidated arcades of Delhi!

Though John Lawrence was equipped with a hard inner core and a leathery mind he responded slightly to the overtones of vanished power and the perfume of a great past that lurked amidst the garbage of this fabulous city.

In those days [he wrote] many of the chiefs about Delhi still held houses and gardens in the city, to which they constantly resorted, partly to pay their respects to the representative of British power, and partly to enjoy the pleasures and luxuries of social life. There were then living also in Delhi old men of rank and family, who had served in one capacity or other in the late wars; men who had been employed in the irregular fashion under Sir Arthur Wellesley or Lord Lake, men who used to be fond of telling stories of those interesting times, and to whom the names of Mr. Seton, the first Resident, of Sir Charles Metcalfe, of Sir David Ochterlony, and of Sir John Malcolm were as household words.

John remained at Delhi for four years, 'working regularly and steadily,' and was then appointed District Officer of the northern division with headquarters at Paniput. Here he remained until 1837.

The District Officer in India has always been the immediate instrument of rule. He was nearer to the people and was caught to some extent in the web of their troubles. To rule the turbulent peoples of Delhi was no armchair exercise in theoretical administration. This was the 'real' India, the India of justice on horseback, for the D.O. was, in many instances, the only British officer in the territory and the symbol of rule must always be in sight.

Charles Raikes, a contemporary of John, has described the life of continuous pressure and movement.

Early in the year 1835 John Lawrence was stationed at the ancient and historically famous town of Paniput. He was 'officiating' as magistrate and collector of the district. He had also to conduct a settlement and survey of the lands comprised in his district. Let us glance for a moment at the details of the sort of work and duty confided to this young Irishman. Paniput is situated on the high road from Delhi to the Punjab, about seventy miles north-west of Delhi. The district is inhabited by Jats, industrious Hindu peasants, devoted to agriculture, and attached by the strongest ties to the land; by Gujurs, who were given to cattle-lifting; and by Ranghurs (Rajputs converted to a nominal form of Mohamedanism), who were as jealous of their land as the Jats, still worse thieves than the Gujurs, with a taste for promiscuous robbery and murder into the bargain. These men, it is to be remembered, are not at all the typical 'meek Hindu', but on the contrary are tall, strong, bold fellows, determined and ready to fight for every inch of their land and every head of their cattle. In those days they never went out to plough or to herd their buffaloes without sword, shield, and often a long matchlock over their shoulders.

View of Delhi from the Palace Gate

Lucknow

Over some 400,000 of a population like this, scattered in large villages through an area of 800,000 acres, John Lawrence ruled supreme. He himself in those days had very much the cut of a Jat, being wiry, tall, muscular, rather dark in complexion, and without an ounce of superfluous fat or flesh. He usually wore a sort of compromise between English and Indian costume, had his arms ready at hand, and led a life as *primus inter pares*, rather than a foreigner or a despot, among the people. Yet a despot he was, as any man soon discovered who was bold enough or silly enough to question his legitimate authority—a despot, but full of kindly feelings, and devoted heart and soul to duty and hard work.

As magistrate he had charge of the police—a handful of *sowars*, or troopers, mounted on country horses and armed with sword and pistol, and mostly retained at headquarters, and the ordinary constabulary force stationed at the various *thanahs*, or police-stations, dotted over the district. Each of these stations was under the charge of a *thanadar*, or chief of police, with a *jemadar*, or sergeant, a *mohurrir*, or scribe, and a dozen or so of police *burkundazes* (literally 'hurler of fire'), who, armed with sword and lance, formed the rank and file of the force. But these were supplemented by a nondescript but very useful village official, a *choukedar*, whose duty was that of a watchman or parish constable, and a reporter (to the *thanadar*) of all crimes, sudden deaths, or other noteworthy events which happened in his village. This was the framework of the district police, little changed from the system which had prevailed for centuries under the Emperors of Delhi. It was a system sufficiently efficacious to protect the public under a just and energetic magistrate, and an apt engine of oppression under a venal or, above all, under a careless and slothful official. Suffice it to say that John Lawrence at Paniput was the right man in the right place, and for the following reasons.

First, he was at all times and in all places, even in his bedroom, accessible to the people of his district. He loved his joke with the sturdy farmers, his chat with the city bankers, his argument with the native gentry, few and far between. When out with his dogs and gun he had no end of questions to ask every man he met. After a gallop across country, he would rest on a *charpoy*, or country bed, and hold an impromptu *levée* of all the village folk, from the headman to the barber. '*Jan Larens*,' said the people, '*sub janta*,' that is, knows everything. For this very reason he was a powerful magistrate, and, I may here add, a brilliant and invaluable revenue officer.

Secondly, he was never above his work. I have an indistinct recollection of his arresting a murderer, on receiving intelligence of the crime, with his own hand. At all events, when the report of a

6—T.N.H.

murder, an affray with wounding, or a serious robbery came in, John Lawrence was at once in the saddle and off to the spot. With greater deliberation, but equal self-devotion, he proceeded to the spot to investigate important disputes about land, crops, water privileges, boundaries, and so forth. The Persian proverb, 'Disputes about land must be settled on the land'—'*Kuzea zumeen buh dir zumeen*'—was often on his tongue.

Thirdly, owing to this determination to go about for himself and to hear what everybody had to say about everything, he shook off, nay, he utterly confounded, the tribe of flatterers, sycophants, and informers who, when they can get the opportunity, dog the steps of the Indian ruler. What chance had an informer with a man who was bent on seeing everything with his own eyes?

All this might have been said of Donald Macleod, of Robert Montgomery, and of other friends of Lawrence who became great Indian administrators. But John Lawrence had in addition a quality of hardness, not amounting to harshness, but not short of severity, which made the malefactor tremble at his name. He might or he might not be loved—this seemed to be his mind—but respected he would be at all events.

I have said enough to show that in the early days of his Indian career John Lawrence was a most energetic and vigorous magistrate. To do any sort of justice to the training of those days which prepared him for future distinction, I must now turn to Lawrence as a revenue officer. The good old East India Company which he served, and which called the young men sent out to rule her provinces 'writers', called the chiefs who gathered up her lakhs of rupees and ruled her landed millions 'collectors'. John Lawrence then was a 'collector', as well as a magistrate, and just then the collector's work was in a transition state, which entailed severe labour and tested every faculty. The great survey and settlement of the land was in progress; boundaries were to be marked, every village measured and mapped, and registers of the area, the soil, the cultivators, the rent, the land-tax in short, of all the facts and figures affecting the land, were to be made.

How it happened that Lawrence was expected single-handed to accomplish so vast a work I cannot tell. All that I can say is that when I was sent to help him, I cannot remember that he had anyone to share his burden except his native officials, who in those days had purely ministerial powers in the revenue departments. For seven or eight months he lived amongst the agricultural classes in his tent, and thus mastered the detail of revenue work.

I was younger than Lawrence, and had been only three or four years in India when I went to join him at Paniput. For very good reasons I shall never forget my first interview with my chief. He was, I was going to say, in his shirt sleeves, only I am not sure that he wore a shirt in those days—I think he had a *chupkun*, or native undergarment—surrounded by what seemed to me a mob of natives, with two or three dogs at his feet, talking, writing, dictating—in short, doing *cutcherry*.

After some talk with me he summed up thus: 'Now look at this map. Paniput district is divided into nine *thanahs* (police circuits): I give you these three at the north-western extremity, including the large cantonment of Kurnal. I put the police and revenue work under you. Mind, you are not to get into rows with the military authorities. If you behave well to them, they will be civil to you. If you can keep crime down and collect your revenue in your share of the district, I will not interfere with you. If you want help, come to me. All reports of your own *thanahs* will be sent to you. I shall soon know what you are made of. Go, and do not be hard on the *zemindars* (landowners). Government revenue, of course, must be paid, but do not be hard: "The calf gets the milk which is left in the cow." Come and see me sometimes.'

John himself has also left a view of his life and what he learned from it. There could have been no better training for the future 'saviour of the Punjab'.

During my charge of the Paniput district, I completed my training as a civil officer. It was a hard one, it is true, but one which I had no cause ever to regret. It has facilitated all my subsequent labours, no matter how varied, how onerous. I had become well acquainted with the duties of an administrator both in a large city and in an important agricultural district. I had come in contact with all classes of the people, high and low. I had made acquaintance with most of the criminal classes, and understood their habits of life. I had seen all the different agricultural races of that part of India. I had learned to understand the peculiarities of the tenure of land, the circumstances of Indian agriculture, canal and well irrigation, as well as the habits, social customs, and leading characteristics of the people. During this period, I defined and marked off boundaries between village lands, which had been the cause of sanguinary feuds for generations; I revised the revenue assessments of the land; I superintended the collection of the revenue; I had charge of the treasury; I sought out and brought to justice a number of great criminals; I managed the police, and, in fact, under the humble designation of magistrate and collector, was the pivot round which the whole administration of the district revolved. In the discharge of my multifarious duties I visited, in all cases of more than ordinary difficulty, the very locality itself. For the most part, my only aids in all this work were the native collectors of the different subdivisions of the country. In addition to all these duties, I did what I could to relieve the sick. In those days we had no dispensaries, and the civil duty of the medical officer was limited to the charge of the jail. I used to carry about a good-sized medicine-chest, and, when the day's work was over, was constantly surrounded by a crowd of people asking for relief for most of 'the ills to which flesh is heir'. Many a poor creature I had thus to send away, simply from fear of doing him harm.

Such was my daily life for nearly two years, and such were the lives of my brother civilians in adjacent districts. Half our time was spent in tents; and every portion of our charges would at one time or the other be duly visited, so that in the event of any untoward accident, or serious crime, we could judge pretty correctly as to the peculiar circumstances connected with it. These were very happy days. Our time was fully occupied, and our work was of a nature to call forth all our energies, all our sympathies, and all our abilities. Our emoluments were relatively small, but the experience and the credit we gained stood us in good stead in after years. During this period I saw little of English society, finding that I could not enjoy it and also accomplish my work. Thus I seldom visited the cantonments except on urgent business, and then only, as a rule, for a single day. In those days I met with many curious adventures, and on some occasions was in considerable peril of life, but good fortune and careful management combined brought me successfully out of them all.

His adventures were many and curious. A characteristic episode was the murder of William Fraser, the Commissioner of Delhi, and the nightmare pursuit of his murderer.

On hearing of the murder John Lawrence rode to Delhi. There no clue had been found, though trackers had traced the murderer's horse. A chance remark that the Nawab of Ferozepur might be involved set John on the road to that prince's house. His biographer has described what followed:

They found no one in the courtyard, nor did any voice from within answer their repeated calls. Simon Fraser entered the house, and, during his absence, John Lawrence, sauntering up to a spot in the yard where a fine chestnut horse was tethered, began to examine his points, and soon noticed some nail-marks on a part of the hoof where they are not usually found. It flashed across him in an instant that it had been reported that Dick Turpin had sometimes reversed the shoes of his horse's hoofs to put his pursuers off the scent, and at that same moment one of the Goojurs, picking up a straw, measured carefully both the hind and fore hoofs. 'Sahib,' he cried, 'there is just one straw's difference in breadth between them, the very thing we observed in the tracks on the road; this must be the animal ridden by the murderer.'

While this was being said and done, a trooper in undress lounged up and, in reply to a question or two, told John Lawrence that he was an orderly of the Nawab of Ferozepur, and that he had been sent by his master on a special mission to the city. 'This is a nice horse,' said Lawrence. 'Yes,' replied the man, 'he is a fine horse, but he is very weak and off his feed; he has been able to do no work for a week.' The appearance of the horse, so John Lawrence thought, gave the lie to this, and espying at a little distance its saddle and other harness lying on the ground, he went up to it and, finding that the nosebag underneath the heap was full of corn, quietly slung it over the horse's head. The 'sickly' animal began to eat greedily. Here was one link more, and, without saying anything to excite the trooper's suspicion, he induced him to accompany him to the *cutcherry*, where he ordered his immediate arrest.

Some fragments of note-paper, which Simon Fraser had meanwhile picked up in a bucket of water in the house, were now fitted together by the two men. The ink had been all but obliterated by the water, but some chemicals revived it, and revealed the words written in Persian, 'You know the object for which I sent you to Delhi; and I have repeatedly told you how very important it is for me that you should buy the dogs. If you have not done so, do it without delay.'

It hardly needed John Lawrence's penetration, with the threads which he already held in his hands, to discover that 'the dogs' were the Commissioner, whose life the trooper had been too long in taking, and, on his suggestion, a message was sent to the Nawab saying that his presence in Delhi was necessary, as a servant of his, Wassail Khan by name, was suspected of the murder of the Commissioner. The Nawab obeyed the summons, but of course he backed up the trooper in his denial, and disclaimed all knowledge of the murder.

Inquiries which were set on foot in the Nawab's territories, while he was detained in Delhi, soon showed that a second man on foot, whose name was Unyah Meo, was believed to have been present at the time of the murder. He was a freebooter, well known for his extraordinary strength and fleetness of foot. He had disappeared on that very night, and had not been seen since. Colonel Skinner, the well-known commandant of Skinner's Irregular Horse, was charged with the duty of searching for him. His whereabouts was soon discovered, communications opened with him, and promises of pardon made if he would give himself up and turn King's evidence against the murderer. Not long afterwards a man appeared by night and said, 'I am Unyah Meo, I will go with you.'

His story was soon told, and, simple truth as it was, it reads like a story from Herodotus about the ancient Persian court, or like a tale from the *Arabian Nights*, rather than what it really was. He had been sent, as it appeared, by the Nawab, with instructions to accompany the trooper on all occasions, and should the first shot fail to kill the Commissioner, who was not likely, with his well-known character, to die easily, he was to run in and despatch him with his sword. Wassail Khan's first shot had passed clean through the 'sacred body' of the Commissioner, so Unyah Meo's services were not required; but he hurried off at once to tell his master that the deed was done.

All that night and a good part of the next day he ran, and towards the evening arrived at the Nawab's fort at Ferozepur, ninety miles distant. He went straight to the door of the Nawab's room, and demanded immediate admittance, as he had news of importance to communicate. A thick curtain only shut off the presence-chamber from the ante-room, and as the orderly entered, Unyah Meo, with the suspicion natural to one of his profession, lifted up very slightly a corner of the curtain and bent down, all eye, all ear, for what might follow. He heard the Nawab give orders that on leaving the room he should on no account be allowed to leave the fort. Well knowing that, now that the deed was done, his death would be more serviceable to his master than his life, Unyah felt that this order was a sentence of death, and the moment he had told his story, and had been promised a large reward—for which he was to wait till the following morning—he slipped quietly down a back way, managed to leave the fort unobserved, and ran for his life to his cottage in the jungle, some seven miles away.

He was tired out by the ninety miles he had run already; but fear gave him fresh strength and speed, and he reached his home just in time for his wives—of whom he was blessed with a pair—to take him up to the flat roof of the house and conceal him under some bundles of straw. Soon the troopers, whose pursuing feet he had seemed to hear close behind him, appeared on the scene. But the wives, Rahab-like, kept the secret well, and Unyah, after a night's rest, escaped, like the spies, to the hills, and defied every effort to

find him till he gave himself up of his own accord, in the manner I
have already described, to the commander of Skinner's Horse.

His story was borne out by the accidental discovery of the
carbine which had been used by Wassail Khan, under circumstances
which were quite in keeping with the other marvellous features of
the case. A woman was drawing water from a well close to the Kabul
gate of Delhi; the rope broke, the bucket fell into the water, and the
hook used to recover it brought up, not the bucket, but the missing
carbine! Other people deposed that they had seen the trooper return
on the night of the murder with his horse—the horse which could
neither work nor eat!—in a tremendous lather, as though from a
long or rapid ride. The Nawab and his trooper still stoutly denied all
knowledge of the crime, but they were tried by a special commissioner, found guilty, and hanged together before the Kashmir
gate of the city.

In 1838 John was posted as Settlement Officer in Etawah,
which he described as a 'hole'. The end of the first stage on his
Indian career was upon him however, as sickness soon compelled
him to return to England.

There he married, and with his wife, Harriet, returned to
India in 1842 as Civil and Sessions Judge, then Magistrate and
Collector, of Delhi.

The first Sikh war lay barely hidden over the horizon and the
notes of the call to the Punjab were already being rehearsed.

THE FIRST MAN IN INDIA WHO WANTED NOTHING

HENRY LAWRENCE'S career between 1830 and 1846 when the two brothers came together in the Punjab, and *we* reach the hub of our story, was chequered and involved.[1]

Two important events that took place between 1830 and 1838 had a profound influence on Henry's future life: his appointment as Assistant Revenue Surveyor in the North-west Provinces in February 1833 and his marriage to Honoria Marshall in August 1837. The first gave him intimate acquaintance and knowledge of Indian ways and thought and the second the strength a lonely man acquires from a wife who truly loves him.

Honoria Marshall, a sort of cousin almost in the Scots manner, met Henry Lawrence in 1827 when he was home on sick-leave, and there is, in Herbert Edwardes' words, a delightful laced-edged Valentine description of their subsequent meeting.

In September of the same year they met again for a few hours, when Henry went to Ireland, and called at Fahan to deliver some presents for Mrs. Heath.

In the spring of 1828 both Honoria Marshall and Letitia Lawrence were staying with their relatives the Josiah Heaths at Twickenham; and here, Henry, coming to and fro, saw more than ever of the fair Irish cousin. Most fair and loveable indeed she was. Her home,

---

[1] As only the highlights of Henry Lawrence's career are dealt with here, the reader may find valuable a brief chronology of his life between 1830 and 1846.

February 1830. Arrived in India after leave.

September 1831. Transferred to Horse Artillery.

February 1833, and for five and a half years afterwards. Assistant Surveyor, then Surveyor, in the Survey Department.

September 1838. Placed at the disposal of the Commander-in-Chief for employment in the field.

January 1839. Officiating as assistant to the Political Agent at Ludhiana.

March 1840–December 1842. Promoted to rank of Captain. Assistant to the Governor-General's Agent for the North-West Frontier; at Ferozepur until November 1841, afterwards at Peshawar and in Afghanistan.

1843. Resident in Katmandu, Nepal.

January 1846. Agent and Resident at Lahore, Punjab.

since she was four years old, had been with her uncle and aunt at
Fahan; and her childhood was passed on the lovely but lonely shore
of the 'Lake of Shadows'. The open air, the sky, the fields, the sea,
these were her playfellows; and in after-life she used to say she got
her schooling mostly from the pebbles on the beach. Truly here she
learnt a deep love of nature, a high romance of feeling, a habit of
self-communion, and a content with solitude, which would have
made poetry of any lot. And so thought Henry Lawrence as he
looked and listened. Soon he opened his heart to his wise sister,
and wondered at her not anticipating his story. But how humble he
was! It was of course not to be expected that Honoria Marshall
could ever care for him. He was not good enough for her. But he
would consult Angel Heath. Alas! *she* thought it most imprudent.
They were little better than children. Cruel Angel! You were like a
frost in spring. The coming flowers went back into their hearts.

Next year, the cousins all met again at the 'Josiah Heaths' in
Bedford Square. Do look at those two, walking about the streets of
London, hand-in-hand, like two children—Honoria staring at the
shops and Henry at Honoria! What a rustic she is—fresh from her
Irish wilds, perfectly happy in new cotton frocks. Angel is older,
and, though an angel, knows worse (nobody said 'better'). Kind,
foolish Angel robes the girl in silk. Of course, she is beautiful—but
she was just as beautiful before. Did you hear that man in the street
say to his friend as she passed, '*She's* well painted, at any rate!' Yes,
she was indeed—by the master-hand that made the rose red and the
lily white.

It is a sad and touching thing and though there is no evidence
for it, probably true, for Henry had the sentimental soft-centre
of his times.

Out of this experience emerged Henry's determination to
achieve a standing in India that would justify him in asking
Honoria Marshall in marriage. With single-minded purpose between 1830 and 1839 he marched, sometimes tripping but always
carrying-on, towards his goal. His opportunity came in the
Revenue Survey.

On arriving in India Henry Lawrence was posted to a company
of Foot Artillery at Kurnaul, where now lived his brother
George, Adjutant of the 2nd Cavalry regiment, and settled down
to study the Indian vernaculars. In 1831, on brother George's
recommendation in the Commander-in-Chief's ear, he was
transferred to the Horse Artillery.

'Here I am,' he writes to Letitia, 'a gay trooper bumping away in the riding-school!' So much for exultation at obtaining an artilleryman's ambition. Now for reflexion.

I must say I like the quiet humdrum of Kurnaul better than the rattle and gaiety of Meerut. Here I am, of course, obliged to belong to the mess, which, though a very superior one, is not in my way. However, I may be thankful on the whole that I am where I am. When I am posted to a troop I will let you know. There is no knowing where it may be; but all Hindustan is alike; and were it not for the little extra expense of marching, nothing I should like better than a constant move.

Henry always maintained his private face in the public places of his life. He seldom mixed in the pleasures that surrounded him, he was without the social graces and tolerance that make a competent man great.

But changes were at hand.

During 1832 George Lawrence had been again obliged to take sick leave to Simla. Lord William Bentinck, the Governor-General, was there; and as George had been so successful the year before in getting the Commander-in-Chief to put Henry into the Horse Artillery, he thought he might as well now try the Governor-General. Accordingly he sought and obtained an interview. 'Well, what have *you* come for?' asked Lord William. 'Nothing for myself,' answered George. 'What then?' said his lordship. 'I can tell you you're the first man I have met in India who wanted nothing.' George then explained that he wanted his lordship to appoint Henry to the Revenue Survey; and the Governor-General, after asking a few pertinent questions, said, 'Well, go and tell Benson; and, although I make no promises, I will see what can be done.' The inquiries into the qualifications and character of the young artilleryman must have proved highly satisfactory, for on the 22nd February 1833 he found himself appointed an Assistant Revenue Surveyor in the North-West Provinces.

If George Lawrence was the first man in India who asked nothing for himself he merely represented the essential character of all the brothers, for in times of patronage and power they all made their way by genuine personal effort rather than the nepotism of friendships and favour.

The Revenue Survey and Henry's part in it have been described by one of the surveyors, James Abbott.

It was devised by the greatest benefactor the people of India have ever known—Mr. Robert Bird. Many before him had been sensible that the Government was impoverishing itself every year by insisting upon the impossible assessments of preceding Governments: which often amounted to one half the gross produce, and sometimes to more than that. But whereas too many others had shrunk from the duty of pointing out this injustice to their Government, Mr. Bird put forth all his energies to convince the authorities of the necessity of a lower assessment, and for long periods. The misery resulting from the then existing settlements was incalculable. Thousands of cultivators every year sank beneath the weight of the land-tax, and were converted from productive to unproductive members of the community; turned adrift from the lands which their father's father had cultivated time out of mind, to become vagabonds and beggars, and swell the ranks of those robber bands which were one of the plagues of India. . . .

Against the insane assessments then existing, Mr. Bird put forth all his might; and the Government were at length convinced of the truth of his statements, and of the soundness of his views, and ordered a revised assessment for a period of, I think, twenty years. But although it was manifest that, to form a correct assessment, a correct survey of the lands was in the first place necessary, yet the insufficiency of the revenues of India to meet the expenses of Government rendered it difficult to provide funds for the purpose, and after some years' trial of the surveys, their expenses were threatening their abolition. In this emergency Mr. Bird took into council Henry Lawrence, to devise only by increasing the strength of the establishments under a single head, and by diminishing the details of the professional portion of the survey. He suggested that the establishment at present existing in each survey, and calculated for the measurement of 1,000 square miles of area, should be trebled, so as to survey 3,000 square miles in one season of eight months, under a single superintendent with two additional assistants.

Again in the autumn of 1833 Henry Lawrence's health compelled him to Simla. 'It is well I should go,' he said, 'action seems to keep me alive. But the springs must wear out.' But he is still on the look-out for Civil employment.

On my way back [from Simla], if I have time, I may come by Agra, and rap at Sir Charles's [Metcalfe's] door, for I have taken a violent fancy to push myself into a Civil situation.

Oudh, I fear, is beyond my mark. Besides, *it is not ours yet*! However, I'll take anything, political, magisterial, or judicial, and

will willingly give up my claim of firing large guns at the black
people, or blowing off people's heads, as Marcia used to insist was
my delight. No! I would now much prefer preventing them breaking
each other's heads, and be instrumental in leading them into paths
of civilization.

His thoughts of Oudh were prophetic for there he was to die
in the flames of the Mutiny.

At home while Lawrence carried on his survey work Honoria
Marshall, tired no doubt of Henry's silence, for he had written
nothing, became temporarily engaged to a Mr. Briggs. But soon
with the aid of the indefatigable Letitia things were right again
and Henry's appointment as full surveyor made marriage financially practicable. On 8th July 1837, Honoria Marshall arrived in
Calcutta. There was no one to meet her. Henry was on sick-leave
again in Simla. They were finally married in August.

Honoria kept, as was the fashion and the necessity, a journal,
and her impressions give not only a fresh view of the India she
found on her arrival but a revealing opening into the mind that
was to dominate so much of Henry's actions.

> During my short residence in this country I have been struck by
> the depth of colouring with which the scenes of existence are here
> painted. Life is so uncertain, disease so rapid; there are such
> lengthened separations and so many uncertainties in the conveyance
> of intelligence, that I feel quite bewildered at the startling occurrences
> I hear of. Take as a specimen two or three which have occurred
> within the knowledge of the friends I am with [at Cossipur, near
> Calcutta]. When Mrs. H. came out she had, as fellow-passenger,
> Mrs. F., a lady who had gone home for her health. Her husband
> had come to Calcutta to meet her. The Semaphore announced that
> her ship was in the river. He immediately got into a little boat that
> he might go down to meet her, intending to await her arrival at a
> certain point. Not seeing the ship, however, he went gradually on
> till he was many miles down the river. A breeze sprang up, which
> was against the boat and upset it. Mr. F. was never seen again, I
> believe; but the breeze carried his wife quickly up to Calcutta,
> where she went immediately to Mr. Thomason's, at whose house
> the meeting was appointed. There she only heard of her husband's
> having taken boat; and it was many hours before the truth was
> ascertained.
> Here again is another. A friend of Major H.'s had gone home, and
> there met a lady to whom he became attached; but not deeming it

then prudent to marry, he returned to India, and afterwards wrote, asking the lady to come to him. She did so; but by a train of circumstances somewhat resembling my own, the gentleman was up the country at the time of her arrival. She came immediately to Cossipoor, and *he* set out to join her as soon as he heard she was come. Some weeks elapsed before he could reach her, and I can well understand what were her anxious and impatient feelings. He was daily expected, when she was taken ill with cholera, and in two days died. The frightful rapidity of death and all belonging to it, in this climate, obliges immediate interment. She died in the morning and was to have been buried in the afternoon. Just as the funeral was about to start, a boat stopped at the steps leading to the house. The gentleman stepped out, and was barely in time to see her remains and to follow them to the grave. . . .

Then to a rather naïve and surprised note:

I think the system respecting servants in this country is very hurtful to one's own mind. You hire your servant at so much a month. They do your work and you have no further concern with them. If they do not please you, you dismiss them. They make their *salaam*, and next day you are surrounded by new faces. All this is very free from care, but has a sad tendency to make you selfish. At home every conscientious person feels responsible to a certain degree for the moral conduct and religious instruction of his domestics, as well as the duty of consulting their comfort. Here the difference of religion does away with the first; and the habits of life, in a great measure, obviate the second. It is difficult for the master and mistress to recollect that their servants are responsible, immortal beings, or to think of more than their own convenience. I was surprised to find among Europeans the prejudices of *caste*, and that many of them object to a low-caste native (simply on that ground), as much as a Hindu would. This is surely contrary to our faith, though I can easily understand the feeling gaining on one. The obsequious manner of the servants annoys me greatly. I do not mean that they ought not to be respectful, but a man's standing with folded hands, waiting for his master's orders, seems to me more like devotion than service. The train of domestics in an Indian establishment arises from the impossibility of getting any servant to do more than one thing. The *bearer* will not take a teacup off the table, nor would the *khidmutgar* pull the punkah. I asked Mrs. H—— yesterday how many servants they had, She replied, 'I am not sure, but we are very moderate people. I can soon reckon.' The number amounted to nearly thirty: a waiting-maid, an under-woman, a sweeper, a head-bearer, a mate-bearer, six under-bearers, a *khansaman* or house-steward, three table attendants, a cook, a gardener, a water-carrier, a washerman, a tailor, a coachman, two grooms, two grass-cutters, a man to tend the goats, two messengers, and a woman to keep off the bodies which float down the stream past the house. Now, having all these servants, they will only wait on their own employers. Everyone going visiting takes his own. A lady who came here for a week lately, brought two women, two khidmutgars, two bearers, and a tailor. . . . All, when out of doors, wear shoes, generally of yellow or scarlet leather, with turned-up toes; but they never come into the house with them. Indeed a man could not show more disrespect than by coming into your presence with covered feet and bare head. Such are the different notions of politeness! . . .

And, of course, the stories she heard about India, were not *quite* true.

I have not yet seen anything like the violence of the elements that I expected in this climate. Indeed I think our Western ideas of the horrors of India are vastly exaggerated. I have not yet seen a snake, except one in the water, though I am not yet reconciled to the great cockroaches which creep out from the crevices [of the cabin of their boat] of an evening; nor was much pleased to see a scorpion walk deliberately across the floor a few days ago; nor to find a centipede making a bed of the slipper I was about to put on. Still there are nothing like the dangers I expected. . . .

Nor must we forget 'good work'.

I went [in Calcutta] to see the Orphan Refuge of Mrs. Wilson, and was much delighted with her and her labours. She is the widow of a clergyman. Years ago, when educating native females was a thing unheard of in Bengal, this courageous woman came out to try the experiment, and by degrees she gathered round her a few girls. She married Mr. Wilson, and I do not know the successive steps in her course; but at present she is a widow, and has an asylum for female orphans, about eight miles above Calcutta, on the Hooghly. The building is large and commodious, standing within an enclosure, which opens by a flight of steps, on the river. Here we entered, and walking across the courtyard, we found ourselves at the door of a room which is the chapel. It was the hour of evening worship. On the matted floor were seated a hundred girls, their ages varying from three to twelve years, arranged in rows of twenty-five each, the little ones in front, the elder behind. All were dressed exactly alike and exquisitely clean, and not being disfigured with ear-rings and nose-rings, they looked simple and child-like. The dress consisted of one large piece of white muslin. This is called a *sari*. One end is wrapped round the waist and tucked in, so as to form a long petticoat. The remainder is thrown round the shoulders and over the head, covering the whole person with a most graceful drapery, leaving only the face, the left hand and right arm bare. The girls all looked healthy and happy; and either there was, or I fancied, much more intellectual expression in the countenances of the elder ones than I had seen in any other native females.

When we entered they were singing the Evening Hymn in Bengali, and it was very sweet to hear a hundred young voices join in its simple music, especially when one thought from what they had been saved.

Henry and Honoria Lawrence's life in the Revenue Survey was a wandering one. In a letter Honoria describes some of her life with a descant on her own, and the poor natives, spiritual condition.

We landed at Chupia, and were six days marching into Gorruckpoor. This gave me the first taste of tent-life; and the pleasant impression I then formed of it has been since continually increasing. We remained at the station only a fortnight, and I was very glad to leave it. I never liked what is called company, and the commonplace superficialities of society came like a wet blanket upon me, after the preceding weeks, during which I had only heard and said words coming directly from the heart. However, I was glad to be in the place where my dearest Henry had been, and I felt an interest in seeing even the common acquaintances with whom he had been associating.

Having received the needful politenesses we were off to the jungles, where we have been ever since. For the last two months the weather has been as delightful as you can imagine—the very *beau ideal* of climate. There has not been a drop of rain since the first week in October. The mornings and evenings are very cold, and all day the air is so cool that we can sit out of doors. I never had such enjoyment of Nature, and since I came out to camp, we have been constantly moving; sometimes our march begins two hours before sunrise, and the starlight mornings, with the dawning day, are beautiful beyond description. We have been in the northern parts of the district, where it joins the Nepal frontier, and where there are long tracts of forest and jungle. The country in which we are is a perfect plain, but we have been in sight of the Himalayas, and have had some glorious views of them; the lower range undulating and wooded, behind them the sharp peaks and angular outline of the snowy range, looking like opal, or mother-of-pearl.

There are constant fresh sources of interest to me in the plants and animals around us. I could not have conceived the luxuriances of Oriental vegetation till I saw it. The trees are splendid, and in this district very abundant, independently of the forest. The natives, as far as I have seen, have nothing attractive in their character; indeed, as Gil Blas said, when he was with the actors, 'I am tired of living among the seven deadly sins', but those whom we have about us, are, I suppose, the worst specimens of native disposition. There is something very oppressive in being surrounded by heathen and Mahommedan darkness, in seeing idol-worship all around, and when we see the deep and debasing hold these principles have on the people, it is difficult to believe they can ever be freed from it; indeed nothing short of a miracle could change those who have lived in such a system; but there is a leaven of education at work, large in itself, though comparatively small, from which much good may be expected. I believe the Baptist missionaries of Serampore have done more than any other body of Christians to enlighten the people. About Calcutta there are numbers who are not Hindus, but it would be hard to find those who are Christians. I hear it said on every hand that missionaries are not effective, but no one seems to have found the way of making them more so. Simple good intentions do not certainly suffice, at least not for extended good, though they may produce individual conversions. Those parts of the Bible that treat of idolatry have a force, when read here, such as in our land they cannot have.

But you will desire rather to know how I find my own spiritual condition affected by this new world. Certainly I miss very much the outward observances of religion, and its public institutions; but with these we have also left behind much of the wood, hay, and stubble that deface piety, where it is professed by the many. It is a position to try our motives, for situated as we are, there is nothing to be either gained or lost by religion, there is no temptation to profess more than we feel, or to deceive ourselves by setting down excitement for piety. But, in these wilds, the Bible appears to me more than I ever before found it, *the Book*. And so long as we seek God by diligent prayer, I feel that He is with us, and can supply every need; but should we fall into forgetfulness of Him, there is nothing external to reach us. I go into these particulars, for surely if we look to one home, dearest Mary, and walk by one rule, we must be interested to know of each other's road, what are its hindrances and advantages. But perhaps you have not a distinct notion of what our mode of life is. Well then, Henry is engaged on the Revenue Survey, that is, in the work of surveying accurately the country, with a view to the fair assessment of the Revenue, which chiefly arises from a tax on the land. He is the head of a party. Three gentlemen are his assistants, besides an office where there are English and half-caste young men, and some hundred of the Native establishment, for measuring, writing, carrying chains, &c. We take the field about the first October, and remain in camp till May or June. Henry and his assistants have detached camps at different points of the district, from whence, as centres, the business is carried on, and as each part is finished our camps move. Last year Henry surveyed 1,400 square miles. You may believe that he holds no sinecure, and his situation gives him considerable power for benefiting others. It is pleasant to think how many of those about him owe their comfortable and respectable situations in life wholly to him. 'I speak,' as the sweet Meta Klopstock says, 'with all wifely modesty,' but I should like my dear Mary to know from his deeds what sort of a husband her friend has got. I have read very little since I landed, my time being much taken up in learning my new place in life. Imagine me, not only with the new duties of a wife, but in a strange country, a strange climate, all the servants speaking a strange language, and with this complete novelty of living in a camp. Truly it required the strength of affection to make me feel at home among all this. . . .

We are on the eve of a march of 200 miles; this district being finished. Henry is ordered to Allahabad. A change of residence seems at home such a formidable undertaking, that you can hardly imagine what a simple matter it is here, particularly to such plain people as we are.

But events are moving fast and the slow, almost idyllic life (though sometimes it was only the idyll of the sick-room) is near its end. On 9th August 1838 Henry Lawrence was informed that his regiment was preparing for active service. The first Afghan War was soon to break.

Henry's action was characteristic. He applied immediately to be returned to his unit and also drew up a scheme for a Corps of Guides. 'If the passes of Hindu Kush are to be fortified,' he wrote, getting a little beyond himself as well as the Government, 'they will need to be surveyed, and such work will require men who have been accustomed to think lightly of hardship and to make the most of materials.'

7—T.N.H.

The reply was simple and crushing:

'We have lately got full and detailed surveys of the Hindu Kush, the Khyber Pass, and all the country between Kabul and Heraut. The surveyors with Captain Burnes have put us in possession of much valuable knowledge in that quarter, and Lieutenant Leech of the Bombay Engineers is now on his way down from Kandahar to Shikarpoor, while Lieutenant Wood is making a survey from Peshawar to Mittenkote. The whole of the passes through the Hindu Kush are now as thoroughly known as the passes of Kheri and Timlee leading into the Deyra Dhun. The Boolan Pass by which the army advances from Shikarpur towards Kandahar has also been examined,' and furthermore he was still attached to the Revenue Survey and should remain where he was.

This was too much for Henry Lawrence. He decided to rejoin his regiment without orders.

The journey with his wife and three weeks old son, Alexander, lurks on the fringes of a nightmare.

When Henry's troop was ordered to march, he volunteered to join, nor could I object to his doing what was obviously his duty; though I clung to the hope that he would not be allowed to quit his office. But on the 15th August came the order to join the army of the Indus at Kurnaul by the 31st October. . . . I dared not give way . . . and I kept up, by God's help, till the 6th September. . . . I knew, unless I was able to move by the 1st October, I could not accompany Henry even as far as Meerut. On that day we set out, and the whole journey seemed to me like a funeral procession; and that the place of parting was to be the grave of my happiness. We were one week going to Cawnpore, and it would be long to tell you the pains and troubles of that week; baby very ill, myself apparently fast sinking, scarcely able to move, yet obliged to push on, that we might get a nurse for baby and advice for me. We at length reached Cawnpore, where I was fortunate in at once getting a good nurse, and meeting a most kind medical attendant; here I was obliged to stop for a week, when it was impossible for Henry to remain longer, and I was *just* able to accompany him. Another week brought us to Meerut, where we came to the house of Henry's brother, who was likewise ordered off, leaving his wife with four children. . . . She is gone down the river to Calcutta and thence home. At Meerut we had ten days *on the full stretch*—days that I cannot yet look back on without agony; and then both Henry and George went. I immediately came here to the house of C——'s [George's wife] sister, Mrs. Metcalfe, a kind, domestic woman, and here, in perfect repose, with my baby to occupy me, and hearing almost daily from my husband, I regained composure if not cheerfulness. And now, beloved friend, my sorrow is turned into joy. Our troops reached Ferozepur on the 30th November, and orders were then issued for half to remain there, as an Army of Observation, while the other half go to Shikarpur, and, probably, eventually to Kabul. My Henry is among those that remain, and I am setting off to join him. The journey is long and rather formidable, and there will be abundance of discomforts in living in a tent fourteen feet square, pitched on a sandy plain; but the prospect of being once more together counter-balances all grievances. The misery of the time we have been asunder, and the unspeakable pain of looking to protracted separa-tion, make me truly feel that all burdens are light which may be borne together. On the 18th, please God, I set out. Imagine the train, dear Mary! We shall have two palanquins (boxes about seven feet long by three broad, and four high, with sliding doors on each side, and a pole sticking out of each end). In one will be your friend; in the other the nurse and baby. Think that you see us about sunset getting into these; and then imagine sixteen black men, eight for each palanquin; four take it up at a time, and run along at a trot of three miles an hour, changing bearers about every five or ten minutes. Further we have two *mussalchis*, men carrying in one hand a roll of flax and rags made into a torch, in the other a skin bottle of oil, which they keep continually pouring on the torch as they run along. Then there are three or four *banghi burdars*, to carry the baggage, which is packed in small tin or leather boxes called *petarrahs*. Two of these are slung on to each end of a long bamboo, which the man carries across his shoulders. Now imagine the torches lighted, the *banghis* slung on the men's shoulders, Nora issuing out in a wadded chintz dressing-gown and silk cap, and seeing that all is right. The nurse clothed after her fashion, viz. in *pajam-mahs*, or drawers of chintz, a very wide white petticoat, a little shift of white muslim hemmed with scarlet (called a *koorti*), a wadded pelisse, outside gay chintz, inside rose-colour, and over all the *chuddur*, or sheet of white muslin, three yards long and two wide, edged with scarlet, and thrown over the head and shoulders. To her care I give our little treasure dressed very warmly, and wrapped up in a *pushmina*, or shawl like yours. Then see that baby's bed (which is a large basket) is fastened on the top of the *palanquin*, that there are tea, sugar, coffee, wine, beer, biscuits, water, oranges, medicine-chest, writing-desk, work-box, all ready in the palanquin. All this being settled, it only remains to summon the *suwar*, or armed horseman, who is to ride alongside, keeping all the people together; and the *chuprassi*, a sort of policeman, who runs by the palanquin to see that nothing goes wrong (the last two are not a part of the regular train, but given me as a favour); and now I once more go into the house, bid 'good-bye', call out '*chullo-jao*', literally 'run, go', equivalent to 'all's right', and off we go! These bearers will carry us ten or twelve miles, when another set takes us up, and so we shall get forty or fifty miles before sunrise. Then we stop for the day, probably at the house of an utter stranger, to whom we have got a letter of introduction, or else in one of the houses built by Government for the accommodation of travellers, where there is shelter from the sun, probably a cane couch to lie upon, and a man to boil water and dress a fowl if you have the luck to get one. At sunset off we go again, sometimes over execrable roads, sometimes through fields of Indian corn waving higher than our heads, again over a sandy plain. Now we come to a wide, deep body of water— never mind, the bearers will put the palanquin on their heads, and swim over. Now we pass through the close and filthy streets of a native town; where no sound is heard but the barking of dogs and howling of jackals; and through all, strange to say, travelling on the average with more safety than by a mail coach in civilized England. I hope to make the journey in five nights to Ludhiana, where Henry is to meet me, and thence we are to march to Ferozepur.

The whole affair though presumably meritorious in its warlike ardour showed that side of Henry Lawrence's character, impetuousness without consideration and single-mindedness without sense, which was to mar again and again the best of motives and action.

To cap it all his unit was not to move into action but to remain at Ferozepur!

A return to the Survey might still have been possible but again good fortune took a hand. George Clerk, Agent to the Governor-General for the Punjab and the North-West Frontier needed another assistant. Thanks to the influence of Frederick Currie, secretary to Lord Auckland, the Governor-General, Henry Lawrence was appointed assistant with civil charge of Ferozepur in January 1839. There he remained until the end of 1841. Now began his almost life-long involvement in the affairs of the Punjab, which was to see both his triumph and his tragedy.

His brother, John, wrote to congratulate him.

I am delighted to hear of your success. You are well out of the Survey. Besides, the Political is the best line. One can get on in it if he has mettle. There are very few sharp chaps in it, I think. Write and let me know all about it. What pay are you to get? You don't think so much about the last point; however, I think it is one of much consequence.... You should begin and save something now-a-days.

The question of pay was rather important for it turned out that Henry was to lose by his new appointment. Frederick Currie wrote to him on the 28th January:

Lord Auckland says there is a great deal of difference between knocking about with a theodolite all the hot weather, living in tents nine months out of the twelve, and sitting with one's heels on the table, playing civilian, and that he will not give for the Ferozepur appointment more than a consolidated allowance of 700 rupees (a month). You must, therefore, determine whether you will remain at Ferozepur on that, or go back to the Survey. I suspect you will remain, for you are in the way to future promotion and distinction in the political line, which you could not be in the Survey.

A description of the Kingdom of the Punjab and Henry Lawrence's experiences at Ferozepur though out of order chronologically will fit better into the perspective of the next chapter, and we must use our licence further to go back a little in time to the causes and progress of the first Afghan War for its effects were to be felt in the Sepoy Mutiny of 1857.

Lord William Bentinck's administration as Governor-General was followed for a short period by Sir Charles Metcalfe, one of the most distinguished men of the Company's civil service. But the rule of not employing a servant of the Company in the highest office in India was rigidly adhered to, and Lord Auckland was appointed in 1836.

At the time, the Home Government was going through one of its Russophobe periods; and fear of Russian designs on India was the *leitmotiv* of Auckland's bumbling rule. He was, admittedly, saddled with instructions by Lord Palmerston, the Prime Minister, which encouraged him to believe a Russian attack on India was feasible—which it was not—and gave him the authority to indulge in that most irresponsible, and politically disastrous, escapade, the first Afghan War. Palmerston's instructions were explicit; Auckland was to—

... judge what steps it may be proper and desirable to take to watch more closely than has hitherto been attempted the progress of Russian influence in a quarter which from its proximity to our Indian possessions, could not fail, if it were once established, to act injuriously on the system of our alliances, and possibly to interfere with the tranquillity of our own territory.

The irrational fear of Russia that saturated the atmosphere of Simla in the twenties and thirties of the last century dominated the private world of the policy makers of the time. It is the theme of all the apparently insane actions of that nightmare period. It replaced sound judgement with precipitate folly and infected the most intelligent of men with the peculiar madness of those who find themselves surrounded by phantoms.

The historical figures who played the great game ignored facts and relied on instinct. Their policies seem to us cynical and vacillating, but cynicism requires at least something concrete to be cynical about. Their actions were concealed with pompous sincerity. Documents were suppressed without even the consciousness of guilt. Honest men bewildered by affairs and tormented by rumour—that is the charitable explanation. The tragedy lies in the fact that it is probably the truth.

When examining these events, it is sometimes hard to believe that, at the time they took place, the frontiers of British India faced the Sutlej and that the empire of Ranjit Singh and all of Sind lay between it and the frontier hills and passes. A few topographical details supply the background of events.

Ludhiana, the centre of one school of ideas about frontier problems, is almost five hundred miles off Peshawar, and Kabul 191 miles further on. The Central Asian Khanates were even more remote. By the most conceivable route via Balkh, it is well over a thousand miles to Bokhara. Of equal importance are the distances involved from Orenburg, the most advanced Russian base of the period. To Bokhara, eleven hundred miles; to Khiva, eight hundred.

In the framework of these distances Russia and England met in Central Asia. Not with armies, but with intrigue. Not with coherent policies but with speculative adventures that created situations in which the Indian Government had neither the civil nor the military resources to indulge, nor the Russians the means to sustain.

Let us examine, against this geographical landscape, the growth of the conviction that Russian expansion in Asia was a dangerous thing and that something must be done to stop it.

The rulers of eighteenth-century India were not much concerned with the countries that formed its borders. It is not until the administration of Wellesley that the government in India embarked upon a foreign policy of its own.

Between 1796 and 1809 the activities of French agents in Persia and the subsequent belief in the possibility of an invasion of India from the Persian Gulf or the Caspian Sea crystallized fears into action. Wellesley employed an agent in Bushire to foment civil war in Afghanistan which indirectly resulted in a treaty with Persia designed primarily to keep French agents out of that country. Persia was to become the first line of defence against an invasion of India.

The Russo-Persian War in 1826–28 and the inability of England to support Persia meant that the first line had fallen almost overnight, and the menace of Russia replaced that of Napoleonic France.

In 1829, General Paskiewitch, then commanding Russian armies in the Caucasus, speaking openly of the coming war with England, prompted Lord Ellenborough, then President of the India Board, to outline the possible course of such a war.

He believed that Russian forces could march on Kabul and, using Afghanistan as a base, advance into India, but he did not anticipate such action in the near future. Basing his conclusions on the history of the English themselves he assumed that the armies would be preceded by traders and when this took place the government would know that action was at hand.

Civilian opinion at the time in India believed, with Sir Charles Metcalfe, that any invasion should be waited for on the line of the Sutlej, and policy should be one of consolidation within that frontier.

This opinion was, however, by no means predominant, and the mystics of Simla were responsible for adding immensely to the geographical knowledge of the time, almost, it might seem, by accident. They were, however, unable or unwilling to draw conclusion from it.

Central Asia at this period was explored and mapped, political intelligence collected, but the men themselves who travelled, and who were on easy terms with rulers who had reached the top through blood and intrigue, had virtually no influence upon the policy of the Indian Government, for they themselves were incapable of analysing the complex phenomena of Asian politics that they could observe only in detail and not as part of any design.

Men nearer home were sceptical about Russia's ability to move armies through Afghanistan to India and were upheld in their views by the disastrous failure of General Peroffski's attempt to reach Khiva from Orenburg in 1839. But these rational beliefs had little or no effect in India.

Policy became centred on Afghanistan itself and in this the outstanding figure is that of Claude Martine Wade, Resident at Ludhiana on the Sikh frontier. Wade and his disciples held sharply defined views on frontier problems and their opinions reflected the fact that they were more afraid of the Afghans than the Russians, and believed that the real line of British India's defence rested in the empire of Ranjit Singh.

This would have been all very well if the Punjab had been anything like stable instead of being held together solely by the personality of an aging and unhealthy man. If the Sikh Kingdom was to collapse on the death of Ranjit Singh it would be British India that would be attacked and not the Afghans. The obvious answer then was a strong united Afghanistan under a friendly ruler. The tragic figure of Shah Shuja now appears on the stage of history as the expendable pawn in an unworkable policy—a policy carried on in an atmosphere so unreal as to defy imagination.

Shah Shuja, the incapable descendant of Ahmad Khan, the founder of the Afghan monarchy, had been in exile since 1809 and had failed to rally any significant support in his several attempts to regain the throne. In 1833 an attempt had been aided by the Government of India, the only result of which had been the annexation of the vale of Peshawar by Ranjit Singh and the driving of Dost Mohammad, the real ruler of Kabul, into an alliance with the Russians.

Another school of thought, more closely allied to those held by the theorists attached to the Residency at Cutch, accepting the loss of Persia as final and the end of Ranjit Singh's empire as an immanent probability, believed that Dost Mohammad should be

helped to supremacy in Afghanistan and sustained there by sub-
sidy and, what was more important, the hope of bigger ones.
These eminently feasible ideas were rejected by Lord Auckland in
favour of a plan, excellent enough in private theory, but completely at variance with the facts of the outside world. This was
the decision to place on the throne of Afghanistan the wretched
Shah Shuja, by force of English arms and with the aid of the Sikhs.

In the meantime a man whose forward policy had few aspects
in common with that of Lord Auckland had been active in
Central Asia. This was Alexander Burnes, who had travelled
extensively in those parts. He was famous for his ride to Bokhara
in 1832 and his reports on the possible routes of Russian aggression. He was appointed, in 1836, Agent in Kabul, where he
established an intelligence service, and, with his assistants, explored the Oxus. The advance of the Shah of Persia towards
Herat and the arrival of a Russian agent in Kabul in 1837 produced the advice from Burnes that the return of Peshawar to
Dost Mohammad would be to the advantage of the Indian
Government. But this was rejected and one of the chief, though
lately converted, theorists of Simla, William Macnaughton, became the instrument of the disastrous policy of the first Afghan
War. He assumed, with Burnes, that the danger was Russia and
with this view filling his eyes he was unable to see the real effects
of his policy in Afghanistan. The whole of the fear of Russia
should have collapsed with Peroffski's failure to reach Khiva, an
attempt not repeated until 1873, but it did not. Macnaughton
continued in vague speculations in the north, while Kabul boiled
over at his feet, engulfing both Burnes and himself.

The final comment in this extravagant confusion in frontier
policy, of behaviour that can be associated more with the asylum
than the halls of government, rode into sight of the garrison of
Jalalabad on 13th January 1842. It was Dr. Brydon, the sole
survivor of 16,500 British and Indian troops who had left Kabul
exactly a week before and who had been decimated by the
Afghans. The illusions of Lord Auckland and fear of Russia had
drawn blood and sown the seeds of the Sikh wars while Russia
herself *retreated* to Orenburg.

Afghanistan was re-occupied after bitter fighting, and was
ended by an unpleasant and almost irrelevant outburst from the
new Governor-General, Lord Ellenborough in 1842:

Disasters, unparalleled in their extent, unless by the errors in which they originated, and by the treachery by which they were completed, have in one short campaign, been avenged upon every scene of past misfortune, and repeated victories in the field and the capture of the cities and citadels of Ghuzni and Kabul, have again attached the opinion of invincibility to the British Arms.

The British arms in possession will now be withdrawn to the Sutlej.

The Governor-General will leave it to the Afghans to create a government amidst the anarchy which is the consequence of their crimes.

The invincibility of British arms was to be overshadowed by the fact of their initial defeat by a native power.

The Afghan War led like some chain reaction to another quite indefensible excursion against the Amirs of Sind. This expedition was under the command of an honest eccentric, Sir Charles Napier, who described the campaign as a 'useful piece of rascality'.

In December 1841 Henry Lawrence was posted as Political Agent in Peshawar, leaving his family behind him. In July of the same year, while Honoria was at the hill-station of Kasanli, the Lawrences played out a scene so much a part of the private tragedy that lurked behind the public drama of the British in India in the nineteenth century. Honoria has described it in a letter.

> . . . About noon on Sunday, Dr. Steel came in. 'How are the children?' 'I hope Letitia is much better, but Alick is very unwell.' 'Yes, Alick is very ill; but it is for *her* you must be most anxious.' The words hardly conveyed any meaning to me. A heavy blow fell on my heart and brain. Then came the necessity for action— leeching and warm baths for both; Alick's entreaties not to leave him for a moment, and her little arms stretched out to mamma. About four o'clock he was easier, and so was she; but a fearful change had come over her countenance. 'Must my child die?' I said to the doctor. 'I can give you no hope.' 'And Alick?' 'He may live till morning.' I sat down on the couch where he lay, and took her in my lap. I looked from her pale face to his, burning with fever. But a holy calm came over me. I felt the Saviour saying to me, 'Suffer your little one to come to me.' I felt I was carrying her through the dark valley, and *saw* the glory she was entering on. Had God offered to restore her, I would not have taken her back. But oh, when I thought of my Henry hearing he was childless, as I hourly

expected he would be! The evening wore away; she lay perfectly
tranquil, breathing away her spirit. I dreaded to call for candles.
When they came, I saw the terrible change. At half-past eight she
ceased breathing. I laid her down to take up my still living child.
All night he continued apparently dying. The next day he rallied a
little. In the morning I laid my beauteous babe in her coffin. Oh,
Mary, dearest Mary, how do I live to tell it all? For five days my
boy continued as ill as possible; the utmost I hoped was, that he
might live till his father returned. Our doctor is an old and kind
friend, and scarcely left me for an hour. Often I thought my
precious boy was actually dead. The following Friday he had
violent fever, which proved the crisis of the disease, and the next
day there was hope. On Sunday night he slept, and so did I. I did
not think Henry *could* be back before Wednesday; but when I
opened my eyes on Monday morning, there he was sitting beside
me, my own husband, safe and well. We had another week of
dreadful anxiety; but Alick had no relapse, and, to my own astonishment, I did not sink in bodily strength. It was not till the suspense
was over that I fully felt my own bereavement. But oh, Mary! this is
sorrow *without a sting*—no anxiety, no bitter feeling, no earthly
dross. It is a bitter cup, but it comes direct from a Father's hand;
and I say with joy and praise to Him that, on the 21st August, our
fourth wedding-day, we were happier, yes *happier*, in each other
and in our hopes for eternity, than we had ever been. We never
could so have loved, had we not sorrowed together, and together
found peace and joy in believing. . . .

Dazzled by the sun on the sword-blade of the Imperial Hero,
so many of the historians and mythomaniacs of British India have
ignored the essential horror of life and its necessary effect upon
action and thought.

At Peshawar, Henry Lawrence found his duties included
liaison with a Sikh Army sent by the Durbar in Lahore to cover
the lines of the British in Afghanistan. The regiments were
mutinous and almost out of control and the whole area in chaos.
The English had been massacred at Kabul, General Sale was in-
carcerated in Jelalabad, in January 1842 a Sepoy battalion muti-
nied at Peshawar. Everything was ripe for a serious affair. But
Henry Lawrence was at hand.

At this time, although I was only a subaltern [wrote J. R.
Becker, an eyewitness] and necesarily unacquainted with the
political arrangements, I used to meet Henry Lawrence, because

the few artillery and engineer officers lived together, and he frequently joined our mess.

We all recognized in him the leading man of the camp. He was always sanguine and ardent for an advance. One evening when he was sitting with us the Adjutant of the 64th came in. He said 'that his regiment had all day evinced a mutinous spirit—it was pay-day, and they refused to accept their pay; they required increased allowances; it was cold in Kabul—they said they required fur-coats and gloves. They grew more presumptuous—they had gone in a body to their "arms"; they were now in open mutiny.' Just then we heard the bugles sounding a general assembly. 'Yes, all the troops were to parade to coerce these scoundrels.' It was almost dark; but there certainly was the summons. Lawrence, surprised at this announcement, immediately went off to find Brigadier Wild.

We made our men 'fall in'. The gunners got ready the Sikh cannon they had borrowed, and we marched off, sappers and artillery. It was so dark we could hardly distinguish one another. There was a general hum and whisper. We stood there in a great suspense. An order came for the port-fires to be lighted. We could just see Lawrence on horseback, dark and prominent against the sky, vehemently urging, and riding here and there. At length we were ordered back. Lawrence had shown the madness of firing on the regiment, at such an hour, when we could not discern the different corps, and of exposing to the Sikh army our internal discords; and had prevailed on Brigadier Wild to defer taking any measures until next morning.

The following day the matter was arranged under Lawrence's counsel, and the Sepoys accepted their pay. I have heard Sir Henry dwell on the dangers of that night, and the difficulty he had to prevent Wild from the suicidal measure of ordering the other Sepoy regiments to compel the 64th. There may have been a deeper danger than we knew; for there is little doubt but that all the Sepoys were equally averse to the advance.

The local commander, Colonel Wild, was typically incompetent. The key to the Khyber Pass, Ali Masjid, must be relieved before the avenging armies could enter Afghanistan. Could the Sikhs be made to help?

About the 10th of January [Henry Lawrence tells his own story] the Sikh and Mussulman officers met Captain Mackeson and myself at General Avitabile's and made fair promises of co-operation, Captain Mackeson agreeing to advance one lakh of rupees to enable

General Avitabile to settle the claims of the troops. The money was advanced, and it was agreed that the Najib and Mussulman battalions should advance with the British detachment; but when, on the night of January 15th, Colonel Moseley with two regiments moved on Ali Masjid, not a man of the Lahore troops accompanied him, although urgently called on to do so, that afternoon and night, by Captain Mackeson.

On January 16th I was promised that the above-named contingent would accompany Brigadier Wild on the 18th, but, on the 17th, General Avitabile begged for a day's delay, assuring me that everything would be ready for his troops to accompany us on the 19th. On the 18th, I was told that the contingent was quite ready, but at 10 o'clock that night a mutiny broke out in their camp; the officers were driven out, and I then learned that no co-operation could be expected.

I went to General Avitabile, and told him that Colonel Moseley must be relieved, and that Brigadier Wild would advance to Ali Masjid, whether supported or not; but that I looked to him at least to make a diversion by the Jaboki Pass with General Mahtab Singh's Brigade. General Avitabile held up his hands in despair, and told me there was no hope. He was ill at the time, and appeared to me to be under some apprehension of the intentions of the mutineers. What actually happened, when Wild went forward to help the garrison at Ali Masjid, was that the Sikh battalions detailed for duty marched back, first to Peshawar, and then to the Indus, while the remaining half of Wild's brigade staggered forward, in ill order, and worse spirits, to the mouth of the pass, and were there repulsed, more by their own craven hearts than by the enemy. Henry Lawrence, who flung all his energies into the operation, found one of the small guns left with the rearguard, *spiked before it had ever come near the scene of action.* 'I've witnessed a shameful sight to-day,' he scribbled on a scrap of paper to his wife, 'our troops behaving ill before a handful of savages.' Later, after a period of shameful confusion, the Peshawar force, assisted by some Sikh troops, was able to afford the Ali Masjid garrison support as it withdrew a few days later.

All that Henry Lawrence could say of the combatants in this inglorious succession of errors may be taken as justified; that 'with few exceptions there was not a man with a head or a heart in the force', that it was a 'focus of imbecility', and that, in consequence, he had himself to act as general, artilleryman, pioneer, and cavalryman; in every case, it may be owned, with inimitable dash and coolness. But the one thing needed at Peshawar in 1842 was a commander with courage to admit *the things he could not do*, as Pollock did when he arrived. Mackeson and Lawrence must be blamed, not simply for interpreting their advisory powers too generously, but for committing Wild to a line of action which, things being as they were, could only end in serious failure. A letter to the political agent at Jalalabad sums up the situation at the end of January with singular force: 'I grieve to say you can have no assistance from us for at least a month. Yesterday we were beaten back from the pass, our guns breaking down at the first discharge, and the sipahis of the 60th behaving ill. The Sikhs marched back to Peshawar and we entered the Pass; so all hope of them is over. If you can make a push for Lalpura, and there hold out till Pollock reaches us, please God we will help you. But it is best to say the truth, that, until then, there is no shadow of chance, for we cannot even relieve Mackeson in Ali Masjid, that is, we cannot take him supplies, and to go without them would only do harm. . . . I do not hesitate to say that nothing can be done. Reckon, therefore, on nothing from us for a month. I say it with real grief.

Fortunately there now arrived on the scene a Company's officer of unusual vigour and competence. General Pollock knew exactly what he wanted and set about doing it.

But we must hurry to the centre of our drama. The Afghan War was soon to draw to an unhappy close. Henry Lawrence exercised both the skill and the knowledge of an artilleryman in aiding Pollock's advance through the Passes. On 10th September Pollock entered Kabul.

Henry Lawrence's notes give us vivid glimpses of the times and of the death of his brother-in-law, James Marshall.

There seems to be no doubt that the army of reserve is but a demonstration (and a very silly one too), and that we are to return as soon as possible, most likely in October. This seems to be the intention of Lord Ellenborough, at all hazards, and in spite of all that can be said against his measures; indeed he seems to be vindictively violent against all who think or urge otherwise. He has the oddest notions I have yet met with, and as concerns politicals especially. He gave Clerk not long since a severe lecture for mentioning to Mackeson that it was contemplated to give Jalalabad to the Sikhs, although the rumour was at the time in every man's mouth; and yesterday the General, who is easily frightened, got a tart letter, asking him who informed Mackeson that the Bala Hissar had fallen, I having written to Clerk, and he having passed on to Government my letter saying that I had heard privately from M. that Col. Wymer had retired from Kelat-i-Ghilzai, which had encouraged a fresh attack on the Bala Hissar, one having failed the day before. Just fancy the implication that Mackeson and I should not be told such intelligence; it makes me open my eyes and ask what I am here for; not much certainly, for between Lord E.'s absurdities, Shakespeare's jealousies, and the General's nervousness as to being accused of being in the hands of the politicals, I am not troubled in any way.

The dust here is very bad, but the Sikhs, who are just across the river, are much better off: I think of going to them for a few days and getting a shady place. I went to Havelock's chapel in the town yesterday. He had about forty soldiers and ten or twelve officers; he prayed extemporarily, read a few verses, sang to hymns and read a sermon on faith, hope, and charity. We assembled under two united tents, where I fancy, all during the siege, he had thus collected a small congregation. It was blowing a dust storm all the evening and night, but I went home with him to his tent, and sat a couple of hours. He is a strange person, but is acknowledged to be as good a soldier as a man, the best of both perhaps in the camp.

For the first time I heard the other day something of the particulars of poor James's end: the troops halted at Jagdalak and the enemy took possession of the heights above, and annoyed them much. At this time there were few or none of the native troops remaining, and the Europeans were almost a rabble. A party of them, however, volunteered to go up and dislodge the enemy, and James offered to lead them. They went and drove off the enemy, but James was shot from behind the shoulder, the ball going into his breast; he was spitting blood. Though the wound was probably mortal, Brydon says that, the same night, when the troops again moved on the retreat he (Brydon) led the horse on which James rode for two miles, until near the barrier that had been raised across the Jagdalak Pass, the enemy rushed in among them. Brydon was knocked down, and when he rose, missed James and saw him no more. At this time and place many were killed, and most likely, nay almost certainly, your poor brother. He had, after he was wounded, given his watch and a locket of your hair to young Bird, a nephew of Mr. Bird's of Allahabad, to bring to me, but Bird was killed not many miles from this place. I have heard many speak of James in high terms, as a good and gallant soldier. What an amount of misery this Kabul business has caused, and yet how little symptom we see of improving by our experience; the same dotage in every department. We are in the hands of a higher and wiser One than ourselves. It is well that our Government in the East should survive, it will do so; but assuredly it will not be by our own mightiness, by our wisdom, or by our valour.

On 11th October Henry Lawrence left for India with the promise of the appointment of Joint Magistrate in Dehra Dun as George Clerk wrote to Honoria.

The appointment selected for Lawrence, therefore, is the joint Magistracy in the Dehra Dun, the residence being, I believe, in the hills, with a Sudder Amin at Dehra, the salary, 1000 Rs. I came to the knowledge by accident six months ago, that Lawrence, on account of his health, desired to be here or hereabouts, but this you perceive is unattainable, at least just now; so I know the Dehra appointment will not be unacceptable to you, for it commands as good a climate for him, and leaves him more to yourself. Lawrence, wherever he is, in any hills, will greatly develop their resources and improve them, so that though there he has no longer any political duties, he will by no means be in an inactive position, though I confess I would rather have kept him on the frontier. Our lately stirring emergency, however, is probably about to settle down into a stupid enough sort of routine of peace. It is to be hoped so, nor do I despair of getting Lawrence back, some time or other.

But this was not to be. After a short stay in the area the offer of the Residency in Nepal was accepted. There, surrounded by all the intrigue of an oriental court, he was compelled to do nothing. 'When you have to bring the expectations of the British Government, on any subject, to the notice of the Durbar, it should be done in a manner so conciliatory that it may not be felt as an intrusion on the independence of the Maharaja.' What a splendid discipline for a 'wild' Irishman! But it was impossible for him to remain inactive even if his activity must be confined to correspondence.

Hodgson [he wrote to George Clerk in 1845] always told Government that we had everything to lose and nothing to gain by quarrelling with Nepal. I differ in opinion on every point. I am sure we could seize the country in three months, perhaps in one, with 30,000 men, and that it would be more valuable to us than the Punjab, giving us the snowy range for our eastern boundary, and Sanataria all along the Oudh, etc., border. Once in possession of the country an extra brigade with a portion of the Cawnpore, Dinapore, and Benares divisions advanced would suffice to keep it, after we had drafted a few thousand of the Gurkha troops into our local and line regiments throughout India. I can thus see the advantages of the country to us, but I think the fair and honest way of dealing with the Gurkhas is to let them distinctly know our power, so that they may not commit themselves, for hitherto their vanity has been so flattered that they are up to any absurdity.

And next, in a letter to George Clerk:

Matabar Singh's efforts have been unceasing to induce me to declare myself his partizan. At first during December [1843] he tried threats of violence from the Prince and troops, but when he found they were only laughed at, he has endeavoured to melt me by tales of his own danger. Throughout, he has cut off all communication with the Residency, except through himself and his creatures. Bearing the name of Minister until the appointment of another, I have often been at a loss how to refer to him. During the last eight months there has been, according to the Durbar's own message in May, no Minister, and yet the Raja has evidently not liked my addressing him but has gone on neglecting to answer references, more like a spoilt child than the ruler of a country.

The final tragedy he repeats in a letter to Lord Auckland.

In December, Matabar again took up the turban, and for four months was in great feather, daily receiving some mark of favour, khil'ats, letters, and solemn pledges of safety.... All went quietly and probably might have continued so for some time, had Matabar Singh acted prudently and temperately. As far as I consistently could, I warned Matabar that it was impossible the Raja really could be satisfied; but in his vanity he believed that he had effectively frightened all whom he had not gained. The chiefs were certainly meek enough in words, and the troops were found so obedient, that he got them to pull down their old barracks, and carry the materials a mile to build them up again near his own house.

I hinted to him the danger of so employing the soldiers, but he would take no advice. The Raja, however, was not slow to take advantage of the discontent now caused. He sent for him at midnight on urgent business, and had him assassinated in his own presence; some say in that also of the Rani. She was at any rate in the plot, and her principal attendant one of the executioners. Before daylight of the 18th, the corpse was sent off to the temple of Paspatnath to be burned. The sons of the late minister have effected their escape to Sagauli; two or three of the family have been seized, and, twelve hours after the murder, not a word was to be heard in favour of the man, who, the day before, had been everything.

Henry spent his time with his eyes on events in the Punjab and his head in the books he had had no time to read before.

I have been reading desultorily *Herodotus*, *Demosthenes*, Müller's *Dorians*, old *Edinburgh* and *Quarterly Reviews*, *Letters from the Baltic*, *History of the Jews*, Paley. Struck with the extraordinary variety of opinion as to historians in different numbers of reviews, especially *Edinburgh*. In one Herodotus is a child, in another wholly trustworthy. One makes Xenophon an imbecile, another a sage. The *Edinburgh*, more temperate than the *Quarterly*, which, again, is often out of keeping; one number makes Hallam, the historian, all that is untrustworthy, another excellent. I don't like Milman's *History of the Jews*, it is not written in the spirit that might be expected of a churchman of his character. *Letters from the Baltic*, interesting. Paley is a better writer than I thought, most clear and lucid, too cool, too unenthusiastic, but most argumentative, and a writer of excellent English.

He was also contributing articles to the *Calcutta Review* on such matters as Army Reform, and preparing plans for the 'Lawrence Asylum', hill-schools for the children of soldiers.

Soon the summons for the wider stage was to come to the remote fastnesses of Nepal. On 11th December 1845 Sikh Armies crossed the River Sutlej and attacked British territory. On 7th January 1846 Henry Lawrence made the last entry in his Nepal journal.

Last evening, on my return from Molikaree, I found a letter from Government calling me to the North-West. I wished for many reasons to delay a week, but I *ought* to go at once. I therefore wrote off three letters to lay bearers, and in half-an-hour (2.30 p.m.) I started after my palanquin, which went off two hours ago. We have had two most happy years here; and, amidst some discomforts, have had many blessings, and have enjoyed, and, I hope, have not envied others. We have gained some experience, and, I trust, will both be the better for our seclusion. My wife, my darling wife, will support herself, and believe that He who brought us together, and has kept us midst many dangers and many partings, can and will protect us still. May we both trust in our Saviour, and endeavour to show our trust by our conduct.

The call had come from the Punjab. The Lawrences were now to take the stage together.

III

THE TOUCHING OF
THE TREES

Plant trees but don't let them touch
Punjabi Proverb

IN THE LAND OF THE FIVE RIVERS

THE PUNJAB, land of the five rivers, was at that time the largest and most powerful of the independent native principalities. Until 1839 it had been ruled by the strong hand and brilliant mind, the cynical, powerful mind, of Ranjit Singh, the Lion of the Punjab.

There have been many evocations of the land and its ruler, but the journal of William Osborne, Military Secretary to Lord Auckland embraces not only a view of the personality of Ranjit Singh and of the Sikh army, but character sketches of those who were later to intrigue and murder for the succession, and whose jealousies led to the Sikh Wars and the annexation of the Punjab.

Osborne was a member of a mission sent by Auckland for the purpose of 'endeavouring to place our alliance with Ranjit Singh on a more secure and decided footing' in anticipation of the need for Sikh aid in the first Afghan War.

26th May—Two marches from Dinanagar. Here we met Partab Singh, a boy of seven years of age, son of Sher Singh, and grandson of the Maharajah. He had been sent by his father to accompany us on our march through his district. This was the first instance we noticed of Ranjit's jealousy of European influence over his chiefs. According to all precedent and custom, Sher Singh himself, and not his son, should have been sent to meet us; and the excuse for this apparent breach of etiquette was highly characteristic of the customs of the court of Lahore—namely, that the Shahzadah Sher Singh had been a little overcome at a drinking party with the Maharajah the evening before, and was, in consequence, unable to travel.

His father is said to be dotingly fond of this boy; and when he was deputed last year by the Maharajah to escort Sir Henry Fane to the frontiers of the Punjab, took him with him; but such is Ranjit's jealousy of Europeans, that before they had got three marches, a regiment of cavalry was sent after them, with orders from the Maharajah to bring Partab Singh back with them, in order that he might remain as a hostage until his father's return to the court. During the whole of our march through Sher Singh's district, all our servants, camp followers, escort, and cattle, were found in supplies at his expense.

28th May—This morning's march brought us to Dinanagar, the present place of residence of the Maharajah. It is a large garden with a canal running through the centre. There are also several small buildings and a moderate-sized plain palace and zenana scattered about the grounds. By means of constant irrigation, the borders and shrubs are always kept green and fresh; and here Ranjit Singh generally passes the hot weather, amusing himself with drilling and manœuvring his troops, a large body of which always accompanies him.

Five miles from our camp we were met by Rajah Sher Singh, and Suchet Singh, sent by the Maharajah to conduct us to our tents; they were seated upon elephants in golden haudahs, and escorted by about 500 of Ranjit's bodyguards, splendidly dressed in chain armour and thick quilted jackets made of rich silk, of all the colours of the rainbow.

Rajah Suchet Singh, or Malik Adil, as he was named by the ladies of Sir Henry Fane's camp, is the brother of the minister, Dhian Singh, and one of the handsomest of the Sikh chiefs, who are all eminently good-looking. He is high in Ranjit's favour, as well as much respected and admired by all the Sikhs, and about twenty-eight years of age.

Sher Singh is also a fine, manly-looking fellow, and was richly dressed after the same fashion. He is a supposed son of the Maharajah, though the latter strongly denies the paternity. He, however, grants him the privilege of a chair in his presence—an honour he shares with Kharak Singh, the heir apparent to the throne, and Hira Singh, the son of the minister, the only individuals of the court who are so distinguished.

I have before adverted to Ranjit's jealousy of Europeans, and Sher Singh has, unfortunately for himself, shewn so much attention to them, and such attachment to their manners and customs, as effectually to rouse his master's vigilance; and whilst in his presence he hardly dared openly to accost us, which we all saw with much regret, as, when removed from observation, he, of all the Sikh chiefs, appeared most inclined to be on friendly and intimate terms with us. He is supposed to be in rather more than usual *mauvaise odeur* at this moment, in consequence of an occurrence which took place at this morning's Durbar.

Aziz-ud-din is, with Dhian Singh, supposed to possess more influence over Ranjit Singh than any other of the Sikh chiefs. He is a fine-looking man, of about five and forty, not over clean in his person, but with a pleasant and good-humoured, though crafty-looking countenance, and his manners are so kind and unassuming that it is impossible not to like him.

In the evening, the presents from the Governor General to the Maharajah were unpacked and got ready for the morning's interview. They consisted of Lord Auckland's picture set in a star of very handsome diamonds, suspended to a string of large pearls; a pair of gold-mounted pistols; a splendid Damascus sword in a golden scabbard, inlaid with precious stones; and two thorough-bred Cape horses, with housings and accoutrements of gold richly studded with turquoise and enamel.

29th May—About seven in the morning, Rajah Suchet Singh and Sirdar Ajit Singh arrived in camp to escort us to the presence of the Maharajah. We mounted our elephants without delay, and, accompanied by our escort and all the state we could muster, proceeded to the gate of the garden palace. We found two battalions of his disciplined infantry drawn up in front of the gateway, as a guard of honour, with some of his artillery, from whom we received a salute of upwards of a hundred guns. Dismounting from our elephants at the gateway, and entering the garden on foot, we were conducted by the two Sikh chiefs up a broad gravel walk about three hundred yards in length, lined on each side by Ranjit's Ghorcharhas, handsomely dressed in chain armour and quilted jackets, made of rich silk of either a bright yellow, green, or scarlet colour, giving the walk, from the gateway to the palace, the appearance of a border of gaudy and gigantic tulips. On reaching the veranda, Ranjit's minister, Dhian Singh, came forward and conducted us round the palace to the hall of audience, at the entrance of which we found the Maharajah himself in waiting to receive us. After a friendly embrace, he led us to the upper end of the hall, and seated us on golden chairs opposite himself. Rajah Sher Singh was seated on his right hand, and Rajah Hira Singh, his minister's son, upon his left, the only two individuals who are allowed a seat in his presence on public occasions, with the exception of his son and heir, Kharak Singh, though in private that privilege is sometimes accorded to the three Gurus, or priests, who act as his spiritual advisers. The floor was covered with rich shawl carpets, and a gorgeous shawl canopy, embroidered with gold and precious stones, supported on golden pillars, covered three parts of the hall.

The *coup d'œil* was most striking; every walk in the garden was lined with troops, and the whole space behind the throne was crowded with Ranjit's chiefs, mingled with natives from Kandahar, Kabul, and Afghanistan, blazing with gold and jewels, and dressed and armed in every conceivable variety of colour and fashion.

Cross-legged in a golden chair, dressed in simple white, wearing no ornaments but a single string of enormous pearls round the waist, and the celebrated Koh-i-nur, or mountain of light, on his

arm—(the jewel rivalled, if not surpassed in brilliancy by the glance
of fire which every now and then shot from his single eye as it
wandered restlessly round the circle)—sat the lion of Lahore.

On Ranjit's seating himself, his chiefs all squatted on the floor
round his chair, with the exception of Dhian Singh, who remained
standing behind his master.

Though far removed from being handsome himself, Ranjit
appears to take a pride in being surrounded by good-looking people,
and I believe few, if any other courts either in Europe or the East
could shew such a fine looking set of men as the principal Sikh
Sirdars.

Rajah Dhian Singh is a noble specimen of the human race; rather
above the usual height of natives, with a quick and intelligent eye,
high handsome forehead, and aquiline features, dressed in a magnificent helmet and cuirass of polished steel, embossed with gold, a
present from King Louis Philippe of France, he loooked a model of
manly beauty and intelligence. He is about thirty years of age, and
is very high, and by all accounts justly so, in his master's confidence.
He is active, clever, and intelligent, possessed of great influence over
the Sikh people, and in all probability will be one, and not the least
powerful or deserving candidates for the throne of the Punjab on
Ranjit's decease. With enormous wealth and property, and a large
tract of country, which he rules with mildness and justice, he
presents a singular instance of a favourite and a man in power,
whose talents and virtues are more appreciated than his power and
influence are envied. Gentleman-like, manly, and unassuming in his
manners, he is still cold and repulsive to Europeans, whom he both
fears and hates with more than common rancour, and against whom
he loses no opportunity of exerting his influence with the Maharajah.

Rajah Hira Singh, the son of the minister, a boy of eighteen
years of age, is a greater favourite with Ranjit Singh than any other
of his chiefs, not even excepting his father. His influence over
Ranjit is extraordinary; and though acquired in a manner which in
any other country would render him infamous for ever, here he is
universally looked up to and respected.

He is the only individual who ever ventures to address Ranjit
Singh without being spoken to, and whilst his father stands behind
his master's chair, and never presumes to answer him with unclasped
hands, this boy does not hesitate to interrupt and contradict him in
the rudest manner. One instance of the way in which he presumes
upon the kindness of Ranjit Singh was the subject of public conversation at Dinanagar upon our arrival, The yearly tribute from
Kashmir had arrived, and was, as usual, opened and spread upon

the floor in the Durbar for the inspection of the Maharajah. It consisted of shawls, arms, jewels, &c., to the amount of upwards of thirty thousand pounds. Young Hira Singh, without the slightest hesitation, addressed Ranjit and said, 'Your Higness cannot require all these things; let me have them.' The answer was, 'You may take them.'

Hira Singh is strikingly handsome, though rather effeminate in appearance. He was magnificently dressed, and almost entirely covered from the waist upwards with strings of pearls, diamonds, emeralds, and rubies; he is intelligent and clever, and has taken a fancy to learn English, which he studies for some hours every day, and in which he has already made considerable progress, being perhaps the only individual who would venture to do such a thing openly. Good-tempered, gentleman-like, and amusing, he is certainly one of the most amiable and popular persons at the court of Lahore.

Ill-looking as he undoubtedly is, the countenance of Ranjit Singh cannot fail to strike every one as that of a very extraordinary man; and though at first his appearance gives rise to a disagreeable feeling almost amounting to disgust, a second look shows so much intellligence, and the restless wandering of his single fiery eye excites so much interest, that you get accustomed to his plainness, and are forced to confess that there is no common degree of intellect and acuteness developed in his countenance, however odd and repulsive its first appearance may be.

His height is rather beneath the usual stature of the Sikhs, and an habitual stoop causes him to look shorter than he really is. He is by no means firm on his legs when he attempts to walk, but all weakness disappears when he is once on horseback. He has still a slight hesitation in his speech, the consequence of a paralytic stroke about three years ago; but those about him assert that his health is much improved within the last twelvemonth. His long white beard and moustaches give him a more venerable appearance than his actual age would lead you to expect; and at fifty-eight years of age he is still a hale and hearty old man, though an imaginary invalid.

Ranjit Singh possesses great personal courage, a quality in which the Sikhs are supposed to be generally deficient; and until the last few years, always led his troops into action himself.

His character was formerly that of a generous and liberal master, and it was his custom to go into action with his arms covered with golden bracelets, and to reward with a pair of them any act of personal courage on the part of his soldiers which might happen to meet his observation. But the vice of old age, avarice, is fast creeping upon him; and at this moment, two out of three of his regular infantry regiments at Peshawar are in a state of open mutiny for want of their pay, one of them being eighteen, and the other twenty-two months in arrears.

With six millions sterling in his treasury at Amritsar, such is his love of money, that he will risk the loss of his kingdom rather than open his hoards, and disgusts his people and army by this ill-timed and cruel parsimony; at a time, too, when his most bitter enemies, Dost Muhammad Khan and the Afghans, are only watching for the first favourable opportunity to attempt his destruction.

In the course of the afternoon, the Maharajah's head man came by his master's orders to know if we should like to see his dancing girls, adding, that four of them who had lately arrived from Kashmir were very handsome. Accordingly, after dinner, we repaired to a terrace on the banks of the canal, where we found eight young ladies assembled, and a display of fire-works prepared for our amusement on the opposite bank.

The four Kashmirian girls were very pretty; and one of them, Sahbo by name, would have been thought beautiful anywhere. They were richly and gracefully dressed in scarlet and gold embroidered shawl dresses, with large and enormously loose petticoats of handsomely worked silk. Their glossy black hair hanging down the back in a number of long plaits, with gold coins and small bunches of pearls suspended to the ends, enormous strings of pearl for earrings, and large gold rings, with several pearls and emeralds attached to them, passed through their noses. They are very fair, with expressive countenances, and large and lovely eyes, but their beauty is much disfigured by the custom which prevails amongst all the Mughal women of covering the lower eyelid with gold leaf, which gives them a ghastly appearance.

One of these girls, called the Lotus, is rather a celebrated character at the court of Lahore. Ranjit Singh received her with the tribute from Kashmir about two years ago, when she was said to have been very beautiful. He fell violently in love with her, and fancied that his affection was as violently returned. One evening, in the course of conversation with Monsieur Ventura, an Italian officer in his service, when the girl was dancing before them, he made some remark upon her attachment to him, which he declared was purely disinterested, and too strong to be shaken by any offers of advantage or affection she might receive from other quarters. Ventura was incredulous; and Ranjit Singh, highly indignant at this doubt of his powers of attraction, defied him to seduce her, and promised to put no obstacles in his way, further than stipulating that she should be placed in the customary seclusion of his zenana. After several polite speeches on the part of Ventura upon the impropriety of his attempting to rival his sovereign, the challenge was accepted, and the young lady immediately transferred to the royal seraglio, with every precaution to ensure her safety.

> Shakespeare described the sex in Desdemona
> As very fair, but yet suspect in fame;
> And to this day, from Venice to Verona,
> Such matters may be probably the same.

They are so in the Punjab most certainly, for scarce had eight-and-forty hours elapsed ere the hoary old lion of Lahore was aroused from his happy dreams of love and affection by the intelligence that his guards were faithless, his harem violated, and himself deserted, and that the lovely Lotus had, nothing loth, been transplanted from her royal lover's garden to the Italian's, where was then blooming in all her native beauty.

Ranjit Singh bore her desertion with great equanimity, and in a short time she returned to her allegiance, and is now enrolled in his corps of Amazons.

30th May—Returning home from a constitutional canter before breakfast, I was overtaken by one of Ranjit's Ghorcharhas, with a message from his master, begging me to meet him at his artillery practice ground, where he was then waiting for me. On reaching the spot, I found him sitting in a sort of gilded litter with glass doors, accompanied by a few Sikh horsemen, and young Hira Singh, who was in the litter with him.

He immediately commenced his usual string of questions: 'Did you see my Kashmirian girls?' 'How did you like them?' 'Are they handsomer than the women of Hindustan?' 'Are they as handsome as English women?' 'Which of them did you admire most?' I replied, that I admired them all very much, and named the two I thought the handsomest. He said, 'Yes, they are pretty; but I have got some more who are handsomer, and I will send them this evening, and you had better keep the one you like best.' I, of course, expressed my gratitude for such unbounded liberality; and his answer was, 'I have got plenty more.'

Ranjit's passion for horses amounts almost to insanity, at least such was the case a few years ago, though at present, age has tamed that as well as other less harmless passions. Avaricious as he is, he did not appear to regret the enormous sum he had squandered to obtain possession of this animal (upwards of thirty thousand pounds) and still less does he regret the vast loss of life to his people, or of character to himself, which this barefaced and unjustifiable robbery entailed upon him. So determined was he to obtain Laili, that he kept the son of the chief in whose possession the animal was supposed to be, a boy of twelve years of age, a close prisoner in his court. In vain he was assured that the horse was dead; his answer was, 'You will remain a prisoner till he is found.' He kept his word; and not until the horse was delivered to him was the boy permitted to depart.

The more I see of Ranjit Singh, the more he strikes me as an extraordinary man. Cunning and distrustful himself, he has suc-ceeded in inspiring his followers with a strong and devoted attach-ment to his person; with a quick talent at reading men's minds, he is an equal adept at concealing his own; and it is curious to see the sort of quiet indifference with which he listens to the absurd reports of his own motives and actions which are daily poured into his ears at the Durbar, without giving any opinion of his own, and without rendering it possible to guess what his final decision on any subject will be, till the moment for action has arrived.

Though he is by profession a Sikh, in religion he is in reality a sceptic, and it is difficult to say whether his superstition is real, or only a mask assumed to gratify and conciliate his people.

He is mild and merciful as a ruler, but faithless and deceitful; perfectly uneducated, unable even to read or write, he has by his own natural and unassisted intellect raised himself from the situa-tion of a private individual to that of a despotic monarch over a turbulent and powerful nation. By sheer force of mind, personal energy, and courage (though at the commencement of his career he was feared and detested rather than loved) he has established his throne on a firmer foundation than that of any other eastern sovereign, and but for the watchful jealousy of the British govern-ment, would long ere this have added Sindh, if not Afghanistan, to his present kingdom.

He rules with a rod of iron, it is true; but in justice to him it must be stated, that except in actual open warfare he has never been known to take life, though his own has been attempted more than once, and his reign will be found freer from any striking acts of cruelty and oppression than those of many more civilized monarchs.

3rd June—Accompanied the Maharajah to his artillery practice ground, where we found twelve horse artillery guns, of different calibres, but tolerably well horsed and equipped. These guns are the refuse of his artillery, and only used to accompany him when he marches. His great depot is at Lahore, and is said to be very superior, and decidedly his best arm, and the one he takes most interest in. He was trying his own shells; at five hundred yards the practice was indifferent, but at eight and twelve hundred it was excellent. Many of the shells exploded exactly over the curtain; and when one burst with more than usual accuracy, he turned round and

remarked,' I think that will do for Dost Muhammad.' At the conclusion of the practice, we rode with him for a short time, and the sun
getting hot, returned to our tents to a late breakfast.

I asked him [Ranjit Singh] how many troops he had at present
at Lahore; he told me about twelve thousand infantry, and two
thousand cavalry, and added, 'You shall see them all out in a day or
two.' He asked several questions about our mode of paying troops,
and mentioned his having been obliged to disband some hundreds
of men from the regiments at Peshawar for mutiny. I asked
when they had been last paid. 'Eighteen months ago, and yet they
were discontented.' 'Very odd,' I replied. 'What should you do in
such a case?' I explained that it could not have happened in our
service, where the men were regularly paid. He replied, 'So are
mine, and more than that, the rascals have been living on plunder
for the last six months.' I tried in vain to impress upon him that I
did not see exactly how else they could live.

20th June—Several of his European officers came to breakfast
with us this morning. They do not seem very fond of his service,
which is not to be wondered at, for they are both badly and irregu-
larly paid, and are treated with little respect or confidence. He
exacts written agreements from them when they join, and some of
these are curious documents. In one, the individual is bound to
marry a native of the Punjab; to serve faithfully against all Ranjit's
enemies, whoever they may be; and never to quit his country or his
service without special leave obtained for that purpose.

This is one of the many instances in which Ranjit sacrifices his
own interests to his unconquerable avarice. With the finest material
in the world for forming an army, requiring nothing but European
officers to make them equal to the Company's, his love of money
opposes an obstacle that habit has now rendered him unable to
overcome. His distrust and jealousy of Europeans is also another
reason that his army, with all its advantages over other native troops,
is not in the state of training its appearance would lead you to
expect. Ranjit, however, is too advanced in life, and his habits of
avarice are grown too strong, to be easily altered, and unless some
unforeseen accident occurs, which, by proving to him how little
his present force is to be depended on in cases of emergency, shall
induce him to follow a more liberal line of conduct, his army will
continue as it is, utterly useless and inefficient.

22nd June—Went to the parade ground soon after sunrise; Ranjit
came to meet us on his elephant about a mile from it, and we
accompanied him to the right of his line of infantry. It consisted of
about twelve thousand men, and reached to the city gates, above
two miles. I never saw so straight or beautiful a line with any troops.

They were all dressed in white with black cross belts, and either a red or yellow silk turban; armed with muskets and bayonets of excellent manufacture, from Ranjit's foundry at Lahore. Their movements are very steady, but much too slow, and an European light infantry regiment would find little difficulty in working round them. This might be easily remedied, by having a proper proportion of active European officers, but nothing can be worse than the system now in vogue. The commanding officer abuses and beats the major, the major the captains, the captains the subalterns, and so on till there is nothing left for the privates to beat but the drummer boys, who catch it accordingly.

The reports from different persons on the efficiency of the Sikh army, who have been witnesses to its conduct in action vary so much, that it is difficult to come at the real truth; but from what I have myself witnessed of its discipline on parade, I should say that it only requires good officers and regular pay to make it a very powerful and serviceable army. The Sikhs are generally accused of want of courage, of the truth of which accusation I am unable to judge, but that they have fought the Afghans hand to hand, and beaten them on more than one occasion, there is no doubt; what they would do against our own Sipahis must remain a matter of uncertainty; though I confess to think, if equally well officered and led, they would prove efficient troops in every way.

After going down the line of infantry, we crossed the river with Ranjit Singh, in order to inspect his artillery, which we found drawn up on the opposite bank. It consisted of a battery of fifty-three horse artillery, nine-pounders, cast in brass in his own foundry at Lahore, from the patterns of those presented to him by Lord William Bentinck. The only discreditable part of his artillery in appearance is the harness, which is patched and shabby, but the horses, though small, appear to be active, and in very tolerable condition. He is very proud of the efficiency and admirable condition of his artillery, and justly so, for no native power had yet possessed so large and well-disciplined a corps. Rajah Dhian Singh feels a great interest in all pertaining to this branch of his master's army, and under his active superintendence it is daily improving, and has already become by far the best and most powerful arm of the Sikh nation.

His regular infantry have been all raised and drilled by General Ventura, an Italian officer in his service, and to whom this present soldierlike appearance and state of discipline are entirely due. The raising of the regular cavalry was entrusted to General Allard, a French officer; but from all I can hear, his intentions have been so thwarted, and his means so limited, by the parsimony of the Maharajah, that the same success has not attended his efforts with the cavalry which General Ventura appears to have met with in the infantry. They are both invaluable officers to the Maharajah; and he is acting contrary to his own best interests by not treating them with more liberality and confidence than he is said to do.

I took the opportunity of looking at the two squadrons of General Allard's cavalry, who were on the ground. They were the first of them I had yet met with, and I was much disappointed in their appearance. They do not look to advantage by the side of the infantry. They are men of all ages, ill-looking, ill-dressed, and worse mounted, and neither in appearance or reality are they to be compared to the infantry soldier of the Punjab. One reason for this is, that Ranjit personally inspects every recruit for his infantry, whilst the cavalry is generally recruited from the followers of the different Sirdars, and most of them owe their appointments to favour and interest, more than to their fitness and capability.

In 1839 Ranjit Singh died. Anarchy struck the Punjab. The following six years have the improbable quality of an oriental romance—a *Vathek* of blood and intrigue. There was a Queen-mother and a boy-king, an effeminate vizier and a turbulent, arrogant army, trained by French and Italian generals.

The army was ruled by committees something like those in Cromwell's forces, playing King-maker with fingers on the trigger. Many of its leaders were intriguing with the British. The Rani, endeavouring to protect her son pushed the army towards a foreign war to relieve its pressure upon her. On 11th December 1845 the Sikh army surged across the River Sutlej. But sobered by their own temerity they waited, 'an army listening in silence to the beating of its own heart'.

The campaign of the first Sikh war does no credit to British arms. Officered by a Peninsular general of monumental stupidity and incredible bravery the war was almost lost by a pathological belief in the virtue of the bayonet and a fantastic disregard for the efficacy of artillery.

Sir Henry Hardinge, the Governor-General and one of Wellington's officers in the Napoleonic Wars cried from the heart after the defeat of the Sikhs at Ferozepur, 'Another such victory and we are undone!'

Finally the Khalsa was defeated and a Regency appointed in Lahore with Henry Lawrence 'in peaceful viceregal authority over the province'.

MR. LAWRENCE'S YOUNG MEN

HENRY's position as Agent to the Governor-General was one of extraordinary difficulty. In the intrigues following the death of Ranjit Singh most of his actual or reputed sons had fallen. His line was represented by a little boy most certainly not his son and dominated by the Maharani Jindan and her lover Lal Singh. Intrigue continued and administration called for diplomacy of the highest order. The territory of Kashmir had been sold to one of the Sikh leaders, Golab Singh, for the sum of one million pounds and it was necessary to use British influence and power to see that he got delivery of his purchase. This was complicated by the Maharani and Lal Singh's secret endeavours to stir up as much trouble as possible. Henry acted decisively and in person like some mediaeval hero descended with British and Sikh troops on the recalcitrant governor. John wrote to his sister of 'Hal and four young officers going off with 30,000 ragamuffins to bring the rebels to their senses'.

With Henry was a young man, William Hodson, later to become one of the more dubious heroes of the Mutiny. In one of his letters home he has left a miniature of the campaign:

> On the 1st instant [November 1846] we got hold of the rebellious Sheikh, and sent him down to the plains; and yesterday, Colonel Lawrence, Captain Browne, and myself, rode into the valley, amid the acclamations of an admiring population of—beggars! I am writing at sunrise in a little tent, and in spite of two coats and waistcoats, I am nearly 'friz'. We crossed the Pir Punjal Pass on the 4th, 12,000 feet above the sea, with snow all around us, and slept on this side in an old serai; I say *slept*, because we went to bed; but sleeping was out of the question, from the cold, and uproar of all our followers and their horses, crowded into a courtyard thirty feet square, horses and men quarrelling and yelling all night long.

The governor, impressed by a show of force and the personality of Henry Lawrence, capitulated, involving the Sikh Durbar in his resistance. A court of inquiry in Lahore followed and Lal Singh was deposed from his position as first minister. The next step was a statement from the Governor-General:

It was repeated to them [so runs Lawrence's official report] that his Lordship would be best pleased could they assure him of their ability to carry on the government alone, unsupported except by the sincere friendship of the British. But if they thought this was impossible, and called on the Governor-General to interfere and actively assist them, they must understand that his interference would be complete, i.e., he would occupy Lahore or any other part of the Punjab with what force he thought advisable; a stipulated sum of money being paid monthly into the British treasury for the expenses of the same; and further, that the whole civil and military administration of the Punjab would be subject to the supervision of a British Resident though conducted by the Durbar and executive officers appointed by them. This arrangement was to hold good till the maturity of the young Maharajah when the British troops would retire from the Punjab and the British Government recognise its perfect independence.

Henry's position was again, as first Resident, one of great difficulty. Though maintaining control over the administration his hand must always do its work in the ill-fitting glove of a Council of Regency. His position was a diplomatic one, the sterile beauty of tax-returns and land-settlement was left to John, whose tastes were for administration and his capacities more suited for it. Out of the differences of the brothers were to emerge their conflicts. John was ruthlessly for the mathematics of power while Henry placed his reliance on the humanity of personal rule fettered as little as possible by the empty logic of 'settled' administration.

There must be a moment here for a passing glance at the active philanthropy of Henry Lawrence. He and Honoria were horrified, and justly so, at the moral and physical squalor in which the children of European soldiers spent their early life in the vicious surroundings of Indian barracks. In Henry's own words he and his wife wished to provide 'for the orphan and other children of soldiers serving, or having served, in India, an asylum from the debilitating effects of tropical climate, and the demoralizing influence of barrack life; wherein they may obtain the benefits of a bracing climate, a healthy moral atmosphere, and a plain, useful and above all religious education, adapted to fit them for employment suited to their position in life, and, with divine blessing to make them consistent Christians, and intelligent and useful members of society.'

Though the idea was received with indifference defeat was not acceptable and finally the Lawrence Asylum at Sanawar came into being. The subscription list reads like a muster roll of Empire.

The Mutiny nearly destroyed this splendid conception as it did many another, but with the aid of a grant from Government the schools were able to continue and still do as a memorial to the soft, human core behind the mask of the Empire-builder, a thing that will be remembered when the dust of British rule in India has been scattered for ever.

But now we must move rapidly into the violet hues of romance, to the Golden Age of British power in India. To the frontier, to Mr. Lawrence's young men.

Their names are almost forgotten, embalmed in the muniment rooms and specialist libraries, dying slowly in the smell of decaying leather on the second-hand bookstall. What an improbable crew they look imprisoned in the coffin of the daguerrotype, their tight uniforms and frock-coats, their massy heads and arrogant whiskers! Are these the hard riders, the sharp dispensers of justice, the wardens of the cruel marches of North-west India? They look more like the occasional proprietors of genteel houses in St. John's Wood. But no, they are Herbert Edwardes, John Nicholson, Reynell Taylor, Harry Lumsden, names that reverberated in the vicarages and public schools of the nineteenth century.

Their government was without system except the rightness of immediate decision, and the construction and maintenance of peace. No wonder Lord Dalhousie, caught behind the bars of his inexorable logic, looked upon the 'Lawrence system' with amazement and positive dislike.

It is impossible, and possibly boring, to attempt a history of these men, but Herbert Edwardes' pacification of Bannu in 1847–48 is a typical example of what they were expected to do, the manner in which they did it, and the laconic way they reported their success.

We will let him tell the story in his own words:

On the 17th of December the powerful, brave, and hitherto unconquered Waziri tribes resigned their independence, and consented to pay tribute; and as far as I know, and with such occasional exceptions as any one might suppose, have abided by that agreement till this day. On the 18th of December was laid the foundation of the royal fort of Dalipgarh. .... On the 5th of January, 1848, the people and chiefs of Bannu were ordered to throw down their forts, about 400 in number. By the end of the month, in spite of being preached against in the mosques, in spite of two open attempts at assassination, and a third plot to murder me in a gateway, I had carried that measure out, and left but two Bannuchi forts standing in the valley and these two by my permission.

Such were the chief results which had been accomplished by this expedition in less than three months; but besides these, a new town had been founded, which at this day is flourishing; a military and commercial road, 30 feet broad, and 25 miles long, had been undertaken and has since been completed through a formerly roadless valley, and is now, under the protection of ordinary police, travelled by the merchant and traveller in ease and security; tracts of country from which the fertilising mountain streams were diverted by feuds, had been brought back to cultivation by the protection of a strong government; others, lying waste because disputed, had been adjudicated, apportioned, occupied, and sown once more; through others a canal had been designed and begun; while a people who had worn arms as we wear clothes, and used them as we use knives and forks, had ceased to carry arms at all; and, though they quarrelled still, learned to bring their differences to the war of the civil court instead of the sharp issue of the sword.

In a word, the Valley of Bannu, which had defied the Sikh arms for four-and-twenty years, had in three months been *peacefully* annexed to the Punjab, and two independent Afghan races, the Waziris and the Bannuchis, *been subjugated without a single shot being fired*.

It was men like Edwardes, thrown young into the exercise of great power, who consolidated the Punjab and kept it secure during the Great Mutiny. It was the pioneering age of British rule, the final push towards the frontier and the outlines of the India that is part of our own knowledge though that too died in the passions of 1947.

RANJIT SINGH IS DEAD TO-DAY

HENRY LAWRENCE was compelled to leave for England on 18th January 1848. In writing to Lord Hardinge, then Governor-General, he confessed his love for the Punjab and his personal belief that he was the ordained governor of the Sikh territories.

'I hope it is from no abstract love of office. . . . But my heart is with my work here and I would prefer working out the present policy on the frontier to obtaining a seat in the council,' and he added, 'It would be a satisfaction to me, both publicly and privately, to leave my brother John, if your Lordship thinks fit to recommend him to your successor.' Henry and Hardinge left for home together.

Henry returned to India in December of the same year anxious to be at work again. In the meantime the Punjab had burst into revolt. Two British officers had been murdered at Multan, and Mul Raj, its governor, put himself at the head of an anti-British rising. Edwardes acted immediately but the new Resident, Frederick Currie, a decidedly second-rate mind, dithered at Lahore. The views of two inexperienced men, the Commander-in-Chief and the new Governor-General, Lord Dalhousie, prevailed. They, in their comfortable ignorance, decided that nothing could be done until the cool season. It was then April. Things began to drift.

Henry, now Sir Henry and a K.C.B., wrote in October 1848 to Lord Dalhousie, and in doing so left no doubt as to his opinion:

> What I always urged on my brother John and on my assistants was, never to allow rebellion one day to make head, and what I should have done, had I been at Lahore when the recent outburst occurred, would have been to have asked my brother John to take my place, while with two or three assistants, and half a dozen volunteer officers, I pushed down by forced marches towards Multan, at the head of such troops as were at hand, and there joined Edwardes, Cortlandt, and the Bahawalpur Nawab, while the Lahore and Ferozepur moveable brigades followed us by regular marches.

Had such steps been taken, I am convinced that Mul Raj would have surrendered before a British Regiment reached Multan; or, at worst, one week, with half a dozen heavy guns, and as many howitzers and mortars, would have decided the question. No one could surely assert that Multan is one half the strength of Kangra and yet, four months after Sobraon, I was allowed to take four native Regiments, without a single European, against it in the month of May.... Although from want of rain the autumn in the Punjab is very hot, the months of April and May are seldom hotter than February and March in Hindustan. The original movement was ordered with a view to save two officers' lives; surely it was as incumbent to prevent the murder of half a dozen others. I think Currie was perfectly right in not recalling them, and I doubt not he was overruled in his original intention by the croakers at Lahore, who talked of Europeans dying of *coup de soleil*. As if war is to be made without loss of life! As if it was not incumbent to strike a blow for six as for two! And, above all, as if it was not incumbent to break up the nest of rebellion, and destroy the rallying point of the disaffected.

This shrewd appraisal of Dalhousie's policy was hardly the best method of influencing him. It was the first stage in their antagonism.

John, too, was quickly conscious of the dangerous situation as he was to be in the Muiny.

The season, no doubt [he wrote to H. M. Elliot, at the Governor-General's headquarters] is terribly bad for moving troops. But the alternative seems worse. The lives of none of our officers in Bannu, Peshawar, and Hazara will be safe, if speedy retribution does not fall on these scoundrels. It was touch and go in the Kashmir affair two years ago. It was then a question whether the Shaikh surrendered or the troops went over to him. *If we do nothing, the whole of the disbanded soldiery of the Manja will flock down and make common cause with the mutineers.*

But wise councils were of no avail. The rebels were given six months to organize and the British did not even bother to prepare for action.

The second Sikh war was almost a repetition of the first. Lord Gough again commanded like a cavalry officer attacking a tank. A terrible battle was fought at Chilianwala on the river Jhelum in January 1849 in which 2,500 British were killed. Finally the Sikh Army was destroyed at Gujerat in February of the same year.

With it died the hopes of Henry Lawrence for a friendly, independent Sikh state.

The Sikhs gave up their arms.

Sikh soldiers, advancing, one by one, to the file of the English drawn across the road, flung down tulwar, matchlock, and shield upon the growing heap of arms, salaamed to them as to the 'spirit of the steel', and passed through the open line, no longer soldiers.

Each horseman among them had to part for the last time from the animal which he regarded as part of himself—from the gallant charger which had borne him in safety in many an irresistible charge over many a battlefield. This was too much even for Sikh endurance. He caressed and patted his faithful companion on every part of his body, and then turned resolutely away. But his resolution failed him. He turned back again and again to give one caress more, and then, as he tore himself away for the very last time, brushed a teardrop from his eye, and exclaimed, in words which give the key to so much of the history of the relations of the Sikhs to us, their manly resistance and their not less manly submission to the inevitable, 'Ranjit Singh is dead to-day!'

So was the Punjab of Henry Lawrence.

I SHALL NOT BE SORRY WHEN HE GOES

'SIR H. LAWRENCE is disgusted, of course, with being a Board, and that Board under strict control. He has tried restiveness once or twice. Lately here, where he has come sick, he began to try the stormy. Upon this I tipped him a little of the "grand seigneur", which I had not given him before, and the storm sank into a whisper in a second.'

So with a characteristic mixture of arrogance and patronage wrote Lord Dalhousie in a private letter of 9th June 1849. This was to be typical of the relationship of these two men.

Previously, on 1st February, after Henry Lawrence had drafted a proclamation to the Sikhs, Dalhousie had shown who was to be master:

> In my conversation with you a few days ago I took occasion to say to you that my mode of conducting public business, in the administration with which I am entrusted, and especially with the confidential servants of the Government, are, to speak with perfect openness, without any reserve, and plainly to tell my mind without disguise or mincing of words. In pursuance of that system, I now remark on the proclamation you have proposed. It is objectionable in matter, because, from the terms in which it is worded, it is calculated to convey to those who are engaged in this shameful war an expectation of much more favourable terms, much more extended immunity from punishment, than I consider myself justified in granting them. It is objectionable in manner: because (unintentionally, no doubt) its whole tone substitutes you personally, as the Resident at Lahore, for the Government which you represent. It is calculated to raise the inference that a new state of things is arising; that the fact of your arrival with a desire to bring peace to the Punjab is likely to affect the warlike measures of the Government; and that you are come as a peacemaker for the Sikhs, as standing between them and the Government. This cannot be.... There must be entire identity between the Government and its Agent, whoever he is.... I repeat, that I can allow nothing to be said or done, which should raise the notion that the policy of the Government of India, or its intentions, depend on your presence as Resident

in the Punjab, or the presence of Sir F. Currie instead. By the orders of the Court of Directors, that policy is not to be finally declared until after the country is subjected to our military possession, and after a full review of the whole subject. The orders of the Court shall be obeyed by me. I do not seek for a moment to conceal from you that I have seen no reason whatever to depart from the opinion that the peace and vital interest of the British Empire now require that the power of the Sikh Government should not only be defeated, but subverted, and their dynasty abolished. . . . I am very willing that a proclamation should be issued by you, but bearing evidence that it proceeds from Government. It may notify that no terms can be given, but unconditional submission; yet that, on submission being immediately made, no man's life shall be forfeited for the part he has taken in hostilities against the British Government. . . .

The Punjab was to be governed by a Board of Three, Henry as chief, John, and G. C. Mansel. Later Robert Montgomery, who succeeded Mansel, was to describe himself as 'a regular buffer between two high pressure engines'.

The Board, despite its internal antagonisms, was the most un-selfish ruler the Punjab had ever had. These three ruled without pretence, sure in the simplicity of their right to rule. Nothing here of the pomp of the great pro-consuls. How simple was their approach to the exercise of power can be seen in the ludicrous situation of the great Koh-i-noor diamond, one of the spoils of victory.

At one of the early meetings of the Board the jewel was formally made over to the Punjab Government, and by it committed to the care of John Lawrence. Perhaps the other members of the Board thought him the most practical and business-like—as no doubt in most matters he was—of the three, or they deemed that his splendid *physique*, and the gnarled and knotted stick which, fit emblem of himself, he always carried with him—and which the Sikhs, thinking it to be a kind of divining-rod or familar spirit, christened by its owner's name, 'Jan Larens'—would be the best practical security for its safe keeping. But in this instance they misjudged their man. How could a man so careless of the conventionalities of life, a man who never wore a jewel on his person, till the orders and clasps which he won compelled him to do so, and even then used to put them so remorselessly in the wrong place that the court *costumier* exclaimed in despair, that he would lose reputation by him in spite of all his pains, how, I ask, was it likely that such a man would realise the inestimable value of the jewel entrusted to him? And, again, what was the custody of a court jewel compared with that of the happiness of the millions for which he was also responsible? Anyhow, half-unconsciously he thrust it, wrapped up in numerous folds of cloth, into his waistcoat pocket, the whole being contained in an insignificant little box, which could be thus easily put away. He went on working as hard as usual, and thought no more of his precious treasure. He changed his clothes for dinner, and threw his waistcoat aside, still forgetting all about the box contained in it!

About six weeks afterwards a message came from Lord Dalhousie, saying that the Queen had ordered the jewel to be at once transmitted to her. The subject was mentioned by Sir Henry at the Board, when John said quietly, 'Send for it at once.' 'Why, *you've* got it!' said Sir Henry. In a moment the fact of his carelessness flashed across him. He was horror-stricken, and, as he used to describe his feelings afterwards, when telling the story, he said to himself, 'Well, this is the worst trouble I have ever yet got into!' But such was his command over his countenance that he gave no external sign of trepidation: 'Oh, yes, of course; I forgot about it,' he said, and went on with the business of the meeting as if nothing had happened. He soon, however, found an opportunity of slipping away to his private room, and, with his heart in his mouth, sent for his old bearer and said to him, 'Have you got a small box which was in my waistcoat pocket some time ago?' 'Yes, Sahib,' the man replied, '*Dibbia* (the native word for it), I found it and put in in one of your boxes.' 'Bring it here,' said the Sahib. Upon this the old native went to a broken-down tin box, and produced the little one from it. 'Open it,' said John Lawrence, 'and see what is inside.' He watched the man anxiously enough as fold after fold of the small rags was taken off, and great was his relief when the precious gem appeared. The bearer seemed perfectly unconscious of the treasure which he had had in his keeping. 'There is nothing here, Sahib,' he said, 'but a bit of glass.'

Fortunately for the Punjab the two masterful brothers managed to keep together for four years. Between them they produced, for a little while, the highest point of British rule in India.

What they did together can best be described by Henry himself in a letter to his old friend J. W. Kaye:

The system introduced by Lord Hardinge into the Cis and Trans Sutlej States in 1846 was followed in 1849 in the Punjab. The country was divided into four Commissionerships, and each of the latter into four or five districts. The Districts of Peshawar and

Hazara were, until this year, kept directly under the Board. Colonel Mackeson is now Commissioner over them. The Depty. Commissioners over Districts perform all the functions of magistrates and collectors in the Provinces, with some of the duties of a judge. Each District has one or two assistants, according to size and importance, as also an uncovenanted, called extra, assistant. All these Officers work in all the courts, civil, fiscal, and police. Natives are eligible to these last named appointments, and it has been our aim to get as many natives of the Punjab into these offices, and also into berths of *tahsildar*, etc., but as yet it has been uphill work, as the Panjabis are not acquainted with forms and rules which are unfortunately thought too much of, though happily not so much so as in the Provinces. We wish to make the basis of our rule a light and agreeable assessment; a strong and vigorous though uninterfering police, and a quick hearing in all civil and other cases. We are therefore pushing on the Revenue Survey (you know I was for several years a revenue surveyor), and the revised Settlement. We have hunted down all the dacoits. During the first year we hanged nearly a hundred, six and eight at a time, and thereby struck such a terror that dacoity is more rare than in any part of India. In civil justice we have not been so successful, or in putting down petty crime; but we are striving hard to simplify matters and bring justice home to the poor. In seven years we shall have a splendid canal with four great branches from the hills close down to Multan, and in two years we shall have a magnificent trunk road to Peshawar, and in every direction we are making cross roads (in the Lahore District there are eight hundred miles of new road), and in many quarters small inundation canals have been opened out or old ones repaired. Col. Napier our civil engineer is a great man in this department.

The defence of the frontier alone has been no small work, considering we have done it in spite of Sir Chas. Napier. We have raised five regiments of as fine cavalry as any in India, and as many corps of splendid infantry; also six regiments of very good military police, and 2,700 cavalry police in separate troops. These irregulars and military police have kept the peace of the country; the regulars being in reserve. There are, besides these, the ordinary *thanah* police, employed as detectives, and on ordinary occasions they may amount to 6,000 men. Not one shot has been fired *within* the Punjab since annexation. The revenue has been reduced by the summary assessments about three lakhs or about twenty-five per cent on the whole; varying from 5 and 10 to 50 per cent. The poorer classes have reason to be thankful; not so the Sardars, and those who used to get employment under the Durbar; of these, hundreds, perhaps thousands, are out of employ. Liberal *life* pensions have been granted; but still there is distress in the higher circles, especially where parties were connected with the outbreak. In the Panjab there is not much less than twenty-five lakhs of *jaghir*, nearly all of which has been enquired into and reported. In this department, we have done more in three years than was done in fifty years in the N.W. Provinces.

Perhaps I expedited matters by prohibiting in the Cis and Trans Sutlej in 1846 any resumption until the case was reported and orders issued. This was reversing what some of our officers wished, viz. first to resume, and then to enquire, perhaps in ten or twenty years afterwards!

We have planted thousands of trees, so that in a few years, the reproach of want of verdure will be wiped off. Serais are at every stage on new main roads, and police posts at every two or three miles. We are enquiring as to education and have got up a good English and vernacular school at Amritsar, where 160 boys and men attend; many of whom already speak and write English. I am very anxious to extend vernacular education and educate Punjabis for the public service, and for engineering and medical and surgical offices.

Difficulties continued in the relations of the two brothers. 'We differed much,' wrote Henry to Lord Hardinge, 'as to the treatment of the old Durbar officials, military and civil, and especially as to rewards to those who had served us well in the war. We also differed in practice, though not much in theory, as to the employment of the people of the country, and indeed as to nominations of officials generally. I wished to employ Panjabis wherever they were at all fit. I also wished to help sons of old officers. My brother, on the other hand, stood out for giving all the uncovenanted berths to natives employed in the settlement, which was tantamount to excluding Panjabis and gentlemen altogether. The opposition I met on all such questions, and as to the treatment of *jaghirdars* was a daily vexation. The chiefs and people of the Panjab had been accustomed to come to me for relief, aid, and advice. Now I could literally never say or do anything without almost a certainty of my order or wish being upset or counteracted by my colleagues.'

In the end the two took to writing to Montgomery instead of direct to each other. One of the brothers would have to go.

Dalhousie, as far back as 1849, had long ago made up his mind. Of Henry he wrote:

I shall not be sorry when he goes, although he has many fine qualities, I think his brother John . . . is a better man . . . antagonism of opinion has, as I suspected, brought the brothers into violent collision . . . and John Lawrence is a good deal distressed by it, and would not willingly get away.

The last words show that there was an understanding between Dalhousie and John.

In December 1852 both brothers offered their resignations asking for the Hyderabad Residency. Henry's was accepted in an insulting letter.

Henry's departure, not to Hyderabad but to the inferior post of Rajputana, shocked his 'young men' and when he left Lahore he was escorted for many miles by Sikh chiefs.

His last letter to John was characteristic:

As this is my last day at Lahore, I venture to offer you a few words of advice, which I hope you will take in the spirit it is given in, and that you will believe that, if you preserve the peace of the country, and make the people, high and low, happy, I shall have no regrets that I vacated the field for you. It seems to me that you look on almost all questions affecting *Jaghirdars* and *Mafeedars* in a perfectly different light from all others; in fact, that you consider them as nuisances and as enemies. If anything like this be your feeling, how can you expect to do them justice, as between man and man? I am sure if you will put it to yourself in this light, you will be more disposed to take up questions affecting them in a kindly spirit. I think we are doubly bound to treat them kindly, *because they are down*, and because they and their hangers-on have still some influence as affecting the public peace and contentment. I would simply do to them as I would be done by.

As Henry moved towards his exile at Mount Abu, Dalhousie wrote the epitaph to his rule in the Punjab:

I have so often mentioned the trouble I had at Lahore with Sir H. Lawrence, and the differences between the two brothers, that you will be glad to hear I have managed to get him moved away without doing anything ungracious. When the G.-G. agency in Rajputana became vacant, he wrote voluntarily to ask that either he or his brother should be removed to it. When he wrote, I opine he had not the least intention that he should be the one to go. I closed at once, told him he might go, as the Government would not consent to appoint him, or any one who was not a trained civilian, to the *sole* charge of the Punjab, but added that he was at perfect liberty to stay if he pleased, in which case things would remain as they were. He was very much disgusted, as I expected, but he at once accepted, and he has left Lahore. The Board of Administration will now be abolished—the government of the Punjab will be confided to a Chief Commissioner (John Lawrence), aided by a judicial and financial commissioner under him. J.L. has really done the work since 1849, while his brother has got all the credit—a position which Mr. John, a very ambitious man, has felt to be very galling.

There was now only one King in the Punjab.

IV

NO SHARING OF CHAIRS

Lawrence has been greatly praised and rewarded and petted and no doubt naturally supposes himself a king of the Punjab but . . . I object to sharing the chairs. . . .

LORD DALHOUSIE to SIR G. COUPER ;
5th February 1849

THE EXILE OF MOUNT ABU

HENRY was to spend four years in the Rajputana. This area of the size of France was a relict of mediæval life. By its strength and vitality, by the vigour and chivalry of its people it had survived as the only ancient political structure that the Moguls and their predecessors had been unable to destroy.

The princes of Rajasthan have had their chronicler in Colonel Tod. He pictures a world of elemental extravagance, of the arrogance that is made of passion and pride. Rajput history is enriched by the improbable and the exotic, its commonplaces more incredible than the wildest dreams of Hollywood.

There is in the Rajput traditions the tale of the fall of Chitor to the Mogul Emperor Akbar.

Scarcely [wrote Colonel Tod] had Akbar laid siege to Chitor, when the Rana was compelled to quit it. Chitor, however, did not lack brave defenders. Sahidas, at the head of a numerous band of the descendants of Chonda, was at his post, 'the gate of the sun'; there he fell resisting the entrance of the foe, and there his altar stands on the brow of the rock, which was moistened by his blood. Rawut Deola led the descendants of Sanga. The feudatory chiefs of Baidla and Kotario, descendants of Prithvi Raj of Delhi, the Tuar prince of Gwalior, the Rao of Jhalawar, the chief of Deola, and many others sacrificed their lives for the sacred city.

But the names which shine brightest in this gloomy page of the annuals of Mewar, names immortalised by Akbar's own pen, are those of Jaimal of Bednor and Patta of Kailwa, both of the sixteen superior vassals of Chitor. The first was a Rahtor of the Maitria house, the bravest of the brave clans of Marwar; the other was head of the Jugawats, another clan descended from Chonda. Their names, 'Jaimal and Patta', always inseparable, are as household words in Mewar. When Sahidas fell at 'the gate of the sun', the command devolved on Patta of Kailwa. He was only sixteen. His father had fallen in the last siege, and his mother had survived but to rear this child, the sole heir of her house. Like the Spartan mother of old, she commanded him to die for Chitor; but, surpassing the Spartan mother, she illustrated her precept by example; she armed his young bride with a lance, and the defenders of Chitor saw the fair princess descend the rock and fall fighting by the side of her brave mother.

When their wives and daughters performed such deeds, the Rajputs became reckless of life. Patta was slain; and Jaimal, who had taken his place, was grievously wounded. Seeing there was no hope of salvation he resolved to signalise the end of his career. The gates were thrown open, the work of destruction commenced, and few survived to make their surrender. All the heads of clans, both home and foreign, fell, and 1,700 of the immediate kin of the prince sacrificed their lives for the sake of their home. Nine queens, five princesses, with two infant sons, and the families of all the chieftains who took part in the defence perished in the flames, or at the hand of the enemy. And many another fantastic episode.

To this bizarrerie came Henry Lawrence and though his appointment was an order of exile no better man could have been found in India for his imagination and understanding of the Oriental mind. And, as Henry was grudgingly to admit, it permitted him to have his headquarters in the hill-station of Mount Abu.

Our house here [wrote Honoria Lawrence to her son Alexander] stands on a high granite rock, round the edge of which are some flower-beds of artificial soil not much bigger than cheesecakes. With diligent watering these produce roses, geraniums, passion-flowers, Cape heath, petunia, and a few others, *one* thriving honeysuckle. From our own bedroom is a door leading into a little thatched verandah and out upon the tiny garden, which is in shade till 8 a.m. Here I greatly enjoy sitting, looking over our rock down into the lake, surrounded by rock and wood. There is a delightful variety of birds, all very tame. I like to watch the kites sailing in circles high up and the busy little swallows skimming zig-zag among them unmolested. There is a sweet little bird, just the size of a robin, and as tame; but our bird is of a shiny purple black, with scarlet under the tail and white bars on the wings, seen when he flies. Then we have a lovely little humming-bird, not so tiny nor so brilliant as the West Indian, but the same form. I love to see it hovering like a butterfly over a flower, then plunging in its long, slender beak, and sucking the honey. Altogether, there is great enjoyment here, of which the greatest to me is the tranquillity and the quiet enjoyment of your father's society, such as we have never known since we left Nepal. We do miss many dear friends in the Punjab; but to me this is more than made up by having more of papa. The society of the place consists of about a dozen families belonging to this Agency and about twenty of the officers belonging to H-M.'s regiment now at Deesa.

But despite his pleasant surrounding his heart ached for the activity of the Punjab days. He was even thinking of quitting India altogether.

I was aware [he wrote in 1854] that I was exalted beyond my merits or rights. No one knew this better than I did. But I worked hard, and was successful, quite successful. Peace and prosperity crowned my efforts—efforts made in the midst of opposition; and yet that was the time taken to degrade me. I cannot forget all that, and it prevents me perhaps taking a proper interest in present duties. And yet if it gave one extra peaceful day to my wife, I do not regret the change, but I fear it did not, and that, little as she said (indeed we did not, after the first few days, half a dozen times talk on the subject), it preyed on her mind, not on her own account, but mine. But why have I written thus? I hardly know, but that I write as I would speak to you. Had we come here [Mount Abu] from Nepal, we should have had little to desire—peace and quiet with full occupation in a good climate, for both. It is only that our hearts were in the Punjab, and that we were rudely thrust from it, that prevented the full appreciation of this otherwise pleasant place. Lord Dalhousie has been very civil to me, but I like him not, and he likes not me. I sometimes think of trying for one of the cold colonies, the Cape, New Zealand, or Canada. . . . I am vain enough to consider myself well suited to be governor of a Colony, as I am ready to work hard, and to reward those who do, and am quite willing to let people manage their own affairs, and to require little more of them than loyalty. If my sons had any turn for a settler's life, I would much prefer putting them down on plots of ground in New Zealand or South Africa, and laying my bones there, than either remaining in India, or retiring to England.

But his appointment was no sinecure to be idled away in the fairytale of Rajasthan. He was soon to be deeply involved in the affairs of Karauli, one of the northern Rajput states. J. L. Morison in his life of Lawrence describes the case.

The chief of Karauli, Narsingh Pal, a boy of fifteen, had died, adopting in his last illness an infant, Bharat Pal, 'descended through half a dozen generations from the third son of a common ancestor'. The adoption had in it some irregularities, and Dalhousie was only too keen an advocate of annexation, when the conditions of adoption did not square with his own dogmatic views. Karauli might easily share the same fate as Satara. But the most interesting feature of the case was that the heads of the main Karauli families, fearful of another case of annexation, and supported both by the proper Ranis of the chief's house and by the feelings of the people, had chosen a grown man, Madan Pal, who possessed much the same genealogical rights as the adopted infant, but who also satisfied the fundamental condition laid down by the thakurs: 'This is the reason for adopting a grown-up person—the splendour and government of the State are preserved, but by adopting a child injury and evil come upon the State.'

There is no better proof of Henry Lawrence's genius for understanding the India point of view—in this case obscured by Tod's feudal theories—than the speed with which he reached the heart of the dispute. Already, by April 14th, he had seen that Rajput problems demanded an understanding of *clan* customs. 'I gather that the general law *prefers* the nearest of kin, but does not object to any members of the parent stock being adopted. Further, that the practice of Rajputana has given the thakurs a voice in the adoption.' Then, in a masterly report to the Government, which summarised both what his assistants had reported, and the evidence of earlier books and Government papers, he defined first the legality of the thakurs' decision, and secondly in anticipation of action by the Governor-General, the question of the annexation of the State through lapse. His formal dispatch left no doubt that he favoured the candidate of the clan heads: 'It remains for me to give my decided opinion in favour of Rao Madan Pal, and my recommendation that, as nearest of kin to Narsingh Pal, and as accepted by the Ranis of Karauli, and by *all* the most influential thakurs, who under a strictly native régime would probably be the electors; also by more than three-fourths of the 38 chiefs who in Lieut. M. Mason's opinion are alone entitled to vote in important state matters, and, as far as can be judged, by the almost general feeling of the country, he be nominated.' Another part of his summing-up can hardly have been acceptable to the Governor-General, for it was a plain statement of the rights of Indian States to avoid annexation through legal or diplomatic processes. 'I am pleased to find,' he continued, 'that the opinion I had formed as to Rajputana rules, from a careful perusal of every document in my office bearing on the question, coincides in the main with the recorded views of such men as the late Mr. Thomason, Lord Metcalfe, and Colonel Sutherland, that opinion being that by *the existing laws* a Rajputana chiefship, great or small, can never escheat to the suzerain, except by

rebellion, and indeed that a Rajputana suzerain seldom excludes an
heir for the offence of his progenitor.' Although the letter and report
had not influence on the decision reached by the Directors, it is
interesting to note that, while Dalhousie had intimated his inclination 'to declaring the State of Karauli a lapse to the British Government', the Company after full consideration of the case came to the
conclusion that the State should continue under a native ruler.

Karauli was saved the fate of other Indian states and because of
it the Rajputana remained quiet in the Great Mutiny of 1857.

There is no place here for a detailed description of Henry
Lawrence's activities in Rajasthan. His life was as it had been for
any district officer. Problems of land-tenure, petitions and
decisions, of administration by presence and the showing of the
person of Government.
He made his particular interest the problem of jails.

In the matter of Jails [he wrote to his friend Kaye], by simply
going once into every jail during a rapid tour, and, on my arrival
here last year, writing a circular remarking that in different jails
(without mentioning names) I had seen strange sights, that must,
if *known* to beneficent Rulers, revolt their feelings, etc., etc., I
suggested that all Princes who kept jails should give orders somewhat to the following effect: classification so as to keep men and
women apart, also great offenders from meaner ones, tried from
untried: to give ventilation, places to wash, and the like. Well, in
the course of two or three months I got favourable answers from
almost all, and heard that at several places including Jaipur they
propose to build new jails. At Udaipur, my brother told me that
they released two hundred prisoners, on my circular, and certainly
they kept none that ought to have been released; for, when I went
to Udaipur last February, I found not a man in jail but murderers,
every individual of whom acknowledged to me his offence, as I
walked round and questioned them. The Durbar don't like such
visits, but they are worth paying at all risks, for a few questions to
every tenth or twentieth prisoner gives opportunities to innocent or
injured parties to come forward, or afterwards to petition. No
officer appears before to have been in one of these dens.

The inefficiency of his assistants worried him, particularly one
who 'allowed his own people and the durbar people to plunder
right and left, and the Maharaja to be brought up in the lowest
debauchery.'

And then to add to his troubles came the bitterness of his wife's death.

My dear sons [he wrote on 15th January 1854], By the side of the remains of what, five hours ago, was your fond mother, I sit down to write to you, in the hope that, weak as may be my words, you will both of you, Alick and Harry, remember them as the dying message of your mother, who never passed a day, indeed an hour, without thinking of you, and the happiness of whose life was the fortnightly letters telling her that you were good, well, and happy. Two hours after her death, which occurred at twenty minutes to twelve today, your letters of December reached me. She had been looking out for them, as she was accustomed to do, from the earliest date of their being due; and her pleasure, nay delight, was always great when all was well and her sons seemed to be trying to do their duty. Her daily prayer was that you might be good boys and live to be good men—honest and straightforward in word and deed, kind and affectionate, and considerate to all around you, thoughtful and pitiful for the poor and weak and those who have no friends. . . .

It is time, Alick, that you make up your mind as to your future career. Tell your uncles about it. Even Addiscombe will require exertion. You think now that you would not care to be a civilian, and that it is not worth the trouble of trying for; but ten years hence you will assuredly regret if you now let go by the opportunity. To the qualified man the Civil Service is a noble field; to an unfit person it and every other field will be a field of vexation and degradation to himself and friends. . . .

Half an hour before I began to write on these two sides of this sheet I had taken my last earthly look at my wife and your mother. Corruption was gaining on her. I had slept on the verandah, as near as the doctor would permit me. . . . So I went and took my last look of her dear sweet face, and prayed for the last time by her side— prayed that what I had neglected to do during her life I might now do after her death, prayed that her pure spirit might be around you and me, to guide us to good and shield us from evil. . . .

Mamma said little to me during her last illness. She knew I weakly feared to part with her. She welcomed Mr. Hill as having come to see her die; and about midnight told me she would not be alive twelve hours. Again I say, my boys, remember with love, and show your love by your acts: few boys ever had such a mother.

It was a different Henry who was to write to his friend Donald Macleod later the same year.

I am sorry to say that time has not improved my opinion of the Rajputs. I am almost in a fit frame of mind to write a leading article in *The Friend of India*, insisting on the duty of annexing all Rajputana. The kings are tyrants, the thakurs are rebels, and at the same time hardly less tyrannical than their sovereigns. We have interfered mischievously far enough for harm, not far enough for good. Jaipur is financially at a deadlock, eaten up with silly conceit, and at the same time without what deserves the name of an administration. It is only by constant threats that I can keep the roads clear of gang robbers. Half the revenue is not collected. Boundaries are only put up to be knocked down. Jodhpur is a little better, but the thakurs are all discontented, and a force is now out against one of them. The king ... was a petty chief in Gujerat ten years ago, but now assumes nearly the full quantum of Rajputana airs. I say nearly, for last cold weather he did pay me an unceremonious visit here, and actually walked half way up the hill, after a trip of 50 or 60 miles. But he spoilt all by putting me to sit on the ground while he sat on thick quilted bedding. On his coming to me the first day I had a *razai* laid out for myself about an inch lower than his, which caused a sensation. Such is Rajputana. It has been petted while other states have been bullied. For years past Mewar has been in tacit rebellion. Four-fifths of the thakurs have cut the Rana, and now that all parties have begged our interference, the thakur gentlemen tell my brother, and indeed me, that they will abide by no decision that does not give them all their own rights, meaning thereby all they want and have been contending for the last 50 years. I have just fined Jaipur 45,000 rupees for knocking down boundary pillars, and have got a lot of thakurs in jail and have pitched into the Mewar thakurs frightfully as also into the Alwar raja. I suspect I am considered a perfect tiger after the gentle Low, who let every man do much as he liked, and Sutherland, who rather encouraged them in following their own pursuits. Sati was put down only in name, and was hardly punished; in Mewar, Bikanir, and Alwar it was not even forbidden. I have just written that if it be not so now I will cut their acquaintance. I thought I came here for peace, but from the day I joined them there have been little wars going on sometimes 2 or 3 at a time. ... In Dungarpur a sati took place two months ago, though a fresh proclamation had only a few days before been published on the subject. I fined the villagers 500 rupees, sentenced 2 Brahmins and the thakur's son, the three active agents each to three years' imprisonment in irons, and the thakur to pay a fine amounting to half his revenue for 3 years. He was absent, but evidently had only gone that very day, to avoid, as he thought, responsibility. Well, the gentleman, his son, and followers, have taken to the jungle. His country is wild, and heretofore such gents after a few months' outlawry got all they wanted. Not only forgiveness but favours. This fellow, I hear, talks of old grievances. I have given him warning that if he do not instantly come in, his estate will be forfeited for good. Fifteen of the Saroli thakurs, after being in the hills for nearly a year, when we hunted them with the Jodhpur legion, and finally starved them into surrender, are now in jail. I hope the new system will do good. We want good boundary settlements and surveys—the work heretofore has generally been badly done, and has increased rather than diminished disputes. We want a map of the country and at least one road through it. The Derajat was as well off under Ranjit for roads as Rajputana is now. The daks are the worst I know of in India, 6, 7, and 8 days from Agra—350 miles; from 8 to 14 days to Bombay, and so on. We are, in short, benighted, and I feel will get little help from Government, as the Governor-General cares not a straw for us, and Colonel Low probably thinks we are uncommonly well off, and that I am a troublesome meddler. In January last the district of Nimach was made over to me as Commissioner. It belongs to Sindhia, but is managed by us. The mode we have, during our incumbency of 8 years, dispensed the blessings of the British Government has been by raising the revenue 30 per cent throughout and in many villages 60, 80, and 100 per cent. Colonel Sleeman never visited the district, and though Mr. Bushby did, it was to very little effect. When I went to Nimach in February I was overwhelmed with complaints.

Yet behind the old benevolence and kindliness remained. His house was always open to guests, his wisdom and experience to those who asked for it. There is a description of him at the time by Major Oldfield who had served under him.

A tall, thin, wiry-looking man, with hollow cheeks, a haggard face, restless eyes, and a long grey beard which extended nearly to his waist. The lines of care and hard Indian service were deeply stamped upon his brow and face, and he looked at least ten years older than he really was. He received me cordially, asked me to dine with him in the evening, and then going into the bungalow was soon immersed in business details. One constant tide of visitors, almost all natives, were making their way to him, with various petitions, requests and remonstrances. All were received and patiently heard, but none could boast of an audience of more than a few minutes.

But we must leave Henry for a while and return to the Punjab of John's rule, undisputed, unshared and—successful.

KEEPING THE TEAM TOGETHER

'I SHOULD like to fix my own impress on administration [of the Punjab],' wrote John Lawrence. 'I desire earnestly to show what a man bred and educated as a civilian can do in a new country.' Let us see how he did it.

His instruments remained that brilliant group of men, India has never seen a finer, left to him by his brother Henry. They were all young men, yet old in the subtleties of rule. It was very much a young man's country, this India before the Mutiny. Dalhousie, the Governor-General, was only thirty-seven in 1849, Edwardes, little more than thirty, John Nicholson in his early twenties, John Lawrence forty-two when he was made Chief Commissioner.

There was no shirking of responsibility, only a tendency to act on their own initiative, a trait that angered Dalhousie into a pro-consular temper.

'I will not stand it in quicker times for half an hour and will come down unmistakedly upon any one of them who may "try it on" from Major Edwardes C.B. down to the latest General-Ensign-Plenipotentiary on the establishment.'

The Punjab was a Non-Regulation Province, i.e., the Regulations of Government were administered in the spirit and not in the letter. This method permitted an essentially empirical approach to the problems of everyday administration. The principles characterizing the Non-Regulation system adopted by John Lawrence were simple. *First*, the country was divided into Districts small enough to make it possible for the officer in charge to know it intimately. *Secondly*, every civil officer held judicial, fiscal, and magisterial power, concentrating in his person authority and undivided responsibility. *Thirdly*, the laws and procedure used were of the simplest kind based, as far as possible, on native customs and institutions.

The concentration of powers meant quicker and more informed decisions unfettered by the shibboleths of western law and practice. The grip of the central authority on the country was firm and informed.

John Lawrence's advice to a young civilian thrown into a badly neglected district is simple and instructive:

> Work away as hard as you can, and get all things into order. If you succeed you will establish a claim to early promotion which cannot be overlooked, and which, as far as I go, shall not be passed over. I made my fortune, I consider, by being placed, in 1834, in a district in a state similar to Leia, in which I worked for two years, morning, noon, and night, and after all was superseded! Nevertheless, all my prosperity dates from that time. Your charge of Leia will prove a similar one in your career. . . . I would throw my strength into putting things straight for the future, and leave off complaints of the past, as much as possible, weeding out bad officials, and making an example in a summary but legal way here and there. . . . Without being too formal and technical, put on record all that occurs, and be careful that you act in accordance with law and justice. . . . You may give such reductions as you may consider fair and reasonable. Don't give it merely because people scream, but where it is necessary. Better give a little too much than too little; it will be true economy in the end.

With others, John Nicholson and Robert Napier, John had many a passage at arms but the team kept together. Roads were built, wages were good, peace and prosperity almost filled the canvas.

A treaty was signed with Afghanistan in 1855 which kept the frontier quiet in the Mutiny. John signed it but against his own judgement. On 3rd June 1854 he had written:

> I dare say I am quite wrong in my views about a treaty with the Amir. With the Governor-General, you [Courtenay], and Edwardes all of a different opinion, it would be very bumptious of me to stand out. But I cannot help thinking that if ever the Russians get to Herat we shall have to fight our battles with our own right hands. I do not see clearly why the Afghans should side with us from motives of interest. Give what support we like in money they could not defend their country so as to prevent the Russians overrunning and occupying it; though after this was effected they might give immense annoyance. Kabul is much more assailable from the Herat side than from this. But we could go there tomorrow, with 10,000 men and a good commander, and hold it also. Not that I advocate

such a measure, which would be most unwise. But, if we like to spend a couple of millions annually on such an insane act, we could hold it.

The golden age of British rule set firmly upon the Punjab while in the villages and palaces, along the roads and in the caravanserai, in the barracks of the sepoys and in the minds of the discontented, the murmurs of revolt rumbled quietly like summer thunder.

A CLIVE MAY NOT BE AT HAND

HENRY in his exile and the depression that followed his wife's death turned to writing as an activity. In the *Calcutta Review* of March 1856, in the course of an article on the 'Indian Army' he foresaw, though almost accidentally, the coming of the Mutiny.

Ninety in a hundred Sepoys have every reason to be delighted with the service. Several of the remaining ten are satisfied. One, two, or three are dangerously discontented. The reason is plain. They feel they have that in them which would elsewhere raise them to distinction. Our system presses them down. . . . We must not wait until, in a voice somewhat louder than that of the European officers in the days of Clive, the 'excellent drills' and the 'tight-pantalooned' combine to assert their claims. What the European officers have repeatedly done may surely be expected of Natives. We shall be unwise to wait for such occasion. Come it will, unless anticipated. A Clive may not be then at hand.

The revolt lay hid in the heart of the Sepoys and yet it could be seen by those that wished to see. Kaye, the historian of the Mutiny, has summed up what he describes as the 'deteriorating influences' in the Bengal Army.

Looking, then, at the condition of the Native Army of India, and especially at the state of the Bengal regiments, as it was in the spring of 1856, we see that a series of adverse circumstances, culminating in the annexation of Oudh, some influencing him from without and some from within, had weakened the attachment of the Sepoy to his colours. We see that, whilst the bonds of internal discipline were being relaxed, external events, directly or indirectly affecting his position, were exciting within him animosities and discontents. We see that as he grew less faithful and obedient, he grew also more presuming; that whilst he was less under the control of his officers and the dominion of the State, he was more sensible of the extent to which we were dependent upon his fidelity, and therefore more capricious and exacting. He had been neglected on the one hand, and pampered on the other. As a soldier, he had in many ways deteriorated, but he was not to be regarded only as a soldier. He was a representative man, the embodiment of feelings and opinions shared by large classes of his countrymen, and circumstances might one day render him their exponent. He had many opportunities of becoming acquainted with passing events and public opinion. He mixed in cantonments, or on the line of march, with men of different classes and different countries; he corresponded with friends at a distance; he heard all the gossip of the Bazaars, and he read, or heard others read, the strange mixture of truth and falsehood contained in the Native newspapers. He knew what were the measures of the British Government, sometimes even what were its intentions, and he interpreted their meanings, as men are wont to do, who, credulous and suspicious, see insidious designs and covert dangers in the most beneficent acts. He had not the faculty to conceive that the English were continually originating great changes for the good of the people; our theories of government were beyond his understanding, and as he had ceased to take counsel with his English officer, he was given over to strange delusions, and believed the most dangerous lies.

But in taking account of the effect produced upon the Sepoy's mind by the political and social measures of the British Government, we must not think only of the direct action of these measures —of the soldier's own reading of distant events, which might have had no bearing upon his daily happiness, and which, therefore, in his selfishness he might have been content to disregard. For he often read these things with other men's eyes, and discerned them with other men's understandings. If the political and social revolutions, of which I have written, did not affect him, they affected others, wiser in their generation, more astute, more designing, who put upon everything that we did the gloss best calculated to debauch the Sepoy's mind, and to prepare him, at a given signal, for an outburst of sudden madness. Childish, as he was, in his faith, there was nothing easier than to make him believe all kinds and conditions of fictions, not only wild and grotesque in themselves, but in violent contradiction of each other. He was as ready to believe that the extension of our territory would throw him out of employment, as that it would inflict upon him double work. He did not choose between these two extremes; he accepted both, and took the one or the other, as the humour pleased him. There were never wanting men to feed his imagination with the kind of aliment which pleased it best, and reason never came to his aid to purge him of the results of this gross feeding.

Many were the strange glosses which were given to the acts of the British Government; various were the ingenious fictions woven with the purpose of unsettling the minds and uprooting the fidelity of the Sepoy. But diverse as they were in many respects, there was a certain unity about them, for they all tended to persuade him that our measures were directed to one common end, the destruction of Caste, and the general introduction of Christianity into the land. If we annexed a province, it was to facilitate our proselytising operations, and to increase the number of our converts. Our resumption operations were instituted for the purpose of destroying all the religious endowments of the country. Our legislative enactments were all tending to the same result, the subversion of Hinduism and Mahomedanism. Our educational measures were so many direct assaults upon the religions of the country. Our penal system, according to their showing, disguised a monstrous attempt to annihilate caste, by compelling men of all denominations to feed together in the gaols. In the Lines of every regiment there were men eager to tell lies of this kind to the Sepoy, mingled with assurances that the time was coming when the Feringhees would be destroyed to a man; when a new empire would be established, and a new military system inaugurated, under which the high rank and the higher pay monopolised by the English would be transferred to the people of the country. We know so little of what is stirring in the depths of Indian society; we dwell so much apart from the people; we see so little of them, except in full dress and on their best behaviour, that perilous intrigues and desperate plots might be woven, under the very shadow of our bungalows, without our perceiving any symptoms of danger. But still less can we discern that quiet under-current of hostility which is continually flowing on without any immediate or definite object, and which, if we could discern it, would baffle all our efforts to trace it to its source. But it does not the less exist because we are ignorant of the form which it assumes, or the fount from which it springs. The men, whose business it was to corrupt the minds of our Sepoys, were, perhaps, the agents of some of the old princely houses, which we had destroyed, or members of old baronial families which we had brought to poverty and disgrace. They were, perhaps, the emissaries of Brahminical Societies, whose precepts we were turning into folly, and whose power we were setting at naught. They were, perhaps, mere visionaries and enthusiasts, moved only by their own disordered imaginations to proclaim the coming of some new prophet or some fresh avatar of the Deity, and the consequent downfall of Christian supremacy in the East. But whatsoever the nature of their mission, and whatsoever the guise they assumed, whether they appeared in the Lines as passing travellers, as journeying hawkers, as religious mendicants, or as wandering puppet-showmen, the seed of sedition which they scattered struck root in a soil well prepared to receive it, and waited only for the ripening sun of circumstance to develop a harvest of revolt.

We are now assembling the materials of the Mutiny and to them we must add the Kingdom of Oudh, for soon Henry was to be its Commissioner and to die in his Residency at Lucknow. There was to be no Clive at hand when he was needed, but the Mutiny produced its own heroes, not the least of which was Henry Lawrence.

THE RETURN OF PHILOCTETES

In 1856 Henry Lawrence had decided to return to England. There seemed no place for him in India. But on 19th January 1857 the summons came. He was to go to Oudh. He accepted immediately by telegram and wrote the same day.

> I am honoured and grateful by your kind letter of the 9th, this day received. I am quite at your Lordship's service, and will cancel my leave, and move to Lucknow at a day's notice, if you think fit, after this explanation, to appoint me. My own doctor (my friend Ebden) thinks better of my health than any other doctor—three others, whom I consulted before I came here, replied that I certainly ought to go home. The two staff doctors at this station say the same. But Dr. Ebden and Dr. Lowndes, both of whom know me well, say that my constitution has that elasticity that, in a work so much to my taste as Oudh, I may be able to hold out. Annoyances try me much more than work. I went round Gujerat last month, several times riding 30 or more miles a day, and being repeatedly out all day or night, and sometimes both. I can also work at my desk for 12 or 15 hours at a time. Work therefore does not yet oppress me. But ever since I was so cavalierly elbowed out of the Punjab, I have fretted, even to the injury of my health. Your Lordship's handsome letter has quite relieved my mind on that point; so I repeat that, if on this explanation you think fit to send me to Oudh, I am quite ready and can be there within twenty days of receiving your telegraphic reply.

Soon he was on his way to Lucknow and a common grave. He arrived at the city on 20th March.

The territory of the Kingdom of Oudh was about the size of Scotland, with a population of some three millions. The capital, Lucknow, was the second city of India with between six and seven hundred thousand inhabitants. Originally it had been a Mogul province but on the disintegration of the empire the Nawab Wazirs had made themselves independent princes and, since 1819, had been given by the Company the title of King.

The Company had guaranteed the dynasty, and protected its frontiers from any rapacity other than its own. In 1801 half the

Walls of Lahore

Lord Dalhousie

---

province had been taken over for the payment of debts and for future services. The Kings of Oudh degenerated into a succession of royal imbeciles, sunk into the sludge of debauchery and subject to the whims of fiddlers, eunuchs, and poetasters. The country was dominated by the private pleasure and personal profit of favourites and panders, while the army, unpaid, dissolute, and mutinous, roamed the country terrorizing a populace already milked by ruthless tax-collectors and petty tyrants.

On 7th February 1856 Oudh became a province of British India. Disorder and discontent remained, for the parasites now had nothing to feed on except their hate for those who had driven them into unemployment. But, most dangerous of all, as the Bengal Army seethed with revolt Oudh, its principal recruiting ground, was no longer a place of greater social standing for the Sepoy. 'I used to be a great man when I went home,' said an Oudh cavalryman to Henry Lawrence. 'The best of the village rose when I approached; now the lowest puff their pipes in my face.'

A bad Chief Commissioner, Coverly Jackson, and a pig-headed Revenue Commissioner, Martin Gubbins, contributed to the chaos. British administration in Oudh was singularly inefficient, without either discretion or moderation. Henry Lawrence arrived too late. His own impressions of Oudh in March and April 1857 are better than any second-hand version:

> You will be glad to hear that after seventeen days' occupancy of my new berth I feel myself more comfortable than I expected. The work is *decidedly* not overwhelming and I have less fear of the heat than I had. There is a large town house and another nearly as large in the cantonment four miles off at my disposal. I was never so well housed. All hands seem glad at my coming, the natives especially. For the first time since annexation have the doors of the Residency been open to the nobles and the traders. I have held large darbars for both Classes (separately); and now the individual members of each class come to me daily. General Outram writes to me that he is glad I am come as he is sure 'I [he] could not have restored order'. His wife, a nice gentle creature, writes to me that she too is very glad as, when she was here in January last, 'everyone was wretched, and all wanted a firm kind hand'. The Civil officers, whether civilians or soldiers, may well be glad of the change, for in the whole course of my service I never saw such letters as have issued from these offices. 'Evasion', 'misrepresentation', etc., were common words

flung about right and left. I tore up two drafts of letters that came to me the first day, and altered three others. Mr. Jackson was not altogether to blame. He is a violent but able and kindly man. When thwarted he could not restrain himself and lost his judgement. He stayed eight days with me, and was very amicable though I told him he was very wrong in some of his acts and in more of his expressions. ... He was on bad terms with five out of the six principal officers (civil), and also with the Civil Secretary. The Judicial Commissioner, as also the Revenue one, were at bitter feud with him. The first is not a wise man, jealous of interference, and yet fond of interfering. Mr. Ommaney is his name. ... I cannot say I admire him, but have no fear of his disturbing me. I took an early opportunity, even while Mr. Jackson was here, to let him (Mr. O.) know that he was not to lead me by the nose. The first occasion was regarding a Thuggee jail, in which I found all sorts of people mixed up with Thugs, and the sentries, all with muskets in their hands, at the mercy of the prisoners. *On the spot* I put the sentries into safe positions. Jackson was with me, and expressed surprise at my daring to interfere, an as much as in one of his despatches he had been told by Government that the Judicial Commissioner had *plenary* power in jail matters. As soon as I came in I wrote an official letter to Mr. Ommaney, saying I did not wish to interfere in details, but that the case was urgent as I was mobbed by life prisoners, mixed up with those confined for misdemeanours, and that all could escape when they liked. ... The Revenue Commissioner, a better and abler man, whom I like, though I have never been officially connected with him, may be a more troublesome coadjutor. He has strong views about breaking up estates and destroying the aristocracy. To a certain extent I agree with him, where it can be done fairly. He also *professes* to advocate low assessments, but in some quarters he has enforced high ones. We have however sympathies in common, and he, Mr. Gubbins, was so tremendously mauled by Mr. Jackson that he, even more than the others, has hailed my coming.

The military and political arrangements are perhaps the worst, and mostly owing to General Outram. In the Punjab we were not allowed to enlist the very men who had fought on our side, and were restricted to eighty [a mistake, actually ten] Sikh Regiments of eight hundred. Here every Policeman and every (with few exceptions) Irregular soldier was in the King's service. Outram would not hear of any outsiders being enlisted. This was a great mistake. Besides, the position of the troops, magazine, treasury, etc., are all as bad as bad can be—all scattered over several miles, the Infantry in one direction, the Cavalry another, the Artillery in a third, the magazine in a fourth and almost unprotected. The Governor-

General seems in some alarm regarding the state of affairs, though I hope there is no serious reason. A few days ago he sent me more than a sheet of paper from an officer in Oudh, whose name he did not mention, giving a frightful picture of the state of irritation afloat in Oudh. . . . I fear his picture of the revolutionary schemes of many (i.e. of the officials) is quite correct. A dead level seems to be the ideal of many civil officers, both military and civilian. . . . My health is *better*, rather than worse. I am calmer and quieter than I have been for years, and take intense pleasure in my daily work of looking about this immense city in the morning, and dealing with *authority* all day in matters affecting many millions' welfare. While I write, 200 or more traders are calling out against a new tax attempted to be levied in the city by Mr. Ommaney. They beset me yesterday evening, when I sent for Mr. O. He did not know, or affected not to know their grievance. . . . I have stayed the levy pending enquiry.

Every act he undertook, every reform he attempted was merely Canute against the sea, there was too little time, too much anarchy, too much hate.

Trouble commenced with the greased cartridges. No time now for reforms, for the orderly penetration of 'Punjab methods'. The Mutiny had begun.

Time is everything just now. Time, firmness, promptness, conciliation, and prudence; every officer, each individual European, high and low, may at this crisis prove most useful or even dangerous.

A firm and cheerful aspect must be maintained: there must be no bustle, no appearance of alarm, still less of panic; but at the same time there must be the utmost watchfulness and promptness; everywhere the first germ of insurrection must be put down instantly. Ten men may in an hour quell a row which, after a day's delay, may take weeks to put down. I wish this point to be well understood. In preserving internal tranquillity the chiefs and people of substance may be most usefully employed at this juncture; many of them have as much to lose as we have. Their property, at least, is at stake. Many of them have armed retainers, some few are good shots, and have double-barrelled guns. For instance (name illegible) can hit a bottle at 100 yards. He is with the ordinary soldiers. I want a dozen such men, European or native, to arm their own people, and to make thannahs of their own houses or some near position, and preserve tranquillity within a circuit around them.

But there was to be only the tranquillity of the grave in the Residency.

V

THE WOUND THAT WOULD NOT BE HEALED

*Thoughts of the breezes of May blowing
over an English field,
Cholera, scurvy and fever, the wound
that would not be heal'd.*

The Defence of Lucknow, TENNYSON

A SMALL CLOUD

LORD DALHOUSIE was replaced as Governor-General by Lord Canning who arrived in India in 1856. In August of the previous year he had been entertained at a banquet by the Court of Directors of the Honourable East India Company. His speech was significantly prophetic.

I wish for a peaceful time of office, but I cannot forget that, in our Indian Empire, that greatest of all blessings depends upon a greater variety of chances and a more precarious tenure than in any other quarter of the globe. We must not forget that in the sky of India, serene as it is, a small cloud may arise, at first no bigger than a man's hand, but which, growing bigger and bigger, may at last threaten to overwhelm us with ruin. What has happened once may happen again. The disturbing causes have diminished certainly, but are not dispelled. We have still discontented and heterogeneous peoples united under our sway; we have still neighbours before whom we cannot altogether lay aside our watchfulness; and we have a frontier configuration which renders it possible that at any moment causes of collision may arise. Besides, so intricate are our relations with some subsidiary States that I doubt whether, in an Empire so vast and so situated, it is in the power of the wisest Government, the most peaceful and the most forbearing, to command peace. But if we cannot command, we can at any rate deserve it by taking care that honour, good faith, and fair dealing are on our side: and then, if, in spite of us, it should become necessary to strike a blow, we can strike with a clear conscience. With blows so dealt, the struggle must be short, and the issue not doubtful.

That small cloud was growing every day.

We have seen the dangerous farce of the Kingdom of Oudh, overrun with discontent and disbanded soldiery, annexations had taken place without reason to the native mind, the Santals, aborigines of extreme simplicity, had rebelled against the Hindus who enmeshed them with debts, a rumour was going the rounds that British rule in India would end in 1857—the centenary of Clive's Battle of Plassey. India trembled like almost-boiling water.

The causes of the Mutiny are complex. There is macabre
improbability about the whole affair. To-day with the memory of
our school history lessons tattered in our minds we remember
vaguely the greased cartridges and the well at Cawnpore, the
siege of Delhi and the Relief of Lucknow. Visions must have
come to us of a people in arms, a white skin—the motive for
murder. But the Mutiny was a small-scale business, restricted,
localized, almost only a riot. Minute armies deployed against each
other while disarmed civilians were anxious only to be left in
peace. Yet the Mutiny destroyed the East India Company as well
as the 'casual' era of British power in India, and left a legacy of
misunderstanding and indifference as the unbridgeable gaps between the rulers and the ruled.

Mutinies in the Sepoy Army had been common enough in the
half-century preceding the outbreak of 1857.

Lord Dalhousie records in a private letter of 6th October 1855
an example that was really a rehearsal for 1857:

> In India we are beginning to be less easy every day, and to feel
> more and more the need of some great success in this war, whose
> existence is universally known among the natives, and whose
> course is universally believed by them to have been disastrous to us.
> In Oudh matters are in a very uncomfortable state.
>
> The violent religious feud which I mentioned to you has been
> temporarily allayed by the shedding of blood; but the causes of the
> feud remain unremoved. The Mussulmans are in a state of great
> excitement; the Hindus are equally furious, equally resolved, and
> far more numerous. If this feud should again break out, it is im-
> possible to say how far the religious feeling may spread or to what
> it may not lead.
>
> The most inflammatory pamphlets on the Mussulman side are
> being circulated throughout the country, notwithstanding the
> seizure of them wherever they can be found. Fortunately Outram
> is at Lucknow, and the affair is thus in the best hands. Mohammedan
> fanaticism has produced, since I wrote, another sad tragedy. Colin
> Mackenzie, one of the Brigadiers of the Hyderabad Contingent, has
> been cut down by his own troopers and is now swimming for his
> life. The whole regiment for a time mutinied, but gave in. It is
> alleged that he interfered with the exercise of their religion during
> their great feast, the Mohurrum. However that may be, he certainly
> interfered most unwisely, and personally, with a procession, and
> was attacked directly. All these concurrent instances of Mohammedan

frenzy and violence are indications not to be disregarded. They care nothing that we are fighting for the Moslem interest in the East.

Pre-Mutiny officials were not indifferent to the nostalgias and horrors of Indian life. On the contrary they responded to them with nausea and distaste. They were active in the suppression of the excrescences of Hindu practice, widow-burning, female infanticide and others. The state of mind induced by continuous dislike is hardly one to create intelligent understanding and wise administration. Armed with the breastplate of Christian righteousness, they felt unassailable in the strength of their charity and condescension. But inside the impressive armour of Faith and superiority was a small frightened man.

The hate of the English, and it was an active hate, was not confined to the Indians themselves. It was also directed to those men who had grown up in a wider and more tolerant world. To give us a 'feel' of this world and the reaction of the 'new Indian' to it the life and writings of Matthew Arnold's brother William Delafield Arnold will help us.

W. D. Arnold gave form to the Anglo-Indian tragedy in a curious autobiographic novel published pseudonymously in 1853, under the name of 'Punjabee' and called, *Oakfield, or Fellowship in the East.*

Arnold's life was a short one, and the high-lights are not exciting. He was born in 1828, the second son of Thomas Arnold, of Rugby, and educated at Rugby and Christ Church, Oxford. In 1848 he went out to India and joined the East India Company's Army as an Ensign in the 58th Native Infantry. Later, under the administration of John Lawrence, he became an Assistant Commissioner in the Punjab; and finally, in 1856, its first Director of Public Instruction. While on his way to England on sick leave he died at Gibraltar, in April 1859. His memory was kept alive in the Punjab by the distribution of medals to the best pupils in the schools he had himself founded. His death was commemorated by his brother in the poem, *A Southern Night.* This poem inhabits the fringe of Anglo-Indian melancholy, of Duty, and the early grave.

> For here, with bodily anguish keen,
>   With Indian heats at last foredone,
> With publick toil and private teen,
>   Thou sank'st alone.

An unspectacular life, but well in the tradition of the British in India. The personal tragedy, which was really part of a vast public one.

Before the fitting of the strait-jacket of Victorian morality, men had lived in an India treated as they found it. A strange land, but full of possibilities. Many of them lived on a lavish and exotic scale; intermarried, kept a harem, luxuriated in the trivia of oriental life. These men fought back by allowing themselves to be absorbed into a different way of life. 'Their black wives hang about, picking up a little rice, while their husbands please them by worshipping the favourite idol.' They ruled as conquerors, but in the terms of the conquered. Little or no racial antagonism existed. England was so far away it became an image, not something one went back to after thirty years' service. These men were not transients in vast clubs and cantonments with gardens made to look like English gardens, but the nearest the British ever came to colonizers. The Eurasian population is its only legacy. These men, who had loved India for what it was, were a dying memory when William Arnold arrived in India. They could not survive, with their loose morals and receptive minds, in the birdcage of the Victorian ethos.

A new attitude was in the air. The spirit which was causing a religious and social revival in England was, somewhat diluted, having its effect in India. In England, Wilberforce and Buxton had exposed the horrors of the Slave Trade. A blood-thirsty criminal code was being overhauled in the name of justice and humanity. In 1833, Keble preached his sermon on National Apostacy, and Newman published the first of the *Tracts for the Times*. They started a movement which was to have considerable influence upon many of the pre-Mutiny officials. A new leaven was working within the small English community in India, a new school of officials and officers began to make its influence felt. It was to show itself in a revolt against the lax morality common amongst Europeans in the East, against the patronage of idolatry by the Government, and against certain Hindu customs. The English began to believe they had a moral mission in India; that they represented a higher civilization, a better religion. The younger men came out to India and received the impression of a country where crime flourished and the mass of the people were steeped in a form of savagery.

So began one of the oddest revolutions in history. Like all
revolutions, it existed in a fever of personal tragedy and dis-
illusion. It was played out against a background of singular
bizarrerie, and was dominated by an ideology, at the same time
both formulistic and inchoate. God's Purpose was defined, even
if Man's Destiny was sometimes obscure. The men of the revolution were not revolutionaries; they lacked the conviction and
heroic irresponsibility which are the hallmark of the man of action.
Above all, they were without the passion of the narrow purpose,
the blinkers of the revolutionary. They lacked faith in themselves, and, caught in a web of doubt, acted precipitously, or
not at all.

Their reactions to the immorality of the times inhabits the
world of the hysteric. They withdrew into soul-searching, into a
sort of abstract cruelty, killing the body to save the soul. Personal
confession became their safety-valve. They were Old Testament
prophets, raging at the times, threatening the calamities of the
God of Vengeance, and finally sinking into despair.

W. D. Arnold, with his background of evangelical militancy,
soon recoiled in horror from the realities of the British-Indian
Empire. Misinformed, like most Englishmen, the heat and the
dust revolted him. Others, having felt the same, retired into
liquor, constructing their imaginary England from the bottle.
But all *hated* India. It was an active, horrible hate, consisting
mainly of fear, fear of death, fear of being thought a coward; fear,
perhaps, of being fearful. India, it seems to Arnold, is always a
bad deal, and one that cannot be avoided.

> ... you see, a man ten thousand miles off can't come back [home]
> the first fine morning he wants to; he very soon finds he has got a bad
> bargain, but also one which he must stick to, and is too much of a
> man to howl and complain; ashamed, too, to regret his own act,
> people think, or pretend to think, that he is very happy and so on.
> I tell you, Herby, you would hate India; everybody does. The best
> men such as your own brother, who work hard and, as it is said,
> Get On, hate it; idle, good-for-nothing dogs like myself hate it;
> perhaps the worst like it best; they can get drunk there, and that is
> about all they want; but even they hate a country where beer and
> wine is expensive.

Arnold was not attempting to describe the top-layer of the
British in India, those subjects for biography, presentation swords,

and the monument in St. Paul's, but the backbone of British rule, the younger soldier and civil servant. Arnold's sympathies were always for the poor 'griff', the newcomer raw from England, soon to be caught in the vacuum of Imperial life. Anglo-Indian society was a ruling society increasingly divorced from those it ruled. It cherished its boredoms, and chose as its excitements the futile and the second-rate. Life was an exile, a siege with only the distant chance of relief. In the meanwhile existence became easier by elevating the trivialities—or drowning them.

> The hot dull vacancy of Indian life is grievous to all. Men try to evade it in many ways—some by the excitement of work, and those are the best off; and yet you would call them active or useful or perhaps brilliant rather than happy. Others by the excitement of drink—poor, feeble ones! deserving not of less contempt, but of more pity than they get, these quickly hurry their half-hours of ecstasy and weeks of awful despondency to delirium tremens and the burying-ground. But by far the greatest number seek relief in the petty dissipations of society; these are the men who drink but are not drunkards, bet and play cards but do not gamble ruinously; eat and drink and sleep and gossip and shilly-shally through their day, trying with all the singleness of purpose they possess to steer a dexterous course between the burden of existence on the one hand, and the vacuum of literally doing nothing on the other. This is the great bulk of Indian society, more or less vicious at different times and places . . . but always shallow, empty and contemptible.

Arnold's eye is jaundiced, but there is truth in what he sees. 'Indian society' *was* shallow, empty, and contemptible, though not uniformly so, but it was invertebrate rather than vicious, weak rather than sinful.

But even through the hatred of man comes the irrepressible Victorian admiration for the ideal. As Oakfield's ship is leaving for England, where Oakfield must die in martyrdom, he sees the ship for Calcutta pass with its microcosm of Anglo-Indian society. Some of those on the ship are to be despised, others pitied, all regretted, but they are the flow of blood that makes the Empire. They are all, however, unworthy, shouldering the Imperial burden—following God's Purpose.

> What hopes and fears were being borne on to their fulfilment; what histories of most thrilling interest were being acted there, in

active expectation of the new chapter so soon to open! There were the sailors returning to Calcutta for the hundredth time, looking at every object with the careless eyes of custom, and only glad to have their journey done. There was the old Indian returning with pleasure to the land of curries, marring his own enjoyment by feverish speculations as to what appointment he would get, and whether so-and-so would have superseded him in his absence; there was the wife returning to her husband to share with him the pain of separation from the beloved children she has left behind her; there are the young ladies coming out to their parents, or brothers, or uncles, viewing everything, some with intelligence, some, it is to be feared, with an inquisitive, insipid feebleness; and there, too, God help them! are the griffs—Oh, how Oakfield's heart was filled with sympathy for them. Some were probably in little need of sympathy; coarse, thoughtless, foolish, as ready to take the road to perdition in India as they would in England; others sanguine, bold, ambitious, crowding to the vessel's bows with eager interest to catch the first glance of what had so long been the land of their dreams and fancies; others again trying to veil an aching heart (poor boys, it seems to them well-nigh a broken one!) under a garb of manliness, of indifference, or recklessness; and some few looking upon all things with a piteous vacancy that proclaims them to belong to that class of characterless victims who are the devil's first, and favourite, and easiest prey; but all, probably, more or less hopeful, more or less anxious. What a depth of fathomless interest was centred in each individual case! And, regarded more generally, here was another instalment of English power; a fresh supply of that material from which the soldiers and statesmen of India were to be formed; what Generals, what Council members, what Governors that ship contain. . . .

The Government of the Empire seems to Oakfield-Arnold to rest on 'blackguardism and blockheadism'. What is not downright evil is stupid. But he does not try to avoid the issue of why the British were in India. His contemporaries spoke of 'law and order' and of 'the Imperial mission' but Oakfield believes the British are in India for mechanical as well as moral reasons.

One of the few sympathetic characters in the book is made to criticize the neglect of public works in India, and Oakfield asks: '. . . is the English message to India civil engineering simply?'

'Not quite,' said Middleton good-humouredly. 'But it is an important—I think, *the* important part of it just now. At any rate, the neglect of it has long been a just reproach to us. A few thousand miles more of the Grand Trunk Road, ditto of canals, and people will no longer be able to say that if the English were swept off the face of Hindustan tomorrow, the only trace they would leave behind them would be the broken tobacco-pipes of their soldiers.'

Faith, apparently, should go hand-in-hand with public works!

Under the surface of this melancholy novel there lurks the belief that in the final analysis, the British are in India for India's good; that, in the end, the revolution is to be a revolution in *Indian* life. The evangelical revolutionaries, however much divorced from the realities of Indian life, were dominated by abstract ideas of Indian welfare. The Victorian hero was a man doing something good for someone else, and doing it in God's name. The revolution was to be a Puritan revolution on the Cromwellian model, hard-headed yet deeply emotional at the roots. In the steam-room of India, the hard-headed became light-headed and emotions came to the surface and obscured reason. The Evangelicals were isolated in a world part blackly heathen, part frivolously indifferent. Hatred was, firstly, for their own kind. If the British rulers of India were part of God's Purpose, then they must be pure and purposeful. Until they were, the revolution couldn't get started.

> So long as European Society in India is what it is, gross in its lowest phases and (I grievously suspect), false and Mammonish in its highest, so long the most vigorous government will be nothing more than vigorous 'street-constableship' and all the missionarising, etc., but the binding of a rope of sand.

The Evangelicals aimed at reforming the ruling-class. It was to be essentially a Palace-revolution. Disgust for the standards of conduct of the British in India dominates their work. Arnold was no exception. He makes Oakfield revolt at the manners of the military.

> I do not mean only that the higher elements of the gentlemanly character are wanting. Courtesy to inferiors Heaven save the mark in this country! Fancy talking to an officer of courtesy to a native!— honesty in money transactions, and so on. But there is not even a refinement of outward manners; so, far from being above, they seem infinitely below par in this respect. I had always thought of a

mess as the abode of luxurious refinement; even, it might be, to effeminacy. I find it a bad tavern. I had not expected to hear literary conversation at a mess-table, but still less such appalling ribaldry as I did hear in the fortnight during which I belonged to the mess. I am not likely to be prudish in these matters; I have spent all my life at Winchester and Oxford, and at both places have been in company with boys and men who were noted for this style of conversation; but I am quite certain that a man saying, at a wine party such things as are common at the 81st mess, would have been kicked out of the room as a gross offender—I do not say against morality, but against gentlemanly behaviour. They pride themselves on a very subtle distinction between dinner and after-dinner. A man is supposed to be reasonably decent while the cloth is on the table, but may compensate himself by the utmost licence of blackguardism directly it is off. I stayed in the mess for a fortnight, but could not stand it any longer; so now I live alone. . . . There are more officers than gentlemen; and there are two men who appear to be both!

But he does not revolt *us*. He was probably more successful with his contemporaries, but all it can convince us of is his essential naïvety. Arnold is by no means alone in this fault. It was a characteristic of the Evangelical Revolution in India. As a revolution, it lacked a sense of place; as a reformation it overlooked the climate of the tropics. A soldiers' mess, anywhere, at any time, can never be a vicarage tea-party. In a tropical climate, immorality is seldom a positive recreation but the negative response to eternal boredom.

But has Arnold something constructive to suggest—a remedy, perhaps?

Oakfield's idea of man's duty in India is ' . . . to help in the work, or try to set it going, of raising the *European Society*, the great influence of Asia, first from the depths of immorality, gradually to a state of comparative Christian earnestness. I am quite certain that nothing less than Christianity, in the Cromwell or some other shape, will have any effect on the awful *vis inertiae* of Asiaticism. The protection of life and property, of which we hear so much, is of course a clear good; hardly, though, a very disinterested boon of ours to this country, for if life and property were insecure, whose throats or purses would go first? But for any purpose beyond protection to life and property (I, for one, will not believe that God gave England the Indian Empire for police purposes only) an eating and drinking, money-getting community is inefficient.'

Arnold was a prolix but not altogether woolly thinker. He disregarded what Kipling later made his especial fetish—the Law, the *pax Britannica*, the Queen's peace over all. The British were in India for some other reason. The Evangelicals, failing to find it on earth, discovered it in Heaven. God's Purpose was the reason, England's Destiny the instrument. But they were never quite sure of themselves; for God at times was inscrutable, and the individual inadequate.

Essentially, their failure was a failure of communication. In attempting to reform the rulers, they isolated themselves from the realities of the ruled. And yet they could never divorce themselves from climate and disease. These, too, enhanced the isolation. The revolutionary always operates in some sort of a vacuum, incomplete but essential. In a tropical country, there is a physical as well as an emotional isolation. This isolation from the other dimensions of living drove the Evangelicals to introspection and doubt, and the irresponsible action that originates in them.

These men saw themselves condemned by fate when in reality they had constructed their own tragedy. The Empire-builders existed in a conscious agony; they were consolidators with doubts. Trying to avoid the propaganda of heroism, they searched for its moral equivalents. They attempted to bring together man's actions and God's purpose, to fabricate an ideology. Once they succeeded, they became its victim, and the victim of the hero-makers. Duty seemed nonsense without sacrifice, England's sacrifice for India.

But Oakfield's contemporaries were sure of one thing at least —the superiority of their Faith. Evangelical officers, even those nearest to the realities of everyday life, believed it right to attempt to convert their sepoys.

These beliefs and others more obvious were the causes of the Mutiny of 1857.

Native rulers trembled under the shadow of annexation, the sepoys under the fear of a crusading evangelism. Without this fear the affair of the greased cartridges is without meaning and probably would have remained so.

General John Hersey, a Company's General of considerable

Henry Lawrence.   From a miniature by Gholam Khan, 1852

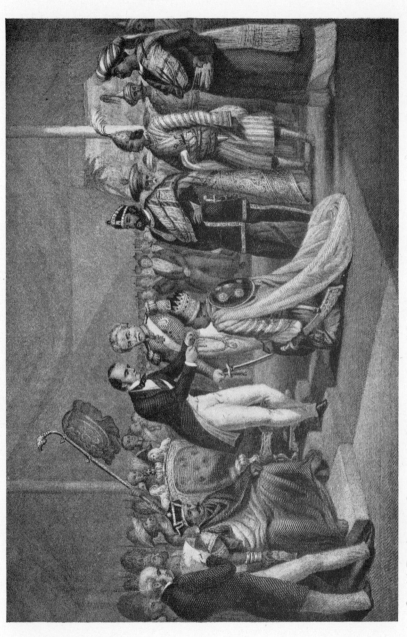

Grand Durbar at Cawnpore after the suppression of the Sepoy Revolt. Lord Canning investing the loyal Rajas with decorations and proprietary rights

character and foresight wrote officially to the Commander-in-Chief, General Anson on 28th January 1857:

> A report [he wrote] had been spread by some designing person, most likely Brahmins or agents of the religious Hindu party at Calcutta ... that the sepoys are to be forced to embrace the Christian faith. ... Perhaps those Hindus in Calcutta who are opposed to the marriage of widows are using underhand means to thwart Government in abolishing the restraints lately removed by law ... and conceive that if they can make a party of the ignorant classes in the ranks of the army believe that their religion or religious prejudices are eventually to be abolished by force, and that by force they are all to be made Christians and thus by shaking their faith in Government, lead them to lose the confidence of their officers by offences such as incendiarism ... they will gain their object.

Soon the meeting of this gallant and percipient old General and Mungul Pandy, a young sepoy, would herald the hell of the Mutiny.

UP AMONG THE PANDIES

At the end of 1856 the Bengal Army murmured with disaffection. Agents of the deposed King of Oudh and of the Nana Sahib moved amongst the sepoys. 'A consciousness of power,' wrote the Commissioner of Meerut, 'had grown up in the army which could only be exercised by mutiny and the cry of the cartridge brought the latent spirit of revolt into action.'

The new Enfield rifle was being introduced into the Army. It was necessary to bite a greased cartridge before loading the rifle. The sepoys believed that the grease was made of cow or pig fat and that an attempt was being made deliberately to break the caste of Hindus and to insult the religious prejudices of the Muslims. Regiments began to refuse to obey their officers.

Kaye has given with little exaggeration the story of how the story originated.

Now, it happened that, one day in January, a low-caste Lascar, or magazine-man, meeting a high-caste Sepoy in the Cantonment, asked him for a drink of water from his lotah. The Brahmin at once replied with an objection on the score of caste, and was tauntingly told that caste was nothing, that high-caste and low-caste would soon be all the same, as cartridges smeared with beef-fat and hog's lard were being made for the Sepoys at the depots, and would soon be in general use throughout the army.

The Brahmin carried this story to his comrades, and it was soon known to every Sepoy at the depot. A shudder ran through the Lines. Each man to whom the story was told caught the great fear from his neighour, and trembled at the thought of the pollution that lay before him. The contamination was to be brought to his very lips; it was not merely to be touched, it was to be eaten and absorbed into his very being. It was so terrible a thing, that, if the most malignant enemies of the British Government had sat in conclave for years, and brought an excess of devilish ingenuity to bear upon the invention of a scheme framed with the design of alarming the Sepoy mind from one end of India to the other, they could not have devised a lie better suited to the purpose. But now the English themselves had placed in the hands of their enemies, not a fiction, but a fact of tremendous significance, to be turned against them as a deadly instrument of destruction. It was the very thing that had been so long sought, and up to this time sought in vain. It required no explanation. It needed no ingenious gloss to make the full force of the thing itself patent to the multitude. It was not a suggestion, an inference, a probability; but a demonstrative fact, so complete in its naked truth, that no exaggeration could have helped it. Like the case of the leathern head-dresses, which had convulsed Southern India half a century before, it appealed to the strongest feelings both of the Mohammedan and the Hindu; but though similar in kind, it was incomparably more offensive in degree; more insulting, more appalling, more disgusting.

The tale spread like a bush-fire.

The next stage in the development of the Mutiny was now at hand. The 19th Native Infantry were marching from Berhampore towards Barrackpore, apparently in a state of torpid resignation; but, day by day, as they approached, the excitement increased in the minds of the Barrackpore sepoys, and on the afternoon of Sunday the 29th of March, when the 19th were only some 18 miles away, the storm broke. The story of Mungul Pandy, the young sepoy who fired the first shot of the mutineers, is a hackneyed one, but cannot well be omitted in the story of John Hearsey's life.

Mungul Pandy was a soldier of good character but of an excite-able disposition, and on the 29th of March he was under the influ-ence of an intoxicating drug. He therefore suddenly became imbued with the belief that the hour of the destruction of the sepoys by the English was at hand, and that he, Mungul Pandy, must be up and doing. He then put on his accoutrements, and seizing his musket went out of his hut, calling upon his comrades to follow him if they did not wish to bite the cartridges and become Kafirs. Mungul Pandy then walked up and down in front of the Quarter Guard of his regiment, the 34th Native Infantry, and ordered a bugler to sound the 'assembly'. The bugler did not comply with this order, but neither the native officer on guard nor any of his men attempted to arrest Mungul Pandy, and when presently the English sergeant-major appeared on the scene they allowed Mungul Pandy to fire at him with impunity. The shot went wide. Mutiny was, however, not yet universal, and a corporal hurried to tell the adjutant of the regiment, Lieutenant Baugh, what was going on. Baugh at once rose to the occasion, buckled on his sword, loaded his pistols, mounted his horse and galloped down to the Quarter Guard. As he pulled up, Mungul Pandy, hiding behind the gun which gave the station time, fired at him and again missed his aim, but brought down Baugh's horse. Baugh then fired at Mungul Pandy, but also missed. The 34th were perhaps not a good shooting regiment. Baugh then drew his sword and fell upon the mutineer and as the sergeant-major also joined in the fray they had odds in their favour. Mungul Pandy, however, showed himself more skilful with the sword than with the musket, and presently wounded both his assailants. He would doubtless have killed them but for the loyal assistance of a Mohammedan sepoy named Shaikh Pultu, who seized Mungul Pandy, and averted his blows. Far different was the conduct of the guard, who struck at the wounded adjutant and sergeant-major on the ground with the butts of their muskets, while one of the guard fired at them, but, as usual, missed.

Meanwhile General Hearsey heard of what was going on—that a single sepoy was defying the State and that no one could grapple with the emergency—and immediately ordered horses to be saddled for himself and his two sons, John and Andrew.

As Hearsey rode on the ground his quick eye took in the situation, and he made straight for the Quarter Guard, accompanied by his sons, who rode on either side of him, and by Major Ross, a staff-officer. As the General passed by, it is recorded that an officer called to him warning him to take care, as Mungul Pandy's musket was loaded. 'Damn his musket!' responded Hearsey, and the bluff sentence has passed into history.

He then ordered the native officers and the sepoys of the Quarter Guard to arrest Mungul Pandy, and, awed by the revolvers of the General and his sons, which they could see ready for instant use, the guard reluctantly moved after the three Hearseys. Mungul Pandy now brought down his musket as if to shoot the General, and John Hearsey cried out, 'Father, he is taking aim at you.' 'If I fall, John,' said the General, 'rush upon him and put him to death.' Mungul Pandy's resolution, however, now gave way. He saw that the game was up and attempted to commit suicide, but only suc-ceeded in wounding himself slightly. Hearsey then rode among the excited troops and fearlessly reproached them with their conduct in allowing a single man to disgrace them. Some of the sepoys excused themselves by saying that Mungul Pandy's musket had been loaded, but Hearsey scornfully rejected this plea and ordered the men to their lines.

This exploit was to give the mutineers the nickname of 'pandies'.

But punishments were mild. The officers did not believe that their 'children' were really bad.

At Meerut troops had refused to use the cartridges and in this case sentence of ten years' imprisonment had been given to eighty-five men of the 3rd Cavalry. The next day, Sunday 10th May, the three Indian regiments in the station shot their officers, broke open the gaol and set off on the road to Delhi. No one stopped them, despite the fact that there were two British regiments and some artillery in the station. The Indian Mutiny had begun and the testing of John and Henry Lawrence was at hand. On them the future of British dominion might largely depend. We must watch them at work.

RETAKE DELHI!

ON 11TH MAY a last message came along the telegraph line from Delhi. 'The sepoys have come in from Meerut and are burning everything—Mr. Todd is dead and we hear several Europeans—we must shut up.' Delhi had fallen to the mutineers and the old King, Bahadur Shah was proclaimed Emperor of Hindustan.

Lord Canning was obsessed (not unnaturally) by the thought that the Sikhs of the Punjab might rise and pay off the old scores of the Sikh wars and the annexation. He had little to fear. John Lawrence was away from Lahore taking himself to a well-earned rest in the Hills, but on receiving the news from Delhi he acted with decision and effect.

The position in the Punjab, however, was pregnant with danger. At the moment of the fall of Delhi there were some 58,000 trained native troops in the Punjab. European troops, numbering some 10,500, were broken up into two sections at the extreme ends of the province, one in the valley of Peshawar on the north-west frontier and the other in the Simla Hills, with miserably weak outposts scattered at intervals between. Of the native troops some 36,000 belonged to the Bengal Army—each a potential mutineer. The remainder were irregular troops and military police raised in the Punjab. On them depended the safety of the province. Would they make common cause with the Bengal sepoys? What was to be done?

There was no way of playing off Muslim against Hindu—the greased cartridges had seen to that. Sikh against Muslim? Though obsessed by active hatred for each other these two had combined only a few years before in the greater hatred of the British.

Here, the 'Punjab system' paid off. Security, prosperity, some sort of justice. Protection from tyranny, vigorous and beneficent rule—because of these the people waited. And while they did so John acted.

On the 12th of May the terrible news of the disasters at Meerut and Delhi was received. Before twenty-four hours were over, the

Native troops at Lahore, who were on the watch for the signal
from below, were disarmed, three thousand well-trained soldiers
piling their arms, 'with silent and angry astonishment', before some
four hundred European infantry with twelve guns; the fort at
Lahore was secured; the great magazine at Ferozepur, containing
upwards of seven thousand barrels of gunpowder and immense
stores of arms, was saved; the fort of Govindgarh, the key of the
Manjha which Ranjit Singh had made almost impregnable, was
occupied; the arsenal at Phillaur with the siege train was transferred
to the guard of European troops; and every District Officer was
made alive to the magnitude of the crisis and warned to secure his
treasure, to deal firmly with the first symptoms of disorder, but to
be quiet and calm and show no sign of alarm or excitement.
'Nothing,' said Sir John Lawrence, 'conduces more to overawe the
Natives than a quiet, resolute demeanour.' And so, all over the
province, except for a short time in the Cis-Sutlej States, the work
went on as if nothing were wrong.

No precaution was omitted to prevent the spread of the treasonable infection. A system of passports was introduced; guards at the
ferries were doubled, with orders to prevent the passage of suspicious characters, especially fakirs and mendicants; letters addressed
to mutinous regiments were opened; the Native Press was put
under censorship; District Officers and their Assistants did nightly
patrol work, and showed themselves more than ever in the remote
parts of their Districts; every officer had to be at his post, and no
leave of absence was granted except for certified sickness. Peshawar
'stood in a ring of repressed hostilities'. Here a Council of War
assembled, of which the moving spirits were Herbert Edwardes,
John Nicholson, and Sydney Cotton who commanded the troops.
In communication with Sir John Lawrence at Rawal Pindi, measures
were at once planned for the preservation of order. Here was
devised, on Nicholson's initiative, the famous Movable Column of
picked men, European and Punjabi, to patrol the country and swoop
down on mutiny at the first signal of alarm. It was destined to
execute terrible vengeance upon revolted Sepoys and in due
time to be the last bolt which John Lawrence was to hurl against
Delhi.

By the 17th of May it became manifest that the rebels would
receive no help from the people of the Punjab. The bold measures
taken at Lahore on the morning of the 13th of May by Montgomery
and Corbett quieted the Sikhs of the Manjha and secured for us
Amritsar on which the loyalty of the Khalsa depended. At Peshawar
the leading men held aloof and watched events. 'If Peshawar holds
firm,' said a sagacious old Native, 'it is well; otherwise——' and he

rolled up the skirt of his muslim robe significantly between his finger and his thumb. When the enlistments at Peshawar first began, not a hundred men could be found to join our cause. On the morning of the 22nd of May the Bengal troops were to be deprived of their arms. 'As we rode to the disarming,' says Sir Herbert Edwardes, 'a very few chiefs and yeomen of the country attended us; and I remember judging from their faces that they came to see which way the tide would turn. As we rode back, friends were as thick as summer flies; and levies began from that moment to come in.'

But the lynch-pin of India lay in Delhi. The city must be recaptured—a demonstration made of the power of the British, otherwise all would be lost. 'Delay was only a less misfortune than a repulse.'

Camels, coolies, carts, bullocks, were collected from every quarter. The country and the loyal Chiefs were put under requisition. And on the 17th of May, a week from the outbreak, the avenging force began to move forward from Ambala. Joining with the troops from Meerut, who fought two successful battles on the way, the united force was at Badli-ki-Sarai, six miles from Delhi, on the 8th of June; defeated the mutineers; drove them back into the city; and occupied, the Ridge.

This was a positive and grandiose gesture, for the force in front of Delhi numbered only 3,600 men and the Ridge they occupied was open at the rear and exposed on the flanks.

John did not expect much resistance from the city, in the pride of his success he underrated the strength of Delhi and the stubbornness of the mutineers.

To this puny David was matched a Goliath seven miles in circumference, supported by some 60,000 men[1] And reinforcements still reached the city.

The opposing forces on the Ridge racked by disease, guerrilla attacks and the formidable incompetence of its successive commanders hung on by its fingernails with the quiet heroism of thin-red line.

John Lawrence made superhuman efforts to re-inforce the little army before Delhi. First to arrive were the famous Guides. They owed their origin to Sir Henry Lawrence. The characteristic features of this distinguished corps, as Edwardes observes, 'do not strike us now-a-days. But in 1846, to set Poorbeahs aside and to raise a corps of sharp-shooters or sportsmen of all nations, and say

[1] This figure is open to dispute.

they should wear their own clothes and be hampered with as few
accoutrements as possible, that they should have loose, dusky shirts
instead of tight red jackets, sun-proof turbans instead of sunstroke
Glengarry caps, and wide pijamas instead of pantaloons and straps
and braces—a change like that was literally a stroke of genius. It
was an invention.' Starting from Mardan on the 13th of May, six
hours after they got their orders, the Guides, under command of
Captain Henry Daly, reached Delhi on the 9th of June, covering 580
miles in twenty-two marches with three intervening halts. It was
the hottest season of the year, and the rate of marching could not
have been performed by the infantry on foot. But a camel was
allowed to every two men which enabled them to keep up with the
cavalry, and to get over thirty or forty miles between sunset and
sunrise. They marched into camp as light of step as if coming
off parade, and three hours after arrival they engaged the enemy
in a fight, in which the Second in Command was killed, and
two other Officers were wounded. During the four months of
the siege these magnificent soldiers were constantly in action,
sometimes twice a day, and out of 800 men 350 were killed and
wounded.

By the beginning of July the besieging force amounted to 6,600
men—quite enough to beat the rebels in the open field; but it had
made no impression on the city. Not a single gun of the enemy had
been silenced. The siege train that had been sent from Phillaur was
altogether too weak. British fire was returned four shots to one,
with a precision which showed that the enemy had got the exact
range of every point of the camp. There had been ten fights, in
seven of which the whole force was employed. In every one the
British were victorious, but the capture of the city was as far off as
ever. It was the policy of the enemy to wear the little force out.
False alarms served this purpose as well as regular attacks, for the
men had to turn out and got no rest. The mutineers chose the hottest
hours for their assaults, when the sun was their strongest ally.
Losses were very heavy. In one week twenty-five Officers and 400
men were killed or wounded. Ague, fever, dysentery, sunstroke,
and cholera too were doing their fatal work. 'A regiment which had
come in 600 strong was in three weeks brought down to 242 out of
hospital.'

At this rate the little force on the Ridge would disappear.
Withdrawal was even considered.

It was now July and the failure to retake the city had its reper-
cussions in the Punjab. Revolts took place but decisive action

destroyed the mutineers—the British apparently were not yet dead.

But Delhi must be taken. 'Recollect,' wrote John on the 24th July, 'if you fall back from Delhi our cause is gone; neither the Punjab nor anything else can stand.'

Then out of his despair came the last bold venture.

On 23rd July John Lawrence issued a peremptory instruction to the Sikh chiefs to supply men. The sword was back in the hand, tempered and sharp. 'I would not put up with any delay or hesitation on your part.' Men were forthcoming and were hurled into the assault. Nicholson's Movable Column came in. On 4th September a heavy siege train drawn by sixteen elephants, and 548 wagons bursting with ammunition 'sufficient it was said to grind Delhi to powder' arrived at the Ridge. Troops poured in from all sides. 'We have sent,' wrote John to Lord Canning, 'every man we could spare, perhaps more.' On the Ridge all was ready for the assault. Sustained only by their determination the British now felt their power. All was not lost—and inside the city the strength of the mutineers was crumbling. Women and children began to leave the city.

Events moved with speed. On the night of 7th September the first breaching battery was laid. By the 13th the breaches were ready for the assault, and Nicholson at the Kashmir Gate died to live in the martyrology of Empire. By the 20th the city was in the hands of the British.

> In the name of outraged humanity, in memory of innocent blood ruthlessly shed and in acknowledgement of the first signal vengeance inflicted on the foulest treason, the Governor-General-in-Council records his gratitude to Major-General Wilson and the brave army of Delhi.

So wrote Lord Canning, underlining ironically that 'innocent blood' was still to be shed, for the city of Delhi was put to the sword, looted, and sacked. 'All the city people found within the walls when our troops entered were bayoneted on the spot; and the number was considerable, as you may suppose when I tell you that in some houses forty or fifty persons were hiding.' The mutineers had purposely left vast quantities of liquor and maddened by drink British troops went berserk. 'The troops,' wrote Sanders, the Commissioner of Delhi, 'were completely disorganized and demoralized by the immense amount of plunder that fell into their hands and the quantity of liquor which they managed to discover. . . .'

The whole population was driven out of the city, Prize Agents were digging for buried treasure, drum-head courts-martial tapped their horrors in summary hangings. Delhi had been retaken—with a vengeance.

SIR HENRY, ARE YOU HURT?

THE CRISIS in Lucknow came in the evening of 30th May. Colonel Inglis, commanding H.M. 32nd Regiment has left his opinion that Henry Lawrence was warned by a native that the mutiny would come at gunfire. As Henry was sitting down to dinner at his house in the cantonment the nine p.m. gun was fired, and Sir Henry said with a laugh, 'Wilson, your friends are not punctual.'

I had hardly replied, when we heard the musketry in the lines, and some chuprassees came and reported the firing. The horses were at once ordered, and Sir Henry stood outside in the moonlight, on the steps of the Residency, impatiently awaiting his horse. There was a guard of a native officer and sixty Sepoys on duty in the Residency, and immediately on the alarm, the native officer had drawn them up in line about thirty yards distant, directly in front of where Sir Henry Lawrence stood. And now the soobahdar came to me, and, saluting, said, 'Am I to load?' I turned to Sir Henry, and repeated the question; he said, 'Oh, yes, let him load.' The order was at once given, and the ramrods fell with that peculiar dull sound on the leaden bullets. I believe Sir Henry was the only man of all that group whose heart did not beat quicker for it. But he, as the men brought up their muskets with the tubes levelled directly against us, cried out, 'I am going to drive those scoundrels out of cantonment: take care while I am away that you all remain at your posts, and allow no one to do any damage here, or enter my house, else when I return I will hang you.' Whether through the effect of this speech and Sir Henry's bearing, I know not, but the guard remained steadily at its post, and with the bungalows blazing and shots firing all round, they allowed no one to enter the house, and the residence of Sir Henry was the only one that night in the cantonment that was not either pillaged or burnt.

Henry Lawrence immediately set out to engage the mutineers. Insurrection broke out in the city. But still the civil power maintained its rule. Finally the sepoys left for Delhi.

The city still trembled under the threat of disturbance. Troops and civilians were withdrawn into the Residency grounds.

Batteries, parapets, fortifications were erected. There was to be a rock in the flood.

On the 9th June Henry's health gave way and he was temporarily succeeded by a Council presided over by Martin Gubbins, a wilful man in love with the extremities of action who attempted to get rid of all native troops from the Residency area.

On 12th June Henry resumed command.

We still hold the cantonment [he wrote] as well as our two posts, but every outpost (I fear) has fallen, and we daily expect to be besieged by the confederated mutineers and their allies from Cawnpore, Setapore, Secrora, &c. The country is not yet thoroughly up, but every day brings it nearer that condition. . . . All our irregular cavalry, except about sixty Sikhs of Daly's corps, are either very shaky, or have deserted. The remnant of Hardinge's corps, numbering 130 men, must be excepted, and their gallant commander thinks they will remain staunch if got out of Lucknow. They therefore march tonight in the Allahabad direction, though we can ill spare them. The remnant of the Native Infantry regiments have behaved well since the outbreak. Mr. Gubbins has been almost insubordinately urgent on me to disband these remnants; but the fact is, they consist of men who either joined us on the night of the *émeute*, or who stood to their guns on that occasion. If not better, they are certainly not worse, than the irregulars and the military police, on which Mr. Gubbins places, or affects to place, implicit reliance. He is a gallant, energetic, clever fellow, but sees only through his own vista, and is therefore sometimes troublesome. . . . The irregular infantry are behaving pretty well, but once we are besieged, it will be black against white, with some very few exceptions. More than 100 police horse deserted last night, and since I began this page I have received the report of the military foot police having deserted the great central gaol over which they were specially placed. . . . Then again, we ought to have only one position.

Henry was pre-occupied with the strengthening of the Residency but still made sorties against the mutineers.

Three or four days before the end of June a concentration of mutineers was reported at Nawabganj, some twenty miles northeast of Lucknow. Gubbins called for action and when Henry refused to weaken his defence, exclaimed hysterically, 'Well, Sir Henry, we shall all be branded at the bar of history as cowards.'

Under pressure from the militants, confused by Gubbins'

faulty Intelligence that the enemy force was some five hundred foot and fifty horse, yet knowing through his own sources that they were at two or three thousand, Henry permitted himself to be harried into action.

The expedition was a ghastly failure.

> This morning [he wrote to General Havelock on 30th June] we went out eight miles to Chinhut to meet the enemy, and we were defeated, and lost five guns through the misconduct chiefly of our Native Artillery, many of whom deserted. The enemy have followed us up, and we have now been besieged for four hours, and shall probably to-night be surrounded. The enemy are very bold, and our Europeans very low. I look on our position now as ten times as bad as it was yesterday; indeed, it is very critical. We shall be obliged to concentrate *if we are able*. We shall have to abandon much supplies, and to blow up much powder. Unless we are relieved quickly, say in ten or fifteen days, we shall hardly be able to maintain our position. We lost three officers killed this morning, and several wounded.

The siege of the Residency had begun.

After the successful withdrawal of the outposts into the Residency area and at about eight o'clock in the morning of 2nd July, Henry Lawrence returned to the main building to rest. A shell had already penetrated his room the day before. He had shrugged it away saying that 'he did not believe the enemy had an artilleryman good enough to put a shell into that small room.' He promised, however, to change his quarters the next day. But too late.

> Towards 8 a.m. 2 July [records Captain Wilson, an eyewitness] he (Sir Henry) returned greatly exhausted—the heat was dreadful—and laid down on his bed with his clothes on, and desired me to draw up a memorandum as to how the rations were to be distributed. I went to the next room to write it, but previous to doing so I reminded Sir Henry of his promise to go below. He said he was very tired and would rest a couple of hours and that then he would have his things moved. In about half an hour I went back into the room with what I had written; his nephew, Mr. George Lawrence, was then lying on a bed parallel to his uncle's, with a few feet between them. I went between the beds and stood on the right side of Sir Henry's, with one knee resting on the bed. A coolie was sitting on the floor pulling the punkah. I read what I had written ... and he was in the act of explaining what he wished altered, when

the fatal shot came—a sheet of flame, a terrific report and shock, and dense darkness is all I can describe it. I fell down on the floor, and for perhaps a few seconds was quite stunned. I then got up, but could see nothing for the smoke or dust. Neither Sir Henry nor his nephew made any noise, and in great alarm I called out, 'Sir Henry, are you hurt?' Twice I thus called out without any answer; the third time he said in a low tone, 'I am killed.' The punkah had come down, and the ceiling, and a great deal of the plaster; and the dust and smoke were so great that it was some minutes before I could see anything, but as it gradually cleared I saw that the white coverlet of the bed was crimson with his blood.

George Lawrence ran into my house [continues Dr. Fayrer], and said that his uncle had been seriously wounded, perhaps killed, and begged me to go over at once and see him. At that moment there was a heavy fire of shot and shell on the Residency house; I went immediately and found Sir Henry laid on a table in the drawing-room with several officers about him; you, I think, and Sir G. Couper were of the number. Sir Henry was faint and depressed by the wound he had just received, and his first question to me was 'How long have I got to live?' I replied, that I hoped for some time; but on removing the torn dress and having ascertained the extent of the wound, I said, as he pressed for an answer, that I thought about forty-eight hours. The upper part of the left thigh was lacerated by a piece of shell which had passed through it, comminuting the head of the bone, and causing extensive injury of the soft parts.

We gave him cordials and endeavoured to rouse him; he rallied considerably, though perfect reaction never came, but he spoke fast and freely, and not only then, but during that day and the next, he talked much, and on important subjects.

As round-shot and shell were striking and entering the house, all thought it better to remove him, lest he should be hit again, or those around him should suffer; we accordingly carried him over to my house, which was just across the road, and placed him in a bed in the northern verandah, which at that moment was somewhat sheltered from the heavy fire of shot, shell, and musketry raining on the Residency.

We got him over without injury to any one, but he had hardly been placed in the verandah before a terrific fire was opened on it, and it was only by the greatest care in keeping within shelter of the pillars and end walls that our party was protected. The following day, indeed, the round-shot had so crumbled the walls of the end rooms which sheltered the verandah, that we had to remove him into the drawing-room, which, though exposed, became less so than the verandah.

When he had sufficiently rested to bear further examination, I and my friend Dr. Partridge, with Dr. Ogilvie, examined him thoroughly under the influence of chloroform, and we found that the injuries were, as I at first supposed, so grave, that even amputation at the hip joint offered no hope of saving life, and we accordingly then thought only of the *euthanasia*, endeavouring to relieve pain, and make the inevitable passage to the grave as painless as possible.

He remained perfectly sensible that day and for great part of the next, the 3rd. He died from exhaustion on the morning of the 4th, at about eight o'clock. I was there, and his last moments were peaceful, and, I think, almost painless. You remember how much he said during the first day, when he gave instructions concerning his successor, about what he wished us to do, and what he thought of the coming troubles; how thoughtfully he dwelt on every point of importance in reference to the defence of the garrison; and also when speaking of himself, how humbly he talked of his own life and services.

I have no doubt you remember that he several times said, he desired that no epitaph should be placed on his tomb but this: 'Here lies Henry Lawrence, who tried to do his duty.'

Before the news of his death had reached London, the Directors of the East India Company had, on 22nd July, passed a resolution unanimously proposing 'to appoint Colonel Sir Henry M. Lawrence, K.C.B., provisionally to succeed to the office of Governor-General upon the death, resignation, or coming away of Viscount Canning, pending the arrival of a successor from England.'

The honours were empty. Henry Lawrence would have appreciated the irony of their timing.

VI

THE PEN AND THE SWORD

By which will ye be governed—the pen or the sword?

Inscription on the statue of John Lawrence,
Lahore, 1887

THE END OF THE MUTINY

HENRY was dead. To John it remained to end the Mutiny—and to see the collapse of the Company's rule in India. To see, in effect, Imperial India take the place of the adventurers' and traders' India. But we must briefly scan the dying fire of the Sepoy Revolt after the capture of Delhi.

The capture of the city, and without doubt the ruthlessness of its captors, had an immediate effect upon the disturbed north of India. Recruits poured in—fair weather brought its anxious friends. Six per cent Government paper which had fallen to twenty-six per cent *discount* rose rapidly to par.

But the pursuit of the Delhi mutineers lingered in the tragedy of the stricken city. Soon however the column was moving, swollen by native recruits from all parts of northern India. The scum of the north-west frontier took their place in the avenging forces. 'Indeed,' wrote Herbert Edwardes, 'it must be admitted that one troop alone that is now fighting at Lucknow, contains no less than sixty outlaws headed by the redoubted Mukarram Khan. These men had harried the border for years, and would have undoubtedly rioted in this hour of our weakness, if not suddenly put in the way of an honest livelihood. As the Native gentleman who raised the troop remarked, "whether they kill the Poorbeahs or the Poorbeahs kill them, it will be an equal service to the State!"'

In Delhi, where organized terror remained an instrument of administration, John Lawrence stood out against its excesses. In the temper of the times his actions were characteristically courageous, though fundamentally his reaction was the commonsense of a governor rather than of moral persuasion.

In a letter to Lord Canning on 4th December he writes:

I do not know what your Lordship has resolved to do with Delhi. But if it is to be preserved as a city, I do hope that your Lordship will put a stop to the operations of the Prize Agents. I also recommend that it be freed from martial law. What Delhi requires is a soldier of energy, spirit, and character to keep the troops in order, and a strong police and a good magistrate to maintain the peace. Until there be some security for the lives and property of the natives, tranquillity will not be restored. I am a strong advocate for prompt and severe punishment when such has been deserved. But the systematic spoliation which I understand goes on at Delhi cannot fail to exasperate the natives, and render more wide and lasting the breach which has taken place between them and us.

And to the commander in Delhi, General Penny, who had made no efforts to stop the looting of the city:

My dear General, Has any reply come from Government about Prize property? I wish I could induce you to interfere in this matter. I believe we shall lastingly, and, indeed, justly be abused for the way in which we have despoiled all classes without distinction. But surely, in any case, two months' plundering should suffice! I hear complaints even from Bombay on the subject. I have this day sent you a copy of a letter from a Babu named Ram Chunder, complaining of the way he has been ill-treated by English officers. I have even heard, though it seems incredible, that officers have gone about and murdered natives in cold blood. You may depend on it that we cannot allow such acts to pass unnoticed. If we have no higher motives, the common dictates of policy should make us restrain from such outrages. No man is more ready to hang or shoot mutineers and murderers than I am, but unless we endeavour to distinguish friend from foe, we shall unite all classes against us. A guerilla warfare will spring up, the country will gradually become desolated, and, eventually, will be too hot to contain us.

Soon afterwards action was taken and the city relieved of its reign of terror.

Meanwhile, Havelock with a tiny force, aided by Sir James Outram, had relieved the Residency at Lucknow on 25th September, though he was unable to leave the perimeter. But the capture of Delhi and the relief of Lucknow had established the superiority of British arms once again. Lucknow was finally relieved in November by Sir Colin Campbell.

The battlefield moved to Central India where Sir Hugh Rose finally defeated Tantia Topi and the Rani of Jhansi at Morah and Kotah. On 8th July 1858 Lord Canning proclaimed peace.

John, in some of his letters home, looked searchingly at the causes of the great rebellion and to the future:

January 14, 1858

My dear Lord Dalhousie, I have to thank you very sincerely for your kind letter of November 28. It is a source of very great satisfaction to me to find that my exertions are acknowledged and appreciated by my friends and my countrymen. This is indeed the best reward that any man can obtain, next to that of feeling that he has done his duty and been useful in his generation. Nevertheless, I am well pleased to receive the fresh decoration which has been given me.

We have indeed had a terrible time. Up to the capture of Delhi, the scales were trembling in the balance. The Punjabis of all classes have behaved admirably, and the zeal and the courage of the Punjab troops have far surpassed my hopes and expectations. Still, if Delhi had not fallen, we must have been ruined. Had the troops retreated, all must have been lost. Had indeed the storming not succeeded all must have gone. To Nicholson, Alexander Taylor of the Engineers, and Neville Chamberlain, the real merit of our success is due. Chamberlain was severely wounded soon after his arrival at Delhi, and, until the actual storm, was, in great measure, laid on the shelf. But when our troops got inside, and Nicholson was mortally wounded, Chamberlain again came to the front, and kept up the flagging spirits of our people and directed the movements of the troops. John Nicholson, from the moment of his arrival, was the life and soul of the army. Before he went down he struck the only real blows which the mutineers received in the Punjab, he led the assault, and was the first man over the breach. Alexander Taylor, though only the second Engineer before Delhi, was really the officer who designed and arranged all the scientific operations which led to the success of the assault, and, in the actual attack, was as forward as any man that day.

Since Delhi fell, all has gone well. There has been doubt, and hesitation, and delay, but always progress. The mutineers produced no one man of ability, or even of enterprise. Their fatuity was extreme. They, literally, seem seldom to have advanced until we were ready to meet them. The Jodhpur Legion walked into our hands. The Gwalior mutineers, whose presence at Delhi would have given the victory to their cause, never moved. Had they even confronted the pursuing Column under Colonel Grant, disaster must have occurred. But no; they waited, and attacked Cawnpore when eight hundred Europeans were ready to meet them. I think that the neck of the Mutiny is broken. There is no one military body who have not in their turn been defeated; and none fight with power the second time, except when behind walls. We have taken the greater part of their guns, and the defeat and capture of the rest can only be the work of time. The danger, however, is that guerilla warfare may follow. Then again the whole civil administration has to be reorganised, and a new military system devised. It seems to me difficult to see how all this is to be done.

For myself, my thoughts are bent on home. I can never hope to retire at a more auspicious juncture. There is nothing to induce me to pass the rest of my life in exile. So long as I am useful, I shall be Chief Commissioner of the Punjab. But this will never enable me to keep a son at home in my old age. I say not all this in the way of complaint, but simply to account to your Lordship for my movements. I had arranged to go home with my wife this very month, but a sense of honour and duty has bound me to my post. I trust that the political horizon will be cleared enough to allow me to take my *congé* in another year. My wife left Multan a few days ago for England in very delicate health. I was rejoiced, however, to see her and my children on their way home. India, for many a day, will be no place for English women.

My poor brother Henry died nobly at his post. To his intelligence and foresight the whole of the Lucknow garrison owe their lives. Nothing but these precautions could have enabled our people to make the stand they have done. All our Punjab officers have done well—General Sydney Cotton, Herbert Edwardes, Robert Montgomery, my brother Richard, and Lieutenant-Colonel Macpherson in particular.

I regret much to hear that your Lordship is still so great a sufferer. Should you be at Malta as I pass through, I will make a point of landing and calling. Pray present my compliments to Lady Susan.

In a letter to George Trevelyan, 16th December 1857, he wrote:

I think we have now weathered the storm. The worst seems over. But great and radical changes are necessary, and who is to effect them? We need a man at the head of affairs of great heart and head, and of vast experience. Nothing short of this will do what is necessary. Condign punishment should of course be meted out to all murderers and the leaders of mutiny. But I see every danger of justice degenerating into revenge of a savage character. Already we hear of strange deeds being perpetrated by private individuals at Delhi and elsewhere. Already it looks too like a general war of white man against black. There is little fear that offenders will escape the just penalty of their crimes; there is much that many innocent people will suffer. It was a great misfortune that troops, even in small numbers, were not sent out overland. Thousands of natives who in the first instance kept aloof fell off, thinking that our hour was come. They would have sided with us if they had seen a chance; but with the general defection around, and no aid within hail, it is not surprising if they were carried away also.

We should have a European army of at least double its former strength in India, carefully kept up to the maximum strength. The native army should be no greater than is absolutely necessary. It should be officered by men carefully selected and removable simply because they were not successful in the discharge of their duties. The Mutiny Act, as regards native soldiers, should be abolished—at any rate, made to accord with common sense. No man should escape punishment for technical reasons. The officers should be selected in England by competition, as is done with civilians. They should join European corps and learn their duty and habits of discipline, and selections should be made from this body for native corps. Officers so selected should receive extra pay, and so have a strong inducement to exert themselves and give satisfaction. The cry for numbers of officers for native corps is merely a cry for rapid promotion. The police should be re-organised and divided into two bodies—organised police on military principles for guards of gaols, treasuries and the like, and detective police for other duties. The latter will not be benefited by drill. This does not give discipline and moral training, which is what is wanted. Select such men carefully, pay them properly, look after them thoroughly, reward and punish promptly, and you will have good police. So far from being surprised at their faults, I only wonder they did so much as they did. The Sepoys in the army would never have done one-fourth of their work.

And in another letter to Dalhousie on 16th June 1858, he again returns to the essential matter of the balance of European and native troops:

We are, I conceive, in great difficulties in India, and I do not think that our position is, by any means, known or appreciated at home. England has done much for us, but she should do more, if we are to recover our lost prestige and diminished power. Her delay in sending out reinforcements in the first instance was wellnigh fatal. As it was, it did us immense harm. It caused thousands to become compromised who would otherwise have remained true. We have never recovered this mistake, and the policy which has hitherto been pursued has enhanced our difficulties. All the bad passions of our nature have been excited. It has been a war of extermination against mutineers, and, in many instances, even against insurgents.

It has become, to some extent, a war of races. The consequence has been that we have an uphill part to play—a part which, I may add, is beyond our resources and our power. While denouncing vengeance on our enemies, we have let them slip through our hands on every occasion. . . . At Delhi we had not the means of punishing them. At other places we have allowed them to escape. It has become a great guerrilla war. East of the Jumna we are nowhere secure beyond the range of our guns. Slowly we march our heavy columns after the mutineers; as we come up, they disperse and assemble at another point. Each expedition costs us the lives of many brave men from exposure. We might as well set bulldogs to run down foxes as European soldiers to catch Hindustanis. We require native troops for the purpose, and we have none to speak of, except Punjabis. Old and new ones together, we have already 59,000 on my rolls, and more than 60,000 if we count all classes. More are required, but to raise more would be very dangerous.

We want more European troops from England; a good body of real light Cavalry. We require a thorough change of policy. We want a discriminative amnesty; that is to say, an amnesty which, excepting all cold-blooded murderers, would allow all others to go and live at their homes in peace, provided they obeyed the laws. We require also a man at the head of affairs with real vigour and promptitude, a man who can see what is to be done in the twinkling of an eye, and, seeing it, will have his own way. If a goodly body of troops be sent out by October next, and a proper system of tactics be introduced, coupled with a policy of vigour, combined with consideration, we shall yet do well. Otherwise it is difficult to foresee what may not occur, and I am quite certain that we shall not see the end of this rebellion for several years. People have no idea of our real position. Now, merely as a question of finance, it is far better to spend money now, and by a vigorous effort to beat down opposition, than allow it to extend over a series of years.

Some intelligence was needed in the handling of the dying mutiny. Clemency was not treasonable and romantic weakness but a major instrument of a vital policy. On the same day (16th June) he wrote to Lord Stanley:

I would also say a few words on the policy which has hitherto prevailed. It has all along appeared to me that the press, the European society, and the Government have taken too high a line. With the majority of Englishmen the cry has been, 'War to the knife!' totally forgetting that such a policy requires proportionate power. Now it seems to me that, setting aside all considerations of mercy and humanity, we have not the means of enforcing such a policy. If every insurgent, or even every mutineer, is to be put to death, or transported beyond the seas, we shall require 200,000 European soldiers, and, even then, we shall not put down all opposition in half a dozen years. Is England prepared to send out these troops? Is England prepared to send out from twenty to thirty thousand troops annually to supply casualties? If she is not, it behoves you all to meet the difficulty fairly, and to decide what ought to be done. Our prestige is gone! our power literally slipping away. In attempting to compass an impracticable policy we are endangering our very Empire in the East. I am no advocate for forgiving the murderers of our women and children. I would hunt all such wretches down. But, to do this effectually, we must discriminate between the mutineers. At present, every man who is caught is hanged or shot. Who will surrender under such circumstances? Thus all classes of mutineers or insurgents are bound together by the very desperation of their position. When we advanced on Lucknow with our large and efficient force, with our tremendous Artillery, we should have offered terms to all but the cold-blooded murderers. Entrenched behind their fortifications, few would have surrendered. But our offers would have become well known, and would have led to discussion and dissension and insecurity. When the insurgents had once been driven out of Lucknow, our proclamations would have begun to bear fruit, and, provided only that those who came in first were treated leniently, more would have followed. By this time, thousands of men now in arms would probably be sitting down quietly in their villages. We have missed a good opportunity and have thereby aggravated our difficulties.

Though the Mutiny was, to all intents and purposes, over, there was to be yet another casualty, the East India Company itself, for in 1858 the government of India was assumed by the Crown. The Company made a graceful exit with a farewell message which is almost poignant in its sentiment. Before this, it had defended itself by pointing out, among other things, that it had laid the foundations of the Indian Empire, at the same period at which a succession of administrations under the control of Parliament were losing to the Crown of Great Britain another great empire on the opposite side of the Atlantic! But petitions, even expertly drafted by John Stuart Mill, were useless. So the Company addressed its servants in India for the last time:

Let Her Majesty appreciate the gift; let her take the vast country and the teeming millions of India under her direct control; but let her not forget the great corporation from which she has received them, nor the lessons to be learned from its success. . . . The Company has the privilege of transferring to the service of Her Majesty such a body of civil and military officers as the world has never seen before.

Queen Victoria's proclamation of 1st November 1858 contained within its imperial disclaimers a certain condescension to the heathen, a declaration of amnesty, and the proposition that, with the aid of Providence, a new and happy era was to come.

When, by the blessing of Providence, internal tranquillity shall be restored, it is our earnest desire to stimulate the peaceful industry of India, to promote works of public utility and improvement, and to administer the government for the benefit of all our subjects resident therein. In their prosperity will be our strength, in their contentment our security, and in their gratitude our best reward. . . .

The bland, Victorian sun was soon to shine upon a shattered India, the dried blood to be washed away by the monsoon of paternal government. Or so one might have thought.

ENTR'ACTE AT 'HOME'

It was time for John Lawrence to have a period away from the stage of India. His wife and family had gone to England in December 1857. 'I will go home,' he said, 'and turn grazier or farmer in some quiet corner.'

Rewards had come his way in a G.C.B., a baronetcy, and a seat in the Privy Council. He left the hill-station of Muree in October 1858 and read aloud to the troops at Peshawar the Queen's Proclamation. Richard Temple, his secretary, has described his last visit to the frontier.

As the year 1858 drew towards its end, John Lawrence crossed the Indus for the last time, to visit Peshawar once more, and I was in attendance on him. As we crossed the Indus at Attock, where a grand old fortress overlooks the swiftly rushing river, he repeated his oft-expressed admiration for that position on account of its classic interest, picturesque beauty, and political importance. Recently, the great river, having been, in its upper course amidst the Himalayas, dammed up by a landslide for some weeks, had at length burst its barrier, and then rushed downwards past Attock with a terrific flood, rising, in a very few hours, twenty feet above high-water mark. The Kabul river joins the Indus at a short distance above Attock; this flood banked up the Kabul river, and the refluent water inundated the military station of Noushera, twenty miles above the junction. As we descended from some high ground towards the valley of Peshawar, and commanded a full view of the place, John Lawrence drew attention to the difficulties of the situation. 'Look,' he said, 'at the fertile and populous plains environed on all sides by rugged hills from which implacable foes can, at any moment, emerge to ravage and to slay.' We ascended a neighbouring mountain where it had been proposed to establish a sanitarium for fever-stricken Europeans from Peshawar; but he set his face against the project, declaring that, sooner or later, the helpless invalids would be attacked and slain by the bloodthirsty mountaineers. Arriving at Peshawar, we marvelled at the crowded markets and diversified wares, the mixture of Indian and Central Asian costumes, the clear running brooks and watercourses, the blooming gardens, and irrigated fields. We went as near to the Khyber Pass as was permissible, to gaze into its gloomy recesses, rode through the Kohat Pass with a strong escort lest the Afridi marauders should rush upon us, examined the defensive posts on the Eusufzye, and accompanied Harry Lumsden with a party of his Guide troopers on a hawking expedition.

But it was time to leave and he sent in his final application for fifteen months' leave to begin from 1st January 1859. 'The whole country,' he wrote to Lord Canning, 'from end to end is as quiet as possible. Indeed I never recollect to have seen the people so loyal and contented. The change at Peshawar, in this respect, since my last visit, is quite remarkable. In the interior of the country I have no apprehensions.'

The territories under his command were made a lieutenant-governorship and, as was fitting, a Gazette of the 1st January 1859 announced that 'the Right Honourable the Viceroy and Governor-General of India has been pleased to appoint the Honourable Sir John Lawrence, Baronet, G.C.B., to be the first Lieutenant-Governor of the Punjab and its Dependencies.'

On 25th February he was relieved and he set out for home smothered in addresses of goodwill and prepared for his reception in England by Lord Stanley. 'Your name and services are in everyone's mouth. Be prepared for such a reception in England as no one has had for twenty years!'

Before he left Lahore, Sir John Lawrence had been offered by Lord Stanley a seat in the Council of India which was formed when the Government was transferred to the Crown. He took his place on 11th April 1859, soon after his arrival in London. The freedom of the cities of London and Glasgow was conferred formally upon him. He was saluted as the 'Organiser of Victory', and the 'Saviour of India'. At a public assembly presided over by the Archbishop of Canterbury, an address was presented to him, signed by over 8,000 persons of all ranks in society. Oxford and Cambridge inscribed his name as a Doctor of Civil Law on their honorary rolls. Court favour was directed to him. He was fêted and made a guest in the houses of the great.

There were discussions with Prince Albert and visits to the Queen, all of which were accepted with characteristic modesty.

His work at the India Office was not arduous nor particularly appealing to his dynamic character, being advisory rather than decisive.

His wife has left a description of a typical day, how different from the excitement and tension of his previous life:

We kept early hours in those days. At 8.30 the household met for family prayers, and the large party of children breakfasted with us afterwards. He used to be the life of the gathering, and the merry stories he told and his romps with the children are well remembered. About 10 a.m. he started for the India Office, and did not generally return till late in the evening; but before he left home he was always ready to give help to me in every little domestic matter. It was now that we first became intimate with Captain Eastwick, who has ever since been our dear and valued friend. He and my husband often walked home together. We had many old friends near us, and members of my husband's family were often coming in and out among us. At that time, we did not go out much in the evening. Occasionally he dined out; but, as a rule, he did not care to do so. Nor did he ever spend much time at the Club. He only dropped in on his return home to hear what was going on. The evenings were generally spent in reading aloud. Sometimes he read to himself; but he was so sociable, and so enjoyed the family being all gathered round the fireside, that he preferred this to reading alone in the library. He took great interest in politics, but no active part in them. He occasionally brought home work from the Office, and I remember sitting with him at night and copying out his papers as fast as he wrote them. This was such a pleasure to me, recalling as it did, the old Indian days. There was not much occasion for this kind of work now; only it made me very happy.

There were honours to be received, solemn progresses around his farm and meetings of the Church Missionary Society. He began to feel that his public career in India was over.

His work at the India Board, though he was not happy at it, took up a fair amount of his time. A colleague kept a diary and his entries gave a splendid feeling of the John Lawrence of this time.

11th April 1859—Interview with Sir J. L. Plain, blunt straightforward manner; a man of action; the man to change the system in India. We must get out of the old groove; we must trust more to men and less to regulations.

21st April—Long conversation with Sir J. L. He thinks the system in India must be greatly changed to keep pace with the times. We must get better men forward and give more power to individuals. Several interesting anecdotes of the late eventful times. Evidently, a man of action; full of energy and self-reliance and fearlessness of responsibility.

3rd May—Sir J. L. evidently requires rest; complains of giddiness and pain in his head, if called upon to concentrate his attention on any work. The medical men in India told him he was travelling towards paralysis of the brain. He has the strongest possible opinion on the necessity for a local army in India, removed from all interferences on the part of the Horse Guards. So strong are his feelings on the subject, that he said that if it were ruled otherwise, he would resign his seat in Council, as he was quite sure disaster would be the result! Sees no objection to an optional Bible-class in Government schools in India.

30th May—He is greatly dissatisfied with the state of things in India; looks to the future with anxiety; he says that we ought to have 100,000 men in India, capable of being massed at any point.

7th October—He spoke despondingly of his own health, said he disliked the Council and thought he would resign. He felt that the members had no real power. 'It is my misfortune,' he said, 'to have a decided opinion on most subjects connected with India, and nothing shall deter me from expressing it, whether I offend Royal Highnesses, or Cabinet Ministers, or anyone. I never have eaten dirt, and I never will if I can help it. I have always observed that those who do eat dirt have, afterwards, to expectorate it.' He thought the system of the India House very defective; hated show, but liked to have the power of being hospitable; would wish to go away for a year and recover his health. He spoke freely and unreservedly on all subjects. I like him much; think he is a thorough, honest, energetic man of the Cromwell stamp, full of self-reliance and practical good sense.

17th November—Walked home with Sir J. L. He said he would give much to speak like Gladstone. He thought he should never speak; it was too late in life to begin.

14th December—Sir J. L. said that his brother Henry had told him that he had attended the council of war before Sobraon, and that all he recollected was Lord Gough saying, 'I never was bate, and I never will be bate.'

31st December—In my walk home with Sir J. L. two nights ago he told me that when he quitted the Punjab there was no arrears, he never allowed any; he always read all the papers himself, and despatched them at once. He saw no difficulty in keeping work down, provided only there was method and industry. But then he was obliged to employ every fragment of his time. There was none wasted from the hour he got up to the hour he went to bed, and he was always looking after those under him. Temple was a first-rate man of business, very ready with his pen, and full of talent; Macpherson, steady and methodical; Herbert Edwardes, very able, would make a first-rate Member of Council; Macleod, sensible, with a great knowledge of India. I wish they would make Sir J. L. Governor-General. We need the best man England can give us, and one who can walk alone.

11th February 1860—Sir J. L. offered the Government of Bombay. He refused it.

15th April—Went with Sir J. L. to hear Louis Blanc on the Salons of Paris at the time of Madame du Deffand, etc.

7th July—Called on Lord Stanley, who said he thought it was a mistake that the Council were excluded from Parliament. It would not do to have old stagers who defended everything, but Sir J. L. would be invaluable as the representative of the more advanced school of Indian politicians.

7th February 1861—Sir John Lawrence spoke strongly on the Opposition side on the military question discussed today; division seven to seven; Sir Charles Wood gave the casting vote. Sir J. L. does not think the Indian expenditure will be brought within the income, and is dissatisfied with the way business is done in the office.

25th March 1862—He said that if it rested with him he would emigrate. He did not like the trammels of English life. He did not know what to do with his boys.

24th June—Went with Sir John Lawrence to see the pictures of 'The Derby Day', and the 'Railway Train', by Frith.

24th July—Beat Sir John in a game of chess.

25th February 1863—Went to a meeting at the Society of Arts. Mr. Cheatham read a paper on cotton. Mr. Bailey in the chair. Sir John Lawrence spoke.

16th March—Went with Sir John to the Dean of Westminster to ask permission that Outram's remains should rest in Westminster Abbey.

20th March—To the Dean of Westminster with Sir John Lawrence to fix the hour and select a site for the grave. Engaged in various ways about the funeral arrangements the whole day.

25th March—With Sir John Lawrence and Willoughby to attend Outram's funeral. The sergeants of the 78th Regiment came up from Shorncliffe to bear the body of their old commander to the grave. A touching incident.

28th November—Heard of Lord Elgin's serious illness. Who will be his successor? Will the Ministry offer the appointment to Lawrence? It would be right, and I think it would be popular. It would be a fitting reward for his great services. The only question is whether his health would enable him to bear the weight of such a charge.

1st December—Heard of the appointment of Sir John Lawrence to succeed Lord Elgin. Wrote to him and to Lady Lawrence. Proud as she must feel at the recognition of her husband's gread deeds and noble character, the prospect of a separation of many months must fill her heart with anxiety.

7th December—I took leave of Sir John Lawrence.

After four and a half years the call of Duty was to sound again.

YOU ARE TO GO TO INDIA AS
GOVERNOR-GENERAL

ON THE MORNING of 30th November 1863, Sir Charles Wood looked into Sir John Lawrence's room at the India Office with the pregnant announcement, 'You are to go to India as Governor-General. Wait here till I return from Windsor with the Queen's approval.' It was not till long after office hours that Sir Charles returned with the warm approval which he had sought and had obtained; and now the 'imperial appointment, which is the greatest honour England has to give, except the government of herself', belonged to John Lawrence.

When the news [says Lady Lawrence] of Lord Elgin's death arrived, I remember my husband coming to my room, while I was ill from some trifling ailment, and telling me what had happened. I don't know why, by my heart sank at once, and I said to him, 'Perhaps you will be asked to succeed him.' Neither of us expected anything of the kind. Still the idea took possession of me. He went to the office as usual. Visitors came and went that day. But my thoughts ran on nothing else. He did not come home by his usual train, and I became more anxious, and so restless that I could not keep still for a moment. At last, when he arrived quite late at night, he brought the news that he was to go to India as Viceroy. I suppose few people would believe that this announcement made me miserable. I could think of nothing but our broken-up home, another separation from our children, and all the risk of climate and hard work for him. Naturally, he felt otherwise and was proud of the position offered him. At my earnest request, he consulted two medical men before he quite decided. But their verdict was favourable. And so there was nothing for it but to face the trial, and begin the necessary preparations as soon as possible, for he was to start at once. I was to follow in the autumn. I can never forget those last days; all the hurry and worry, the constant demands on his time, the private arrangements he wished to make for his family, the kind friends so ready to help—Mr. and Mrs. Cater among the most prominent. A very dear and valued friend, Mr. Jay, who had formerly been a chaplain at Lahore, came to see us for an hour or two before he left. He had prayer with us all before he took leave, and a very solemn and impressive meeting it was. At last the parting came. Before starting, we all gathered for the last time round the drawing-room fire, and he made each child say a hymn to him—Bertie, who was little more than two years old, being in his arms. He left home about 7 p.m. to catch the night mail from Charing Cross; and thus, on December 9, 1863, closed one of the happiest chapters in our happy lives.

What had happened in India in those four and a half years? Was the India of 1864 very different from that of 1856?

The Mutiny had shaken the attitudes of both British and Indian into new moulds. The memory of the Mutiny, its ruthlessness and hates, remained for both sides a bed of nails. Imperialist writers with their hands at the throat of British-Indian history have tended to ignore the effect of the occurrences at Cawnpore, Delhi, and Lucknow and the fate of the rebel leaders upon the Indian mind. The Mutiny, one might think from an intelligent perusal of the historians' garbage, ended abruptly with a return to normal. Nothing could be more misleading.

Indians came to realize that British rule was unlike any other before it. Unlike the Moguls and their predecessors it could neither be assimilated nor expelled. Where, at one time, there had appeared the possibility of an Indo-European civilization, now it seemed essentially improbable and morally undesirable. Indians turned back to the orthodoxies of their own religions. The *Brahmo Samaj*, an organization pledged to a synthesis of East and West died before the harsh wind of the proselytizing, revivalist, *Arya Samaj*. As the Indians moved back to the old gods, to the old vitalities and the glorious heroisms of the golden ages, the British retired behind the bastions of their white skins and the conventialities of racial solidarity. But one good thing emerged. No more were Indians' religious prejudices to be subject to the ugly passion of Evangelical paranoiacs The function of the occupying power, and now the British felt themselves as such, was to maintain law and order, balance the Budget, and bring some of the material blessings of European expertize.

The Indian Army, as the primary cause of the Mutiny was radically altered. The East India Company's methods of recruiting by caste were abandoned and an entirely new principle of balancing communities inside the Army was adopted. The European element was also continually increased while the Indian was reduced. Artillery was strictly in the hands of white troops.

At the same time the position of the Indian princes was stabilized and protected, and as an antidote to the optimistic occidentalism of pre-Mutiny times, the States were to act as bulwarks of traditional strength. Lord Canning summed up the prevailing attitude for he had 'seen a few patches of Native Government prove breakwaters to the storm which would otherwise have swept us over in one great wave'. At the same time the indirect power of the central Government was exercised, through Residents whose 'advice' became more and more executive. Truly Imperial India, a vast network of directly administered territories and tributary states, was in the making.

Even in the anarchy of the latter half of 1857 when the foundations of British India still trembled on the Ridge of Delhi, the administration continued, with the orderly indifference which has often been described as traditional British phlegm. Lord Canning summoned his Executive Council to discuss the founding of universities at Calcutta, Bombay, and Madras when European 'culture' seemed in danger of being thrown into the sea.

Indian finances were administered in the 'most happy-go-lucky system that perhaps ever existed in any civilized country'. But in the person of James Wilson and his successor, new accountancy methods were introduced and that symbol of modern government, income-tax, somewhat shyly appeared, though it did not become a regular part of the financial system until 1886. The apparatus of administration more and more conformed to the scaffolding of European practice.

The India that John Lawrence returned to was no longer the almost free and easy administration of traders and men of action. The sword was giving way to the pen, the dynamic to the ordered, the adventurous to the caution of the bureaucrat.

VII

THE QUEEN'S PEACE
OVER ALL

For we must bear our leader's blame,
On us the shame will fall,
If we lift our hand from a fettered land,
And the Queen's Peace over all,
Dear Boys,
The Queen's Peace over all.

'The Running of Shindand': KIPLING

THE FETTERED LAND

THE YEARS of John Lawrence's Viceroyalty were quiet though
not uneventful. The Mutiny was strong in men's minds and because of it the problems which seemed most important were
concerned with Europeans rather than Indians.

This came about because of the rapid expansion of the non-
official European population after the Mutiny. It was found that
tea could be profitably grown in Assam and coffee in the Nilgiris.
A flood of Englishmen swept over India, businessmen and
planters, narrow-minded, race-conscious, contemptuous of things
Indian. They packed juries, subsidized a vicious press and
generally attacked the Government.

John Lawrence shocked people by showing himself *on foot* and
at places where Viceroys were least expected.

He walked [says his Private Secretary] to the Eden gardens in
the gloom of those January evenings, and, like the Sultan in the
Arabian Nights, heard with amusement or with interest remarks
about himself as he mingled with the crowd. He walked to the
Scotch Church or St. John's on the Sunday morning, throwing
down his great white umbrella in the porch, and striding in, to the
dismay of the officials, who were expecting him to arrive in full
Viceregal state at the grand entrance. He walked across the Maidan
at five o'clock in the morning, and, on one occasion, when confronted with a bison or buffalo which had escaped from the Agricultural Exhibition then being held at Calcutta, he amused his Staff
by telling them 'not to run', although his own pace was being
rapidly accelerated, and escape from the huge animal, as he bore
down upon them, seemed somewhat problematical. He walked to
the Bazaar when notice of a fire reached him, and he spent much
time during this, his first fortnight in the City of Palaces, in examining the different sites suggested for a Sailors' Home, the first public
work he took up, and one to which he devoted himself very
assiduously, laying the foundation-stone with his own hand, and
heading the subscription list with a large donation. It was on his
return from one of these pedestrian excursions, late in the evening,
that he met with a personal repulse, which was duly published in

the newspapers on the following morning, and afforded much amusement to the Calcutta community. The south entrance to the Viceregal Palace is considered sacred to the Governor-General, and ingress after dark is only allowed to those to whom he gives special permission. Just as Sir John had passed through this portal he was challenged by the sentry with a smart 'Hooo cum dar?' ('Who comes there?'). Not stopping to reply, Sir John pushed on, when his further progress was effectually barred by the Sepoy, who brought his weapon with fixed bayonet down to the charge. The members of the Staff, who were convulsed with laughter, in vain assured the sentry that it was the Governor-General. He had never heard of, much less seen, the 'great Padishah' or 'Lord Sahib Bahadur' walking on his own feet; and when told that this was 'Jan Larens' of the Punjab, he collapsed with fear, and was only too glad to see him pass on, unruffled, into the house.

John Lawrence concerned himself with internal problems. His foreign policy has been described as one of 'masterly inactivity'. But to compensate there was masterly activity at home. Sanitary reforms, the influence of Florence Nightingale, were put in hand. Death was pushed a little further away. John's regard for the Indian peasantry saw the Punjab and Oudh Tenancy Acts passed during his term of office. In these he championed the ryot against European planters, Indian landowners, most of his Council, and the Secretary of State. 'No more useful or beneficial legislatic,' wrote the Indian historian R. C. Dutt, 'was ever undertaken by the British Government in India ... legislation which respected the great and protected the weak, and which was based on the unwritten customs and ancient rights of India.'

Two severe famines visited India during John's Viceroyalty. A great commercial crisis rocked banking houses in 1866 and many firms crashed. The land was fettered not only by the power of the British, but the instability of its commerce and finance.

In 1864 a Great Durbar was held at Lahore, the capital of the Punjab. John Lawrence returned to the stage of his triumphs and the Chiefs gathered to hear him: John addressed them in Hindustani:

Maharajahs, Rajas, and Chiefs! Listen to my words. I have come among you after an absence of nearly six years, and thank you for the kindly welcome you have given me. It is with pleasure that I meet so many of my old friends, while I mourn the loss of those who have passed away.

Princes and Chiefs! It is with great satisfaction that I find nearly six hundred of you assembled around me in this Durbar. I see before me the faces of many friends. I recognise the sons of my old allies, the Maharaja of Kashmir and Puttiala; the Sikh chiefs of Malwa and the Manjha; the Rajput chiefs of the Hills; the Mohammedan Mullicks of Peshawar and Kohat; the Sirdars of the Derajat, of Hazara, and of Delhi. All have gathered together to do honour to their old ruler.

My friends! Let me tell you of the great interest which the illustrious Queen of England takes in all matters connected with the welfare, and comfort, and contentment of the people in India. Let me inform you, when I returned to my native country, and had the honour of standing in the presence of Her Majesty, how kindly she asked after the welfare of her subjects in the East. Let me tell you when that great Queen appointed me her Viceroy in India, how warmly she enjoined on me the duty of caring for your interests. Prince Albert, the Consort of Her Majesty, the fame of whose greatness and goodness has spread through the whole world, was well acquainted with all connected with this country, and always evinced an ardent desire to see its people happy and flourishing.

My friends! It is now more than eighteen years since I first saw Lahore. For thirteen years I lived in the Punjab. For many years, my brother, Sir Henry Lawrence, and I, governed this vast country. You all knew him well, and his memory will ever dwell in your hearts as a ruler who was a real friend of its people. I may truly say that from the day we exercised authority in the land, we spared neither our time, nor our labour, nor our health, in endeavouring to accomplish the work which we had undertaken. We studied to make ourselves acquainted with the usages, the feelings, and the wants of every class and race; and we endeavoured to improve the condition of all. There are few parts of this province which I have not visited, and which I hope that I did not leave, in some degree, the better for my visit. Since British rule was introduced, taxation of all kinds has been lightened, canals and roads have been constructed, and schools of learning have been established. From the highest to the lowest, the people have become contented, and have proved loyal. When the great military revolt of 1857 occurred, they aided their rulers most effectively in putting it down. The chiefs mustered their contingents, which served faithfully, and thousands of Punjabi soldiers flocked to our standards, and shared with the British troops the glories, as well as the hardships, of that great struggle.

Princes and Gentlemen! If it be wise for the rulers of a country to understand the language and appreciate the feelings of its people, it is as important that the people should have a similar knowledge of their rulers. It is only by such means that the two classes can live happily together. To this end, I urge you to instruct your sons, and even your daughters.

Among the solid advantages which you have gained from English rule, I will now only advert to one more. It has given the country many excellent administrators. Some of the ablest and kindest of my countrymen have been employed in the Punjab. Every man, from the highest to the lowest, can appreciate a good ruler. You have such men as Sir Robert Montgomery, Mr. Donald Macleod, Mr. Roberts, Sir Herbert Edwardes, Colonel Lake, and Colonel John Becher—officers who have devoted themselves to your service.

I will now only add that I pray the great God, who is the God of all the races and all the people of this world, that He may guard and protect you, and teach you all to love justice and hate oppression, and enable you, each in his several ways, to do all the good in his power. May He give you all that is for your real benefit. So long as I live, I shall never forget the years that I passed in the Punjab and the friends that I have acquired throughout this province.

It was both a personal credo and a statement of government policy.

The problem of Afghanistan was an ever-open sore in the Frontier relations of British India. It was to leave John almost unruffled.

Initially, the old Sikh frontier was maintained, and trans-frontier trade encouraged. Lawrence, fresh from the lessons of the 'Mutiny', sought to consolidate India. His policy was of peaceful progress at home and of non-interference in the internal affairs of India's neighbours. He conceived that his duty in India was to centralize and unify, and that these responsibilities were the sum total of British aims and endeavours. He saw the Afghan problem as a will-o'-the-wisp, leading to dangerous swamps, and did not see why, as his biographer puts it, he should 'make the imperial policy of India depend upon the flight of a random bullet or the dagger of a paradise-seeking Ghazi.' Or to 'employ our Indian army on a service which they hate, and so to increase the difficulties of the recruiting officer, which are already formidable enough' and 'to throw away crores of rupees on barren mountain ridges and ever-vanishing frontier lines, while every rupee is sorely needed by a Government which can hardly pay its way, and by a vast population which, living on little more than starvation-rates, cries aloud to be saved from the tax-gatherer on the one hand, and from actual starvation on the other.'

Lawrence's conception of a 'close-border' was typical of the man. He was an administrator, not a dreamer; phlegmatic rather than a visionary. He took his views of strict neutrality, as he did most things, to their logical conclusion. He would support any faction in Afghanistan that appeared stable, but would help no one to achieve the throne. In a letter to Afzul Khan, one of the many rivals for power in Afghanistan, Lawrence blandly wrote:

'My friend, the relations of this Government are with the actual rulers of Afghanistan. If your Highness is able to consoli-date your Highness's power, and is sincerely desirous of being the friend and ally of the British Government, I shall be ready to accept your Highness as such. . . .'

No attempt at a settled administration of the frontier tribes was made. It would have been too expensive for Sir John Law-rence, who practically lived within the bars of the Indian Budget. Instead, refractory tribes were subjected to punitive expeditions, the so-called 'butcher and bolt' tactics, which by destroying their crops, added to their incentive for plunder and unrest.

But the end of non-intervention was at hand. Superficially, it might seem that such a policy had been based upon ordinary commonsense and memory of 1838, or perhaps even upon moral grounds, but this was not in fact the case. Lawrence never forget the lesson of the Mutiny: that the British government in India was maintained by a combination of power and consent, and that a wave of popular feeling and hatred, properly led and supported from outside could drive the British into the sea. The aim of Lawrence, an aim to which all imperial policy must be subordi-nate, was simply to prevent the possibility of another, and perhaps successful, mutiny. This was given explicit expression in his covering despatch to Minutes in reply to Sir Henry Rawlinson's Memorandum proposing measures 'to counteract the advance of Russia in Central Asia, and to strengthen the influence and power of England in Afghanistan and Persia.'

Should a foreign power, such as Russia [wrote Lawrence] ever seriously think of invading India from without, or, *what is more probable*, of stirring up the elements of dissaffection or anarchy within it, our true policy, our strongest security, would be found to lie in previous abstinence from entanglements at either Kabul, Kandahar, or any similar outpost . . . in the contentment, if not in the attachment of the masses; in the sense of security of title and possession . . . in the construction of material works within British India, which enhance the comfort of the people while they add to our political and military strength . . . coupled with the avoidance of all sources of complaint, which either invite foreign aggression, or stir up restless spirits to domestic revolt.

But it was not to be left to Lawrence to settle the Afghan problem. Others more adventurous were to burn their hands in that particular fire.

The fundamentals of Lawrence's administration were empirically sound based as they were on pragmatic experience.

His ideal [wrote a contemporary], which I have often heard from his lips, of a country thickly cultivated by a fat, contented yeomanry, each riding his own horse, sitting under his own fig-tree, and enjoying his rude family comforts, may not have been the ideal of a State in the nineteenth century politically free; but for a people whose destiny it has been for centuries to be conquered, domestic comforts and the enjoyment of their own customs, their own religion and their own language, soften the sting of foreign domination.

The land might be fettered but the fetters were to be the soft guiding hands of paternalism.

BE JUST AND KIND TO THE NATIVES OF INDIA

On 11TH JANUARY 1869 a farewell dinner was given to John Lawrence in the Town Hall of Calcutta. After the speeches the Viceroy rose to reply:

He spoke [writes his biographer] in a low and broken voice, which, more than once, hesitated from emotion, and could be distinctly heard by those only who were near at hand. He, too, reviewed his own career, and with genuine modesty reminded his hearers, that no small part of his success was due 'to the officers with whom he had worked, and to his countrymen in India'. Nor did he forget to pay a warm tribute to the sterling qualities of the natives of Upper India, among whom he had laboured for nearly forty years, those with whom he had sympathised so keenly, and had understood so well. Then, alluding to his foreign policy, for which he had been so much attacked, he declared that 'he had never shrunk from war when honour and justice required it, but pointed out that to have continued the wars in Bhotan and Huzara after their purpose had been answered, would have been neither wise nor merciful.' To the charge that he had followed a supine and inert policy in Central Asia he gave an emphatic contradiction. 'I have watched,' he said, 'very carefully all that has gone on in those distant countries.' It was true that he had set his face against all projects which seemed likely to involve an active interference in Central Asia, because such interference 'would almost certainly lead to war, and end of which no one could foresee, and which would involve India in heavy debt, or necessitate the imposition of fresh taxation, to the impoverishment of the country, and the unpopularity of our rule.' 'Our true policy,' he added, 'is to avoid such complications, to consolidate our power in India, to give to its people the best government we can, to organise our administration in every department on a system which will combine economy with efficiency, and so to make our Government strong and respected in our own territories.' By so doing, and standing fast on our own border, we should be best prepared to repel invasion, if it should ever come. And when as his parting counsel, as the last of his last words, he urged his countrymen 'to be just and kind to the natives of India', his words were received with a storm of long-continued and earnest cheering, such as one who had been present at many public gatherings in Calcutta, from the days of Lord Dalhousie downwards, declared that he had never before witnessed.

The next day his successor, Lord Mayo, arrived.

The reception of a new Viceroy on the spacious flight of steps at Government House, and the handing over charge of the Indian Empire which immediately follows, forms an imposing spectacle. On this occasion, it had a pathos of its own. At the top of the stairs, stood the wearied, veteran Viceroy, wearing his splendid harness for the last day, his face blanched, and his tall figure shrunken by forty years of Indian service, but his head erect, and his eye still bright with the fire which had burst forth so gloriously in India's supreme hour of need. Around him stood the tried counsellors with whom he had gone through life, a silent, calm semicircle in suits of blue and gold, lit up by a few scarlet uniforms. At the bottom, the new Governor-General jumped lightly out of the carriage amid the saluting of troops and glitter of arms, his large athletic form in the easiest of summer costumes, with a funny little coloured necktie, and a face red with health and sunshine. As he came up the tall flights of stairs with a springy step, John Lawrence, with a visible feebleness, made the customary three paces forward to the edge of the landing-place to receive him. I was among the group of officers who followed them into the Council Chamber, and, as we went, a friend compared the scene to an even more memorable one on the same stairs. The toilworn statesman who had done more than any other single Englishman to save India in 1857 was now handing it over to an untried successor; and, thirteen years before, Lord Dalhousie, the stern ruler who did more than any other Englishman to build up that empire, had come to the same act of demission on the same spot, with a face still more deeply ploughed by disease and care, a mind and body more weary, and bearing with him the death which was about to come upon him as the price of his great services to his country. In the Chamber, Sir John Lawrence and his Council took their usual seats at the table; the Chief Secretaries stood round; a crowd of officers filled the room; and the silent faces of the Englishmen who had won and kept India in times past, looked down from the walls. The clerk read out the oaths in a clear voice, and Lord Mayo assented. At the same moment, the Viceroy's band burst forth with 'God Save the Queen' in the garden below, a great shout came in from the people outside, and the hundred and ninety-six millions of British had passed under a new ruler.

On 18th January Sir John Lawrence left India for ever. On arrival in England he was raised to the peerage as Baron Lawrence of the Punjab. He now declines from our story finally to die on 27th June 1879.

No statesman [wrote Lord Lytton, then destroying Lawrence's foreign policy, in the *Gazette of India*] since Warren Hastings has administered the Government of India with a genius and an experience so exclusively trained and developed in her service, as those of the illustrious man whose life, now closed in the fulness of fame though not of age, bequeaths to his country a bright example of all that is noblest in the high qualities for which the Civil Service has justly been renowned; and in which, with such examples before it, will never be deficient. The eminent services rendered to India by Lord Lawrence, both as ruler of the Punjab in the heroic defence of British power, and as Viceroy in the peaceful administration of a rescued Empire, cannot be fitly acknowledged in this sad record of the grief which she suffers by his death, and of the pride with which she cherishes his name.

John Lawrence's last words were 'I am so weary' but his greatest, spoken from his complex heart, were 'Be just and kind to the natives of India.'

EPILOGUE

THE NECESSARY HELL

It may take years—it may take a century—to fit India for self-government but it is a thing worth doing and a thing that may be done.

HERBERT EDWARDES, 1860

THE NECESSARY HELL

FROM the death of John Lawrence the Indian Empire moved inexorably to its fall. The Government of India had become respectable, a puppet on the end of the telegraph wire. No more —except in 1886 in Upper Burma, the last gesture of the good old days—was there to be the flush of adventure, the excitement of expansion. The limits had been reached. All that was left were the satisfactions of bureaucratic efficiency and the monuments of the Public Works Department.

The administration no longer believed in getting its hands dirty. It was mainly concerned with trimming the edges of the *Pax Britannica* and maintaining an Imperial system centred upon India. Because of this dual pre-occupation with peace and prestige the Indian Empire, immense, grandiose, and luxuriant with the appurtenances of power, was ensuring its own disintegration.

While the administration of India remained dynamic all was well. An empire that is caught in the passion of its young men, that still holds a pistol in one hand and a revenue map in the other, is secure. The pioneer spirit is as good as a shot of benzedrine. But the minutiae of government, the despatch-boxes and the impedimenta of routine confine the rulers in the delicacies of *precedent*—there is no place for the eccentric.

But this system which was in turn to die could only emerge from the rough and ready methods of the period of expansion. Even the Mutiny was a functional part of the progress from action to consolidation. The events of 1857 were not only the culmination of the Evangelical revolution, the Reign of Terror which leads to the bourgeois virtues of the Directory, but the last throw of a traditional society. The Mutiny was, in fact, the meeting of two dying systems. British-India as a 'country' power—an oriental government with European overtones and traditional India unwilling and unable to absorb the militancies of the other.

In the history of India under European domination, the hell of the Mutiny and the years of violence and expansion that preceded it was a necessary one. Out of it was to emerge the peace that made the revolution of 1947 a unique ending to a glorious, but by then somewhat tarnished, empire.

The men of the Mutiny, both Indian and British, were no longer the men of the Indian Empire. The aristocrats of the sword and the aristocrats of the land were to give way to the bourgeois civil servant and nationalist. The British could not be fought in the strength of their arsenals but hurt in the speech of their own political institutions and winded in the belly of their self-importance.

The rulers of India in the last ninety years of British occupation were concerned not with power but with prestige. In the essential belief that British Imperialism was different; the product not of coercion but of collusion, not of the secret police and a tank on every street corner but of the right persuasion and the consent of respect.

There is much to be unhappy about in the history of British India, many things of which to be justly ashamed. But we must always look to the larger canvas and the greater good. Ends only casually justify means but they often explain them. The causes of action are usually obscure, the apparent results are in many cases misleading. The necessary hell of British India has led to the freedom of India, a freedom, perhaps to construct its own hells. The tragedy of British India, I have tried to show in this book, was a tragedy shared. That is the paradox and in it lies the pride.

Of the fitting of India for freedom, Herbert Edwardes said in a lecture given in 1860 that 'it is a thing worth doing and a thing that may be done'. There is blood on the pages of British India but in the final analysis no one can deny that it *was* worth doing and that it *has* been done.

SELECT BIBLIOGRAPHY

The material on which this book is mainly based is contained in the following sources:

AITCHISON, SIR C.: *Lord Lawrence*, Oxford 1892.

BOSWORTH-SMITH, R.: *Life of Lord Lawrence*, London 1883.

DIVER, MAUD: *Honoria Lawrence*, London 1936.

EDWARDES, SIR H. B. and MERIVALE, H.: *Life of Sir Henry Lawrence*, London 1872.

The H. M. Lawrence and John Lawrence Collections (papers, correspondence, etc.) in the India Office Library, Commonwealth Relations Office, London.

MORISON, J. L.: *Lawrence of Lucknow*, London 1934.

Other sources

BJORNSTJERNA, COUNT: *The British Empire in the East*, London 1840.

CAVE-BROWNE, REV. J.: *The Punjab and Delhi in 1857*, London 1861.

CUNNINGHAM, H. S.: *Earl Canning*, London 1892.

CUNNINGHAM, J. D.: *A History of the Sikhs*, London 1849.

DALHOUSIE, LORD: *Private Letters of the Marquess Dalhousie*, edited by J. G. A. Baird, London 1910.

EDEN, EMILY: *Up the Country*, edited by Edward Thompson, London 1930.

EDWARDES, SIR H. B.: *Memorials of the Life and Letters of Major-General Sir Herbert B. Edwardes by his Wife*, London 1886.

EYRE, VINCENT: *The Military Operations at Kabul*, London 1843.

GERMON, MRS. *Journal of the Siege of Lucknow*, edited by Michael Edwardes, London 1958.

GUBBINS, MARTIN: *An Account of the Mutinies in Oudh and of the Siege of the Lucknow Residency*, London 1858.

HEBER, REGINALD: *Narrative of a Journey through the Upper Provinces of India, 1824–1825*, London 1828.

HODSON, W. S. R.: *Twelve Years of a Soldier's Life in India*, London 1859.

15*

KAYE, J. W.: *A History of the Sepoy War in India*, London 1864–76.
—— (published anonymously): *Peregrine Pultuney or Life in India*, London 1844.

MAJENDIE, V. D.: *Up Among the Pandies*, London 1859.

MALLESON, G. B.: *The Indian Mutiny of 1857*, London 1891.

OSBORNE, The HON. W. G.: *Court and Camp of Ranjit Singh*, London 1840.

PEARSE, HUGH: *The Hearseys*, London 1905.

ROBERTS, P. E.: *History of British India*, 3rd edition completed by T. G. P. Spear, London 1952.

RUSSELL, W. H.: *My Indian Mutiny Diary*, edited by Michael Edwardes, London 1957.

SLEEMAN, WILLIAM: *Journey through the Kingdom of Oudh*, London 1858.

SPEAR, T. G. P.: *The Nabobs*, London 1943.

—— : *Twilight of the Mughals*, London 1951.

TEMPLE, SIR RICHARD: *Men and Events in my Time in India*, London 1882.

THOMPSON, EDWARD: *The Other Side of the Medal*, London 1925.

—— : *The Life of Charles, Lord Metcalfe*, London 1937

THOMPSON, E. and GARRATT, G. T.: *Rise and Fulfilment of British Rule in India*, London 1934.

TOD, JAMES: *Annals and Antiquities of Rajasthan*, London 1821.

TREVELYAN, SIR G.: *The Competition Wallah*, London 1895.

Selections from the Letters, Despatches and other State Papers preserved in the Military Department of the Government of India, 1857–58. Edited by G. W. Forrest. Vol. I, 1893.

Selections from the Records, Punjab Annual Administration Reports (1849–50, 1855–6).

Calcutta Review, March 1856.
Dictionary of Indian Biography, edited by C. E. Buckland, London 1906.

INDEX